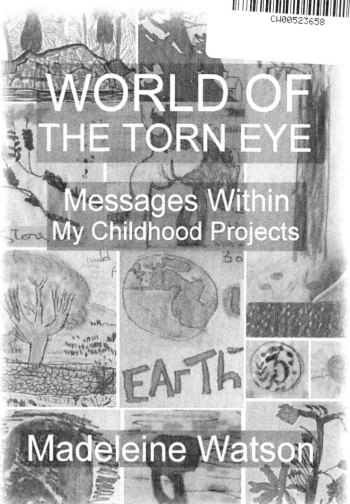

WORLD OF THE TORN EYE

Messages Within My Childhood Projects

Madeleine Watson

To the ghost-girl

ISBN: 9798838279675

At the age of 51, I learned something truly terrible about myself. Unbeknown to me, clues to this horrific truth had leaked into my stories, paintings, poems and other creations. Due to the sensitive nature of this book, names and certain details have been altered in order to protect identities and I am writing under a pseudonym.

INDEX

INDEX (Cont)

Introduction

Everything within this book is true.

This book is about my fact-based projects.

From early childhood, I wrote about the world, nature and science. Once upon a time, I wanted to write the encyclopaedia. I began with 'a' and wrote about aircraft and couldn't wait to get to 'e' so I could get to earthquakes, or 't' to write about the tides. Before long, my project floundered. No wonder. I was just nine.

But my projects wouldn't stop. Before long, I'd be writing about something else, reading a load of fascinating facts about the Earth. I got into countries, capitals, islands and oceans. What causes the Aroura? How high can clouds go? I did quizzes about the airmasses and extremes. In fact, I was running away from something horrible inside. I didn't know what it was. But without my realisation, the answers were seeping onto every page I wrote.

My diaries (1977-88)

This book looks at sixteen projects. There were more, but some haven't survived.

Weather forms my biggest obsession. I wrote about nature's fury, including tornadoes and thunderstorms. I also kept weather records. The weather is 'big'. I have therefore dedicated an overflow book about the weather but have provided a linking chapter here, which forms part of a series.

I was doing a load of other stuff too. I've written children's stories, novels, screenplays and poems. I kept a detailed diary for over eleven years. My artwork is abundant. These have been covered in my other books. Something is evidentially fuelling these projects. At the age of fifty-one, this fuel would finally reveal itself.

This book lays bare my findings.

SECTION 1: THE BEGINNING
Chapter 1: The Human Being
Introduction
Part 1: The Big and Small
Interlude 1: The Codes
Part 2: The Codes in Action
Part 3: Scar in my Chest
Part 4: Motherhood
Part 5: Keratin Growths
Part 6: Bloodied Pages
Part 7: The Neck
Part 8: The Awakening
Part 9: Drowned
Part 10: Plural Writing
Interlude 2: The Background

Introduction

This first chapter of this book is about a project I did on human endurance and extremes. I had called it *The Human Being*. It's in an A5 green notebook. The year is 1980, and I am fourteen.

I had got this information from the *Guinness Book of Records* I had for Christmas 1979. Why this turn, is at first mystifying. I'm usually into the weather, plants or astronomy. The information is accurate as of this time, and of course records since have been broken. I have also retained my occasional misspellings for the purpose of unearthing my findings.

The Extremes

Here, I have written about the tallest giants, smallest dwarfs, the lightest and heaviest person, multiple births, food abstinence, coin-swallowing, underwater feats and more. My felt tip drawing shows the human form.

Part 1: The Big and Small

My project begins with the tallest giants. I had written,

My headings for big and small.

'In biblical times, lived Og, the Amorite, King of Basham and Gilead. In 1450, he stood 9 Hebrew cubits, (13 feet 2½ in). In 1060 BC, stood 6 cubits and a span (9 ft 6½ inches)'.

I would follow this with the tallest recorded man in modern history.

robert pershing wadlow

AGE	HEIGHT ft ins		AGE	HEIGHT ft ins		AGE
5	5	4	14	7	5	21
8	6	0	15	7	8	
9	6	2½	16	7	10½	HEIGHT ft ins 8 11¾
10	6	5	17	8	½	
11	6	7	18	8	3¼	
12	6	10¼	19	8	5½	
13	7	1¾	20	8	6¾	

My table showing Wadlow's growth.

'Robert Pershing Wadlow (I continue) was born 22 Feb 1918 in Alton, Illinois, USA weighing 8½lb at birth. His abnormal growth began almost immediately.'

The Big Preoccupation

I cannot guarantee the accuracy of my transcription, only of what I had put here. But as will be seen, this project isn't really about the *Guinness Book of Records* at all. It's about me. This tall-men preoccupation would provide a clue.

I go straight into other people who exceeded eight feet, as shown in the next image.

The drive for this project is my toddlerhood. This may seem mystifying but is true. I've had a vile toddlerhood. My other projects are the same: fuelled by my toddlerhood.

My choice of topics begins with giants. In the early Eighties, I kept visualising a big man standing at a railway bridge that leads from my childhood village. He has acromegaly (a condition of overgrown bones). This image would eventually lead to the penning of my first novel, *The Lessons* in 1985. It's the same here with the giants – a preoccupation. To a toddler, my rapist would seem like a giant. He was over six feet tall.

Yes, my rapist. He was Mum's half-brother, and he lived in my toddlerhood cottage for most of 1968. I was three. Due to what he did to me, I have become plural. I have a split-self due to toddlerhood rape, and this 'self' has been separated from me. My odd insecurities were mistaken for something else. Not until 2016 when I was fifty-one did a memory come up.

This book examines how my plural has used these projects to sneak a message through. They're like Trojan Horses.

This intermission explains.

Interlude 1: The Codes

There is a lot of data in this project: names, places and dates. This is my plural's doing. She is using streams of data in a bid to find something of relevance to my toddlerhood. I will then write something meaningful, not realising what I am doing. As will be seen, my works are rife with these 'codes', for this is what they would become: codes. This is how it works.

This book begins with Og (King of Amorite). This is 'Go' (spelt backwards). The liar in my head is telling my plural to 'go away'. I have a liar in my head. The liar has formed from trauma and is keeping my plural's truth away from me.

I put the liar there. When my rapist left the cottage, I lied to myself. I was three-and-a-half and wanted the nasty thing to go away. This wish would slip from my conscious awareness and the liar was born. This liar would then work in the dark minus my conscious awareness.

We're back to 'Og (meaning 'go').

The 'Amorite, King of Basham and Gilead' means 'King am-all-right, of be-shaam and gile'd-a' (guiled-her).

How weird. A complex message has emerged beneath my paragraph about this king.

The meaning is 'I'm all right living a sham and the liar can guile me.' I am 'king' of the cottage, while my plural has been outcast. My projects carry a shadow message. My plural has used streams of data to glean out meanings. 'She' is telling me about my vile toddlerhood through these projects.

Giveaway of the Codes

My code-cracking had begun in 2016 with Aidan. Recall had occurred a few weeks earlier and my research was still in its infancy. Aidan is the main character of my first novel, *The Lessons*. I was nineteen and at Uni. My rapist's name forms part of Aidan. Ai-*Dan*. My uncle's name was Dan. So, Aidan really means 'hey-Dan'. Aidan would form the entrance to a labyrinth of other codes.

(***Note:*** *to retain anonymity, I have changed my rapist's name. It's not really Dan. This means changing the character-name of my novel too. But the principle here is the same*).

Riddled with Messages

So, my creations are infested with another meaning. The more I dug, the more I found. A hidden language emerged. Within, I would find expressions for rape, suffocation, and clues to assault sites – expressions for a split-self, too. The word 'elm' and 'ams crop up a lot. Elm is 'me' spelled backwards with a slash through (e/m). Ams is plural for 'am'. Words containing 'rac' (in any form) means me, for forming part of my nickname.

My entire novel was riddled with clues to my vile toddlerhood, and I had never realised. This code runs throughout my children's stories too, and my artwork. These science projects as well. I was distraught at this discovery. *What's happened to me?*

My Saltland Tics

This ghost language is in my body. In my cells.

My tics tell me so.

I suffer tics.

When certain words are uttered, like sat, stain, upon and under, I would flick my fingers away as though to get rid of something. I used to wipe my hands on bedding as a nightly ritual. My body knows something I don't. My imaginary childhood island, Saltland (with its own language), means sat-land. I drew a picture of this island on sugar-paper and invented words. I was nine at the time. But this island was conceived by a child who was mounted (sat) and stained in toddlerhood by an uncle. My response to under-on words tells me so.

Cubits (Og's unit of height) means buc-sit – sit-book. This book (buc) is telling me about the sit. It is telling me why I tic and the Saltland meaning. But I have a lock in my head. I mustn't know. Locks are abundant in my creations. So are lies, trauma, a split-self and oblivion.

Toddlerhood trauma has created another language, another self. I know this for my selection of topics here and how I expressed these words. This 'buc' will show.

Return to Chapter 1: Part 2: The Codes in Action

I'm back to my project on the '*Human Being*'.

Og has been explained. It means 'Go away'. The liar in my head is telling my plural to 'go away' and is guiling me into believing I'm 'all-right'. But the truth will not go away. It can't.

The Sinking

My list of giants includes a man called Myllyrinne from 'Helsinki, Finland'. I know I was sunk in the bath by Uncle Dan, and it was hell. Hell-sink-I. It's in Finland too. Within this same notebook, I have listed French verbs for homework. Fin is French for end. I thought I was going to End-land.

Sulaiman Ali Nashnush (final on the giant list) contains the code sully-I-man, or rather, man-sully-I. I was sullied by a man. Constantine (penultimate on the list) means con-sat-taint. I'm being conned about the stain I carry. The liar is conning me.

New York State, USA, (birthplace of Carroll), ends with 'seat-user,' for this is the sounding of 'usa,' user. I was mounted like a seat (State) and used. Part 10 of this chapter show tics when I write words like these.

My tics show up in how I write words.

Rogan of Tennessee contains my rapist's nickname. And Gabriel (Monjane) means liar-bag – a bag of lies about my life.

8

There's lots more like this. Section 7 at the end of this book provides a list of all the codes found here.

Distortedly Tall

I move onto the tallest women. Abuse brought a distorted perception of myself. I had intrusive thoughts of a large face being used. I felt big and ugly. Here, I would write about Pauline Marianne Wenche (1866-1883) the 'tallest woman of all time'. This troubles me, for I can find no record of this woman. But her name is strikingly similar to my rapist's full sister, my aunt. What's happened here? Where did I get that name?

Wenche's height (I had written) was 8ft 4in, but (I add) her true height was 7tt 4in.

John F Carroll (Born 1932) of buffalow new york state USA (8 feet 7¾ inches)
John william rogan (1871-1905) a negro of Galligatin Tennesse USA (8 feet six inches
Don Koehler (Born 1426) of chicargo illonois USA (8 feet 2inches
Vaino nyllyrinne (1409-1965) of helsinki finland (8 feet 1.2 inches)
Gabriel Estavao monjane (born 1944) of monjacoze mozumboine (8 feet 1 inch)
Constantine (1872-1902) of reutlingen west germuny (8feet 8 inches)
Sulaiman Ali NAShnush (born 1943) of tripoli Lybia (8feet 4 inches)

My table showing men exceeding eight feet in height.

And Anna Swan (another contender, 1846-1888) was 8ft 1in, but her true height was 7ft 5in.

I'm providing two versions of each woman – two different heights. My plurality has just expressed itself. This would happen many times.

I am two.

The Tall Woman and the Chair

I move onto the growth spurt of Dolores Ann Pullard of Dequincy, USA. When she reached 7ft 5in, she was confined to a wheelchair. Her 'sitting height' was 5ft 9.5in.

My children's story, *Horror in the Flat* (1975) is about a woman confined to a wheelchair. I wrote this story when I was ten. Thirty years later, I would write a novel, *Nadia* (2015) about a man (again) confined to a wheelchair.

What's this thing about wheelchairs? The answer is my plural was made to feel like a chair during rape. The chair symbolises my plural, for how she was made to feel. And 'I' am like the oblivious occupant. I can't see my used-self, for I am facing forward.

Chapter 17 shows how this works.

9

AGE	HEIGHT
5 months	25 inches (2ft 1inch)
13½	27 inches (2ft 3inch)
18	30½ inches (2ft 6inches)
30	35 inches (2ft 11inches)
51 (death)	40 inches (3ft 4inches)

AGE	HEIGHT
Birth	8 inches (0ft 0inches)
1	14 inches (1ft 2inches)
6	17 inches (1ft 5inches)
10	21 inches (1ft 9inches)
15	25 inches (2ft 1inch)
25	35 inches (2ft 11inches)
30	39 inches (3ft 3inches)

My tables showing the growth rate of the dwarfs, Stratton and Boruwlaski.

Dwarfs

I move onto dwarfism. In toddlerhood, I was short like a dwarf. Impressions of my toddlerhood are coming out in my choice of topics. I write: 'The shortest type of dwarf is an Ateliotic dwarf, known as a midget. In this form of dwarfism, the skeleton remains in its infantile state. Midgets seldom grow to more than 40cm.'

I have a frozen toddler within me. She can't move beyond her infantile state for the traumas. She is stuck in the past.

Connect-I-cut Stratton

I write about Charles Sherwood Stratton (alias General Tom Thumb) of Connecticut, USA. He is 'the most 'famous midget in history' (I write).

My 'Rac-name and 'sat-on' can be found in his name. The 'alias' means 'liaas' – a liar that makes me plural, hence the 'alias'. And Connecticut means 'connect-I-cut.' I have cut connections to my abused-self for what the 'user' did to me. I have scribbled off the word 'history' (see image). I have erased my history for the rape. I am now oblivious.

Another celebrated midget, Count Boruwlaski, of Poland, means I-all-scar-borrow. I am all-scarred by rape and wish to borrow another identity. I don't want to be me anymore and I would therefore adopt another history. I am 'borrowing.'

Both men grew to the height of an average toddler. Their height reflects a part of myself unable to grow further. This data seems aimed at me but isn't. It just seems that way due to the forces in my head.

I-am Rac-Rac Most-Silly

This bit elaborates upon the divide within me.

'An Italian girl, Caroline Crachami, (born in Palermosicily in 1815) was only 21in when she died in London, aged nine. At birth, she measured 7in long and weighed 11lb.'

Notice the two 'racs' in the name (*Car*-oline and *Crach*-ami). The first rac means lie/lyn'. The second one means I-am (truth).

I-am-Rac-Rac. I have two versions of myself. But the liar latches onto the 'most-silly' (Paler-mos-I-silly) in the placename. The liar is saying my plural is silly. Don't believe the messages stowed within this project.

I add, 'Her skeleton measuring 20 inches is ~~know~~ part of the Hunterian Collection, London.'

I had written 'know' instead of 'now' and scribbled off the 'k.' My 'Rac' *knows* about the rape, and the liar has scribbled off the 'k' and calls her silly. The 'know' has gone.

Heaviest

I'm now writing about the heavy. I have put (abridged): 'The heaviest human was the 6ft 0½in Robert Earl Hughes of Illinois. He reached 76 stone 5lb in February 1958,

robert Earl Hughes

AGE	WEIGHT
Birth	11¼ lb
6	14½ stone
10	27 stone
13	39 stone
18	49½ stone
25	64 stone
27	67½ stone

My table showing the weight gain of Hughes.

and his (final) weight was 74 stone 5lb. He claimed a waist of 122 inches, his chest, 124 inches, and his upper arm of 40 inches. He died of Uraemia (a condition of urinary matter on the blood) aged 32. He was buried in Binville, Illinois. His coffin, a converted piano case was 7 by 4 feet.'

I sigh at this. Clues to my toddlerhood are rife here. *How can this be happening?*

It all begins with the heavy. A big heavy thing was on me. The topics I choose within this project are informing upon sensations of my toddlerhood, and my rapist must have felt a ton.

My Plural's Roleplay

I have learned these aspects would be 'worn' by my plural as she roleplays her toddlerhood experiences. The big man in my novel would be driven by my own used feelings and therefore this man would become me. I could see myself in the big Hughes, incapacitated and suffering of Uraemia.

In my final novel, *Nadia* (2015), a woman survives a car crash. I had put (abridged): 'She found herself slumped upon her bed. Shivers skittered up her spine and her tongue hugged the roof of

13 **HEAVY WEIGHT LIST**

	STONE	lb
MILLS DARDEN (1798-1857) U.S.A. (7ft 6 inches)	72	12
JOHN HANSON CRAIG (1856-94) U.S.A. (6ft 5 inches)	64	11
AURTHER KNORR (1940-60) U.S.A. (6ft 1 inch)	64	4
T.A. VALENZUELA (1895-1957) MEXICO (5ft 11 inches)	60	10
DAVID MAGUIRE (1904-1935) U.S.A. (5ft 10 inches)	57	12
WILLIAM J COBB (1926) U.S.A. (6ft 0 inches)	57	4

My list of heavyweights.

11

her mouth. The drizzle flecked her tongue in measly portions. Her body didn't want to move but she desperately needed a pee.'

I am describing sensations of rape, not a car crash at all. Immense pressure compressed my bladder. I badly needed the toilet, and oral rape left my mouth dry. I would finally write: 'The limo had done something to her quietly.' This limo represents the trauma site (my bedroom), and the internal injuries, the force of rape.

The Burial and the Piano

The face I mustn't see in music.

Hughes was buried in 'Binville.' This is what I have done: buried and binned (the) vile. Bin-vile. Illinois means in-soil. I have been soiled inside and it was vile. A piano is buried too. Throughout the Seventies, we had a piano. I had lessons, but I couldn't get to grips with reading music. The liar doesn't want me seeing 'face' on the stave (see image). My face has been horrifically in oral rape and recall must be avoided. Clues to my toddlerhood keep leeching into my creations and the liar rather I 'bury' the lot. Bury this notebook about the *Human Being* too.

My Inner Twin and My Outer Twin

I'm writing about the heaviest twins now.

This brings me to my twin. I have an identical twin. She was born forty minutes after me, and I have called her Eve for this account. She was abused too. Not until I told her about my recall would memories of her own come up.

So, I have an inner twin and an outer twin. How confusing. This suits the liar. The liar wants me to confuse my plural for my identical twin. I will keep looking to my twin to fill an inner void. This void is my missing toddlerhood. I will keep looking in the wrong place to fill it, never to realise I have a plural. The aim is that I will never know about my toddlerhood rape.

The Heavyweight Twin within Myself

I had put: 'The heaviest twins are Bill and Ben McCeary (b 1948), of North Carolina, USA. In February 1968, weighed 40 stone and 45 stone.'

This just comes to show that I have internalised the heavy and the big. My rapist was a big father-figure, and my young-self was forming a bond with him. My plural has used aspects of his appearance and demeanour to drive characters in my stories. The heavyweight twins are called Bill and Ben. *The*

Flowerpot Men (part of the *Watch with Mother* series 1952-3) are like twins and I saw myself in both. The name Ben recurs in my stories.

These heavy twins are in fact about my plural and myself, not my identical twin at all. Notice the two 'Racs' again – am-Rac. It's in the *MaC*-ea*r*ys (of '*Ca*r-olina').

Bill and Ben, the Flowerpot Men

Due to this finding, I watched an episode of this TV programme on YouTube. I would encounter my inner toddler as I watched the two men in black and white. They are like twins. And 'weed' stands between.' For my plural, 'wee(d)' means semen. The toddler I was, didn't know different. The episode was called *Cabbages*. Here, the flowerpot men appear to roleplay the abuse as they ride on these cabbages. At the end, 'Weed' goes to sleep. I can no longer remember the thing that rode on me nor the semen. Cabbage means back-age, the past. My diaries tell me so.

PTSD has blighted my childhood. I can't watch popular entertainment without inexplicable intrusive thoughts slicing through. Unsavoury notions would well up from seemingly nowhere like this.

Heaviest Twins at Birth

I continue to dwell upon twins, moving onto the heaviest at birth. I had put: 'The heaviest twins were boys, 17lb 8oz (and) 18lb in Derbyshire on 6 December 1884. Another is Jerrald and Jeraldine, weighing 11lb each on Jan 8th.' (No year given).

Each twin weighs the equivalent of two babies. It's like each twin has another twin inside. My birthweight was 8lb 1oz (and Eve, 6lb 11oz). Since toddlerhood, I have a torn-self and she is like my inner twin.

Gerald in Geraldine, Man in Woman and He in She

I have misspelled Gerald and Geraldine. I had begun each name with 'Je'. My plural did this. Je is French for 'I' and I have two 'I's. My notebook contains a list of French verbs. French has entered this Saltland language.

The man's name (Gerald) exists within Gerald-ine. The '*aldine*' contains lie-lied-l'in' (lying).

The word 'man' can be found in 'wo-*man*' too. The principle is the same for 'he'. Notice s-*he* and *he*-r in female pronouns. The male characters of my novels bear female rape scars. All my characters are womb-men: men with wombs who have been raped. And all are (je) me.

What a bizarre thing.

And now for triplets. These are heavy too.

13

Heaviest Triplets (Britain)

'The heaviest triplets in the UK (I write) were born on 8 February 1965. They weighed an aggregate of 21lb 13oz to Maureen Head of Denbighshire (HM Stanley Hospital, St Asaph).'

What am I doing writing about heavy triplets now?

Being plural brings a hall of mirrors effect. I have an identical twin. I also have an inner twin. There are three of us. I used to imagine having an 'extra twin' to fall back on, if Eve and I fell out. I notice my 'Denbigshire.' Isn't this supposed to be Denbighshire? The 'big' has muscled-in. Something big lived in my toddlerhood. A code has just exposed itself within my spelling.

These triplets share my birthyear. And the HM Stanley (hospital), means lye-stain – lie about the stain on my phaas (face), for this is the meaning of St Asaph. Oral rape made me feel dirty.

I move into quadruplets.

Heaviest Quadruplets

'The heaviest quadruplets' (I write) weighed an aggregate of 19lb 13oz. (They were) born by caesarean section to Ruth Becker on 3 August 1962 at the Vancouver General Hospital, Canada.'

For almost fifty years, I mistook my plural for my identical twin. This makes us three. As I see my plural in Eve too, she would naturally have her own plural. This comes to four.

I notice the 'Lynn' (lyin') in Lynn, and 'truth' in 'to-Ruth'. My foray into multiple births ends with Siamese Twins. For reasons that will become clear, I have placed Siamese twins in the following part, 'Scar in my Chest.'

The Lightest and the Slim

And now for the other extreme – the lightest. I would begin: 'The lightest adult was Lucia Zarate (of San Carlos, 1863-1889), an emaciated Mexican midget of 26½in, who weighed 2 1/8 kilograms at 17. She fattened to 13lb on her 20th birthday. Her birthweight was 2½lb.'

'The thinnest adult (I add) is the American exhibitionist Rosa Lee Plemons (b 1873) weighing 27lb at eighteen.' (And) 'Edward C Hagner (1892-1962) alias Eddie Masher is alleged to have weighed 3stone 6lb at 5 feet 7in. He was known as the Skeleton Dude.'

And finally:

'In 1825 the biceps of Claude Ambroise Seurant (1797-1826 of Troyes, France) was 4in. And the distance between his back and chest was less than 3in. He stood 5 feet 7½in at 5 stone 8lb. But in another account was 5 feet 4 inches at 2 stone 8lb.'

14

Allaying the Belly

So.

What explains this lot?

I had a potbelly in toddlerhood. I have photos that show. This belly would flatten go as I grew up. But part of me remembers the potbelly. My plural hates it. She hates anything that reminds her of being used, and this is what the potbelly has come to represent: being used.

In early adolescence, Eve became anorexic. For a time, I joined her in diets, but after a while, didn't bother. I was skinny anyway but would soon develop dysmorphia. I disliked being bloated and hated my post-caesarean belly. I have reason to know the liar in my head wanted me to become anorexic. Part 5 of this chapter explains.

In my 1978 diary, I kept a record of my school lessons. Biology is first mentioned on 22 May when I get a 'new book'. In June, we learn about 'hygiene and got a slim and trim leaflet.' We touch upon 'digestion.'

Remaining Slim and Trim

After studying my diaries, I have learned the liar plugs only the topics it wants me to observe, in this case, 'hygiene and the slim and trim leaflets.' I must become 'skinny' and 'clean' to eradicate the used-potbelly feeling of my toddlerhood. If I become thin, I can escape it.

This brings me to food abstinence.

Hunger Strike

I write: 'The longest reported hunger strike was 94 days (11 august to 12 Nov 1920) by John and Peter Crowley (and eight others) in Cork Prison, Ireland. (Joseph Murphey died on the 7th day). These nine survivors owed their lives to medical attention.'

Programmed to Suffer Anorexia

I am saddened at this. In the Eighties, Eve took strict diets and ended up losing her periods. She fell to 6 stone at 5ft 4in. It seems she was fleeing her toddlerhood. I am appalled such a code can bury itself in the subconscious and cause the sufferer such pain. From this, it seems the liar deems oblivion overrules health. Running away from toddlerhood is the goal.

This research aims to highlight these codes, some of which are harmful to the carrier. In my case, lies about my toddlerhood rape.

Part 3: Scar in my Chest

I have a scar in my chest. My rapist mounted my chest and deprived my lungs of air. My drawing shows a scar on my chest. My plural has used the cases of Siamese twins to show we are joined to this trauma site. This scar would re-emerge in my *Astronomy* project (chapter 15).

My drawing of the human form with a scarred chest. Inset shows my drawing of Uranus in my Space *project of 1974.*

'Conjoined twins (I begin) derived the name 'Siamese' from the celebrated Chancy and Eng Bunker (b 11 May 1811) of Maklong, Thailand (Siam). They were joined at the chest by a cartilaginous band. They married and fathered ten and twelve children respectively. They died within three hours of each other in 1874, aged 62.'

I add.

'There was no evidence for the existence of the publicized Chalkhurst twins, Mary and Aliza of Biddenden, Kent, (b 1550).'

I-Am-mes of Siamese

Siamese means I-am-mes. I have two mes. We are conjoined and this has been conveyed through the word Siamese. It's via an 'us-Rac-tailing' (car-*tilagin*-us) band that we are joined. My plural is telling on the rape through this project, but she is 'banned' from getting the message through.

My plural spotted a parallel between myself and the Bunker twins. She has used this story to tell on my own conjoining and the scar in my chest. It was in *my* chest that I saw a man. It happened one day when Eve and I were four. She cut her face on glass and returned from hospital unconscious. Her inert state triggered a memory of my own inertia after rape. Eve looked like me and I saw myself in her. I then saw my rapist's face in my chest.

This experience is known as a somatic memory. My chest had 'recalled' Uncle Dan yet 'I' hadn't. My rapist sat on my chest before smothering me with his crotch. I remember him doing it and I remember blacking out.

. My *Space* project (chapter 6) explores the planets. Here I had drawn Uranus with what appears to be an 'm' ('me') fastened to a cord. (See inset image). This is like the cartilaginous band. My plural and I are like Siamese twins. We are conjoined. We are two 'mes'.

The Man-Child

So, I had penned over my drawing of a man's chest. This 'man' appears to be tottering. Only now am I beginning to realise this man is a toddler. The 'human being' is me, not a generic man at all. The scarred chest shows. My drawing shows a toddler with a scar of suffocation in her chest. She has become plural due to toddlerhood rape.

The Vanishing

But one set of Siamese twins (the Chalkhursts) have no 'evidence' of existing at all (I had written). The liar doesn't want me to see that I am conjoined or have another me. She only wants me to see Eve. She is the only twin I have, and we are not conjoined. My oblivion hurts my plural, hence 'hursts' (in Chalk-hursts). It hurts that I am plural, and I don't know my inner-twin exists.

Multiple Digits

A few pages on, I report on the person with 'the most fingers.' I had put, 'Voight records someone with 13 fingers on each hand and 12 toes on each foot.' These surplus digits suggest two people in one again. This is like me with a hidden Siamese twin. I have another version of myself, and we are conjoined.

My plural is using *The Guinness Book of Records* to tell on my vile toddlerhood. She would do the same thing with other books that I select for future projects.

Part 4: Motherhood

My topic takes another turn: motherhood. Here, I would write: 'The mother with the most children is 69, by the first wife of Fyodor Vassilet (1816-72) of Moscow, Russia, who in 27 confinements birthed 16 twins, 7 triplets and 4 quadruples.

'So renowned was Mme Vassilet (I continue), she was presented at the Court of Tsar Alexander II.'

Being Barren

My plural feared I was barren. My *Earth* project (chapter 6) says so. In a section on *What the Earth is Made of*, I had written about the oceans. I had put, 'The big seas (meaning oceans) are the Pacific, Atlantic and AraBian (Sea).'

I was nine when I wrote this, and the codes are glaring. But why would I include the Arabian Sea with two oceans? My odd AraBian is the giveaway. It means I-barren. (Read backwards from the 'I': 'I-Bara-an'). My plural feared toddlerhood-rape had taken my fertility. The liar would commandeer this fear with the insistence I remain childless in case labour triggered a memory. Indeed, I had children late and failed to go into labour.

A Wish to Go to Court of the Sat

I note this 'mother' was so 'renowned,' she was presented at the 'Court of the Tsar.' This is what my plural wanted, to take my rapist to the court of 'sat'. (*Tsaa* means sat.) She wanted to testify about the day I was mounted and raped. I wish I had done so, but the liar stood in the way.

I wonder on this next bit: the growth of keratin. Why have I written about this?

Part 5: Keratin Growths

I would begin with nails. 'The longest recorded fingernails (I write) were from Shanghai in 1910 in the case of a Chinese priest who took 27 years to grow nails up to 22¾ inches.'

I follow this with: 'The longest hair was Swami Pandara Sännadhi, the head of the Thiruvadbl Thurai Monastery in Incha (India). His hair (in 1949) reached 26ft.'

And finally:

'Hans N Langseth (1846) in Norway has a beard of 17½ft.'

Why all these growths?

All means lies. The lie in me is growing long. Day by day, it's getting longer and longer.

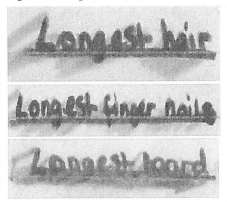

Long hair, nails and beards.

The Liar in Nails

Let's start with the nails. I have come across the 'nails' before. It's in a schoolbook called *Science* (see chapter 3). We explored living and non-living things. For a questionnaire, I had chosen 'snail,' (anagram of 'nails'). Both snail and nails contain 'liar' (lia). It's buried in the word. The 'n' brings lyin.' The lie is growing long. This priest took twenty-seven years to grow his 'nails'. The lie within me has now grown another thirty-five years.

In the early Eighties, Eve got into false fingernails. They were long too. She shoplifted some in September 1980. It's in my diary. Did she do so driven by this liar code? I wasn't immune to the nails, for at the same time, I was toymaking snails. Yes, snails. This means liar too and it seems I was doing the same thing as Eve: living a lie. Chapter 15 looks at my toymaking.

The Liar in Long Hair and Short

The word 'liar' exists in 'long-hair' too. It begins with the 'h-*air*' and rotates back to the '*l*' of 'long.' Switch the words to see it clearly. 'H*air*-

long.' Notice the liar stowed within h-*airl*-ong. Chapter 5 *Lines*, shows the hair-liar-code in an illustration.

In my diaries, I often reported on what I did with my hair. On 14 Apr 1979, I had written 'washed *chair*' (instead of washed hair). My plural did this. She is showing up the codes again. I was made to feel like a chair whilst being mounted and used, and the liar is trying to wash the 'chair' away. My wheelchair stories come to mind.

But the liar creates paradoxes. Short hair means lies too. It contains 'tear' (*t-hair*-s-hort). Being torn means living a lie, just like the long-hair. Long hair and short means the same thing.

Going the Nor-Way

The beard-man symbolises the liar too. He comes from Norway. This means going along with my rapist. I know this for the letters 'Nor'.

'Nor' forms part of my rapist's real name and 'torn' (what he did to me). As explained earlier, I have changed my rapist's name to protect my identity. I have called him Uncle Dan. But part of his real name keeps popping up in proper nouns of my creations. *What can I do about this?* Sometimes, these letters latch onto *c* or *l* (for forming 'uncle'). In writing this account I have little choice but to reveal this Nor-code, for its incidence in these projects.

The Nor-Code

So, Nor means my rapist. These letters appear in many names: Norman, Norbert, Ronan, Norris, Aaron, Conor, Ronald, Roman and more. The Nor appears in nicknames, first, middle or surname. With this in mind, I can reveal this about my rapist. Nor forms part of his name, like Rac forms part of mine.

My plural saw Nor in Norway. She would see Nor in many other proper nouns.

The Liar in Beard

Norway means going the Nor-way, in with my rapist. What an odd turn. My plural has used a country to tell me a liar in my head is letting my rapist get away with it. Norway is a Trojan Horse carrying another meaning, just like this entire project.

The beard is the same: It carries another meaning. Beard is hair and means long-liar again. It symbolises going the Nor-way. It's getting longer, just like the nails. The liar is getting longer with every day.

The Bold of the Bald

Characters with bald and shaved heads speckle my stories. How odd. Bald is a homonym of bold, meaning brave. Shaving the head appears to symbolise *not* going the Nor-way. Of course, this is rubbish. Truth can be observed, regardless of hairstyle. But the liar finds meanings in words of

19

which I am unaware. The liar twists what I do to imply a consent. This consent will be explained in chapter 3. Chapters 11 and 20 returns to the beard in 'whiskers'.

Anorexia and Dyslexia

The snail-nails and the Norway makes me think of Eve's anorexia. This word contains 'Nor' (like Norway). What follows is 'ex-I-her'. This means I-ex-her – a self-divorce. What an odd thing. Anorexia carries a code, and it seems to be fuelling Eve's condition. It means a self-separation due to rape.

But why didn't I get anorexia? The answer is, in a sense I *had*. At the same time, I got obsessed with 'dyslexia'. Aidan (the main character of my novel) contains the Nor, just like my rapist, and suffers this condition. I spent hours reading about 'word-blindness'. In fact, I'm the afflicted one. I can't read these codes, and my Aidan-character is a reflection of myself.

A-nor-exia.

A-nor-~~dysl~~-exia.

Notice anorexia in both words. Both mean a self-divorce. But one contains 'dys' (dies). Suffocation had almost made me die, and I have divorced myself from it. Eve and I appear to be driven by the same code within different words. We are divorcing a part of ourselves due to the Nor of our toddlerhood.

la OLDEST Lived in	Years	Days	Name	Born	Died
Canada	113	124	Pierre Joubert	15 July 1701	16 Nov 1814
United States	112	305	John B Salling	15 May 1846	16 Nov 1959
United Kingdom	111	339	Ada Rowe (Giddings)	6 Feb 1858	11 Jan 1970
Ireland	111	327	Theban Katherine Plunket	22 Nov 1820	14 Oct 1932
South Africa	111	151	Johanna Booyson	17 Jan 1857	16 Jun 1968
Czechoslovakia	111	+	Marie Bernatkova	22 Oct 1857	1968
Channel Islands	110	321	M. Ruth Horlick	15 May 1792	April 1903
Yugoslavia	110	160	D. Philipovitch	March 1818	Aug 1928
Japan	110	114	Y. Itto	Aug 1856	Nov 1966
Netherlands	110	5	B. Kornebek	Oct 1849	Oct 1959
France	109	309	M.A. Flossayer	Jun 1844	April 1954
Italy	109	179	R. Soato	Aug 1847	Feb 1957

Lived in	Years	Days	Name	Born	Died
Australia	109	37	James hall	Aug 1933	Sep
Scotland	109	14	R MacArthur	1952	1961
Norway	109	+	M Oslen	May 1850	Aug
F	1				1959
Tasmania	109	+	M.A Crow	Feb 1653	1945
Germany	108	128	125 Schwalke	Sept 1824	Feb 1858
Portugal	108	+	M.L. Jorge	Jun 1859	Jul 1967
Scotland	107	108	J. Speer	Nov 1842	Nov 1948
Finland	107	+	M Anderson	Jun 1825	1936
Belgium	106	267	M.F. Purnode	Apr 1843	Dec 1949
Austria	106	231	A. Nigschlitz	Feb 1850	Nov 1956
Sweden	106	96	E. Gustaffson	Jun 1858	Sep 1964
Isle of man	105	221	J Linnen	Nov 1942	Jun 1953
Spain	105	217	M.C Cdenes	Feb 1845	Nov 1950

My list of the oldest people on record.

The Oldest People

The previous image shows my table of twenty-five centenarians. This links into the *long* – a long life of lies and oblivion (as symbolised by the nails and hair).

My plural has succeeded (again) in getting me to copy all this data. Section 7 at the end of this book unearths the codes I have found here.

My plural is showing up what the liar in my head is doing. My creations form an imprint to the forces in my head.

Freeing Myself of the Codes

I was horrified at all these codes.

What has my brain done?

But my initial horror would lead to a clearer view. Little by little, I would unearth these codes. Whilst doing so, I would continue to wear my hair how I want and eat what I want. Every code unearthed means a step closer to setting myself free of a gilded cage due to toddlerhood rape. I can free myself of the liar.

This next bit would shake me to the core. Never would I see it.

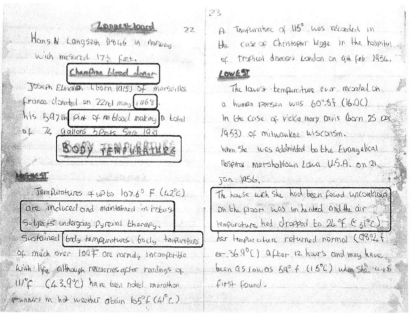

Pages with clues to rape.

Part 6: Bloodied Pages

The image shows the pages that shook me.

The margins appear stained. It looks like blood. My *Guinness* book may have had a blood-graphic, and I was simply copying it in felt-tip. The stippled effect would indicate so. A blood-theme exists here, hence the blood-stained emulation.

I shall begin thus.

Champion Blood Donor

'Joseph Elmalen (b 1915) of Marseilles, France donated his 597th blood on 22 May 1968, totalling 74 gallons, 5 pints since 1931.'

I had written 'm̶ blood,' (scrubbing off the 'm'). The letter 'm' is sounded 'em,' (me backwards). This means me-blood. My plural is trying to tell me it is *my* blood that has been lost, but the liar has scrubbed off the 'me'. A me is missing.

The year of the bleeding was 1968 too, as written on this page. This was the year I was raped.

The donator, Joseph Elmalen contains a me split. Elm means e/m and mal means a/m. Mes and ams have been expressed here. A vowel has been slashed through. This symbolises the slash within me. I am torn. Elmalen's birthplace, Marseilles 'says' my 'ams' is due to the 'rams', for this is what Uncle Dan did, ram into me. My diaries and *Space* project tell me the same thing. Marseilles is sounded *Mars-say*. This means' rams-say'. My plural is saying 'rams' through this word.

On the same page, I write about body temperatures. I would begin with the 'highest.'

The Highest Body Temperature

'Temperatures up to 107.6°F (42°C) (I write), are induced in subjects undergoing pyrexial therapy. Sustained *body temperatures body temperatures* of over 109°F are normally incompatible with life, although recoveries after readings of 111°F (43.9°C) have been noted. Marathon runners in hot weather attain 105°F (41°C).'

I had written 'body temperatures' twice. My plurality has come out again. What follows is the 'pyrexial therapy.' Therapy means the-rape-I. I was raped and it burnt, hence the high body temperature. Pyrexial means I-all-ex-pyre. Pyre means fire and I have exed all memories of the burning. This page is telling me I was raped, bled and it burnt in 1968. I have since become plural.

The Lowest Body Temperatures

And now for the lowest temperature. I would write: 'The lowest temperature recorded was 60.8°F (16.0°C) in Vickie Mary Davis (b 25 Dec 1953) of Milwankee, Wisconsin, when she was admitted to the Evangelical Hospital, Marshaltown, Iowa, USA on 21 Jan 1956.

'The house in which she had been found unconscious on the floor, was unheated and the temperature had dropped to 24°F (31°C). Her temperature returned (to) normal after twelve hours and may have been as low as 59°F (15°C) when she was found.'

The Town of All Sham

I notice the 60-8 (°F) of Davis' body temperature. This means '68, the year I was raped again. My 'Milwaukee' looks like Milwankee. Did I know the word 'wank' at fourteen? My research has shown the brain knows more than it lets on.

I was raped in the guestroom of the cottage before fainting down the stairs. I remember fainting. My rapist slept in that room. Davis was found on the floor. I ended up unconscious on the floor too. She ended up in the 'Evangelical' (Hospital). This symbolises 'going to heaven.' During rape, I thought I was going to die. Instead, I survived and lived in Marshal-town. A town of ams, rams and-all-sham.

Omission of Minus in Temperature

I seemed to have omitted the minus sign of the air temperature. I had written it had *dropped* to 24°F (31°C). This doesn't sound cold at all. Only when inserting the minus sign, does it make sense. -24°F equals -31°C. The temperature had *dropped* to -24°F (-31°C). This is what I had meant.

My plural has omitted the minus sign to flag me.

I was cold in the bath. Uncle Dan dunked me in cold water. I know this for my creations, flashbacks and these projects. The bathroom is located at the foot of the guestroom stairs too and I ended up cold on the floor.

The Pages of Truth

My plural is making a testimony through these pages.

But the liar heads this page (see former image). He is the beard-man of Norway. Remember him? This means going the Nor-way (my rapist) and the long-hair of the liar. I had imagined this man to be big. The liar wants me to. He is big and at the top of this page. The rape is beneath.

Part 7: The Neck

What would I find next? A load of 'neck-stuff.' I'm writing about necks now.

I would begin with hiccoughing. This is what I would write.

Hiccoughing

'The longest record of (an) attack of hiccoughs was Jack O'Leary of Los Angeles. He hicked more than 160,000,000 times which lasted eight years. His weight fell from *a stone*, 12lb to 5 stone 4lb. People sent 60,000 suggestions for cures.

'One worked: a *prayed* to St Jude, the Patron Saint of Lost Causes.'

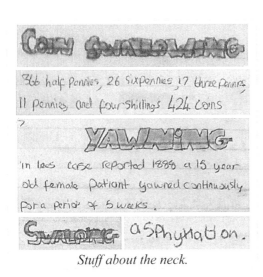

COIN SWALLOWING

366 half Pennies, 26 Sixpennies, 17 three pennies, 11 pennies and four Shillings 424 coins

?

YAWNING

in less case reported 1888 a 15 year old female patient yawned continuously for a period of 5 weeks.

SWALDING   asphyxiation.

Stuff about the neck.

The Neck's-us of Nexus

My final novel, *Nadia* (2015) contains a nightclub called the Nexus. My plural has chosen this name. I am joined to my other self by the neck, for this is where trauma occurred. Nexus means neck's-us, for Uncle Dan orally raped and suffocated me. I would have coughed afterwards, and it would have felt like forever.

Notice the name, Jack O'Leary. His name contains 'oh-really.' This is the liar's scepticism. My plural isn't being believed.

The Not of Stone

I have italicised O'Leary's weight loss. It had fallen from '*a stone*'. My plural has omitted the number of stones like she had the minus sign earlier. She uses aberrations like these to draw my attention.

Stone means not-knows. Notice the central 'not.' This means denial. The 'stone' is further explained in my *Science* project (chapter 3). But the 'oh-really' has fallen from a place of denial, the 'not' of stone. I don't know anything.

The Raped within Prayed

A cure came in the form of a 'prayed' (I had written). I have made another error here, using the verb-form rather than the noun. This is my plural's doing too. My plural sees raped in prayed. What an unfortunate thing. But again, my plural has signposted me.

Patron means Pa-torn. I have been torn by a Pa-figure. I have become a 'lost cause' as a result. Whilst oblivious to the 'stain' (anagram of saint), no one can help me. After almost six years of research, I am coming to learn the complexity of these codes. It's staggering.

Longest Necks

My neck theme continues with the following,

'The successive fitting of brass rings as practised by the Padating people of Burma brought a neck length of 15¾in. (Normal neck length is 3 to 5in). It serves the purpose of enhancing the female's beauty and ensures fidelity.

The neck muscles become so atrophied, the removal of the rings produces asphyxiation.

The Suffocation

I'm astonished at the 'Padating People.' Does this word exist? I checked it out and found I had meant *Padaung*. But this isn't an error. My plural saw Pa-dating in this word and urged me to write it.

Another aberration.

So, I was 'dating a Pa.' This is how my plural sees the liar in my head as doing: complicit with my rapist. Burma looks like Burnna, for the 'm'. 'Burn-her.' I have been burnt during the 'Pa-date'. What an odd way of putting it. My plural has managed to get me to write 'suffocation' too. This father-figure suffocated me.

The stretching of the neck wasn't from the outside (as with the rings), but from within via the penis. Something big was pushed inside and my throat muscles expanded. The inside of my neck felt stretched. I was like one of the 'Pa-dating people.'

The Never-ending Swallowing

The next topic despairs me: swallowing. How could I not see these messages? I would begin: 'The worst known case of compulsive swallowing was reported in the Journal of the *American Medical Association* in December 1969.'

(I continue, misspellings preserved): 'The patiant who complained of swollen anckles, was found to have 258 items in his stomach, including 3lb pieces of metal, 26 keys, 3 rosary beeds, 16 religious medals, a bracelet, a necklace, 3 tweezers, 4 nail clippers, 39 nail files, 3 metal chains and 88 assorted coins.'

The Force and the Sore

That's quite a list! My plural did this. She keeps urging me to write things. The swallowing was forced. It kept going on and on.

The reporting is in 'this' journal, meaning this green notebook. I am writing about it now. The acronym of the 'American' journal, is AMA, a mirror-image *am*. I have two ams and one of them has a load of 'keys' to the rose-ary-beeds – the times I was made sore-bed by Uncle Dan.

The objects are telling. I note the 'metel.' This mean me-tell. But a load of 'nails' gets in the way. This means liars-lyin.' Each is clipping off and filing away the bed-sore.

The swollen 'anckles' is trying to be 'uncle's and it is 'swollen.' Patiant means Pa-taint. See the codes flowing out of how I select and write words?

Coin Swallowing

I conclude the swallowing with 'coins.'

'The worst case of coin-swallowing (I write) was by Sedgefield General Hospital, County Durham on 5th Jan 1958. It was 366 half-pennies, 26 six-pennies, 17 three-pennies, 11 pennies and four shillings. 424 coins valued at (£1.175.5d), plus 27 pieces of wire. A total of 5lb.1oz was extracted from the stomach of a 54-year-old man.'

Endless Pennies

Another endless list, I see. And this time includes a load of 'pennies.' This means penis. Repeatedly, my plural is telling me I swallowed a penis. The contents entered my stomach. The half-penis means half-oblivion. Part of me can't see the penis. Three-pennies mean I was three when it happened. Six pennies mean sex-penis. A penis entered me. But shillings mean she-lying. The 'wire-totalling' means writing-all (and wrote). I am writing about the rape through this project, but the 'shilling' brands, my plural a liar. The following chapter looks at my collation of Mum's coins, which links to this.

My neck-foray ends with yawning.

Yawning Forced

'In a case reported in 1888, a fifteen-year-old female patiant yawned for a period of 5 weeks.'

This one requires little explanation. A female is 'Pa-tained'. A father-figure forced my mouth open, and the yawning felt endless.

Stuff to do with recall.

Part 8: The Awakening

One day, I would recall. These final elements are about the awakening.

Recall occurred on 10.30pm 23 October 2016. I was fifty-one years old and analysing *Nadia*, my final novel. A series of events had led to this moment, and a scene triggered a memory. The memory came up and I saw Uncle Dan suffocating me on my bed. Until that moment, I had assumed I was a childhood virgin and had never suffered sex abuse at all.

This next bit is about the awakening. I would awaken to my toddlerhood abuse, and this means not asleep to the truth anymore. This is what I would write.

Human Memory

'Mehined Ali Halici of Ankara, Turkey (on 14 Oct 1967) recited 6,66 verses of the Koran in six hours. The recitation was followed by six Koran scholars.'

My rapist's Nor is in the word 'Koran.' The letters *n-k-a* brings the uncle-sounding. My plural keeps seeing his nickname in proper nouns and urges me to write them. But the memory-man refutes all. Notice the me-deny (in Mehined), and the 'lia' (in Ali). Six means 'is-x' (is-ex, as in divorced), which rotates back to 's-ex'. I am 'ex' due to the 'sex.'

Sleeplessness

Stopping awake comes next.

'Toimi Arthurinpoika, a 54-year-old of Finland, stayed awake for 32 days, 32 hours from 1st March to 2 April 1967. He walked 17 miles per day and lost 33lb.

'Eustace Rushworth Burnett (1880-1965) of Hose, Leistershire lost all desire to sleep in 1907, so he never slept in a bed again.'

Poker in Author

I note the insomniac's name, Toimi. I think of the dwarf, General Tom Thumb (alias Charles Sherwood Stratton). This dwarf contains the Rac and sat-on. He is small like I once was. I-Tom (Thumb) means me in toddlerhood. I was small like Tom.

His surname begins 'Arthur.' This means author, for I wanted to be one, and I sometimes confused the spellings (as seen in Section 3). Notice the 'poker-in-author' running backwards within Toimi's surname. I-Tom (thumb) poker-in-author. This is me being raped in toddlerhood.

Used Face in Eustace

The second subject, Eustace means used-face. (Topple the 't' to 'f' to bring Eus-face). My face was used in oral rape. No wonder 'Eustace' lost all desire to sleep in a bed. I have misspelled Leicestershire. This shire means lessed-her. I am less, for losing part of myself.

My third novel, *North Window* is about an insomniac. He in fact suffers PTSD. My plural knows this for she drove the character. But the 'author' believed the insomniac, a mere corporate with a shady past.

This data is brimming with codes. Section 7 lists them.

Part 9: Drowned

This project ends with underwater. I begin with 'heart stoppage.' This means stop-age. Stop any memory of my toddlerhood age from entering my conscious awareness. The liar does a lot of 'stopping.'

This is what I had put.

Heart Stoppage

'The longest recorded heart stoppage ~~was~~ is 3 hours in a Norwegian boy, Roger Arntzen in April 1962. He was rescued drowned after 22 minutes under the waters of the River Nideelv near Trondheim.'

I had scrubbed the '~~was~~' and substituted 'is.' I almost became a 'was' (for the Nor). But remain an 'is.' I don't know if my heart stopped or not, but my plural would learn about the heart years after the drowning. She would discover the heart beats when you are alive and stops when you are dead. It can stutter due to cold water or choking. I was drowned and suffocated. But I cannot be sure if my heart stopped or not.

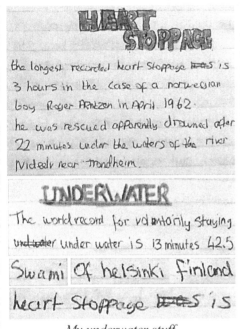

My underwater stuff.

The image shows what I had put about underwater. I notice other references to drowning, like the name 'Swami' which means I-swam (the lie). And Helsinki, hell-sink-I (the truth).

Underwater

My foray into human feats ends with breath-holding underwater. I had put: 'The record for staying ~~underwater~~ underwater is 13 minutes 42.5 seconds by Robert Foster 32, of Richmond, California. He remained 10 feet down in the swimming pool of the Bemuda Palms Motel, San Rafeal, USA (15 March 1959). He hyperventilated with oxegin for 30 minutes before his *descendant*. His longest breath hold without ogedgin was 5 mins 40 secs.'

The Pool

We had a pool in the back garden. Uncle Dan raped me there. My flashbacks of a girl being raped by rockpools tells me so. My children's story (*The Secret of the Shadows*, written 1979) includes a torn swimming costume and a creepy uncle. I have written 'underwater' twice. I have also written 'descendant' instead of 'descent.' My inner-child (descendant) had a 'descent' into water.

After overcoming my terror of water at nine, I couldn't get enough of the baths. My plural worked out it wasn't water I should fear, but Uncle Dan. Even so, the baths evoked seedy feelings within me and spurred odd behaviour.

Oxygen Deprivation during Smothering

My oxygen-spelling is weird. What's got into me?

I had spelled it 'oxegin', and then 'ogedgin'.

The same thing has happened in my *Lines* project four years previously (chapter 5), these odd oxygen-spellings. Combined, the meaning is ex-dogging. On seeing dogs pee and mate in parks, my plural would see her face there. I was sullied and oxygen-deprived by a crotch. The liar in me would then 'ex' it.

My oxygen-deprivation is due to Uncle Dan.

Part 10: Plural Writing

This final part of this chapter looks at further expressions for my plurality. All show what I carry.

Shadow Writing

This initial image shows my shadow-writing. I've come across it before: in my *Science* project (chapter 3). I kept rubbing out sentences and rewriting. Here, I have adopted shadowy titles. I

My shadow-writing in various forms.

keep using blue, yellow and red. These colours carry potent meanings, which can be seen in my school project on *Colours* (chapter 4). The way I write these words would also betray of these meanings.

The leeching of my felt-tip onto the reverse of pages has been used by my plural to tell me I am two. We are like a mirror image, one of which is in shadow.

Split Characters

This second image shows incidences of slashed characters in my writing. These

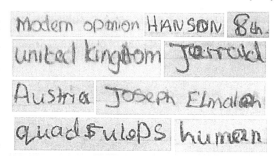

happen in my other writings too, including my diaries. This slashing most often happens to rounded letters like vowels. Notice the 'o' and the 'a' slashed through. The slashing occurs in 'human,' I note. This means me, the '*Human Being*' of this project. Elmaleh, in itself, means e/m. I have been slashed.

Sat-tics in my writing.

I note the United Kingdom. It looks like Kingtom. I am reminded of Tom-thumb, alias of the dwarf, Stratton. Once, I saw myself as small, and only then, was I 'united.' I was once united-king-tom. I am now untied. Plural.

Tics of My Plural

This third image shows tics in my writing. I have a physical tic too. When certain words are uttered, I tic, for an unrealised unsavoury under-meaning.

Notice the 'United Statettes'. This means sat-seat. Mon*sast*ery is trying to spell out 'sat' in the middle. Notice further aberrations with heaviest, waist, lives and lightest.

Words with 'st' bring about an occasional tic. For my plural, the 'tion' suffix means shun. I am shunning the 'sat'.

Pa, Uncle and Taints

The final image shows further expressions for carrying a rape scar. I keep spelling patient, patiant. This means Pa-taint. I was tainted by a pa-figure. The Patron saint of Lost Causes reiterates. I have been

Other tics in my writing.

stained by a pa-figure and the liar deems this part of me, a lost cause. The pa-figure was an uncle (anckle) who raped (prayed) me.

My odd 'maintained' (maintatined) means man-tainted. This tainting was done by a big and long man. My 'length; has been written over. My plurality has come out again. And my 'me-use-um' (see image) means me-use-me. I have been used and become two.

This concludes my analysis of this project on *The Human Being* (me).

Interlude 2: The Background

My *Human Being* project is telling me about my toddlerhood. I was raped, suffocated and drowned by a big man. He was Mum's half-brother.

An interlude has been placed here to explain my situation whilst working on these projects.

Throughout this time, I was living in a run-down cottage with my parents and four siblings, including my twin. I have five siblings in all. The place was noisy and there was always something going on.

The Cottage

My childhood cottage was one of the oldest in the village. Dad purchased it in 1956. It was a two-up two-down affair overlooking a pond with a clear view of the church across the field. Dad spent some months doing the place up. He built a side extension with a guestroom and its own stairs. In the Sixties, a building estate sprouted up, concealing the views. But the place remained idyllic. The garden had several apple trees, swings, lawn and a playhouse. I loved that garden, but the cottage was cramped and winters cold. We would soon descend into poverty when Dad quit nightwork and become mentally ill. He would take the guestroom for himself and never worked again.

My parents' marriage would then turn sour.

The Red Herrings

Throughout my life, I have suffered vile imagery. They were so abhorrent, I simply didn't believe in them. Things like a face relentlessly being used or set on fire, objects stuffed down throats and coma. I had gone to the doctor's a few times in the belief I had inherited something from Dad. Since I was four, he suffered rages and hallucinations for being on medication. I felt horrid for Mum. She was trapped in a terrible marriage and sometimes expressed a wish to end it all.

Seeking Diversions

So, I journeyed into life under the belief my fears borne from this. Nothing but this. I've had a difficult childhood. *So what?* Don't lots of people? And so, I took up diversions as a coping strategy. My diaries say it all, with testaments of writing, painting and doing these science projects. I produced huge oil paintings, as I went to art school for five years and got a degree.

The Memory

But learning of my horrific toddlerhood has changed everything. Recall came when I was fifty-one. I've never experienced anything like it. Suddenly, I saw Uncle Dan on my bed. He was about to eclipse my bedroom window and suffocate me. A complex series of events had led to this moment. When the memory came, I simply lay down.

So those horrible notions were from something real, all real. I couldn't bear the thought. I wondered how I was going to live. How am I going to *exist*? I have lived almost fifty years carrying something monstrous in my subconscious and I didn't know. What else has Uncle Dan done to me? How many times had he done that?

Wallpaper Memories

Other memories came up.

They advanced from wallpaper. By this I meant they were always there, but the trauma aspect had been torn off. These 'flicker' memories fell into the background for evoking no feelings whatsoever. They slipped from notice.

He was in the bathroom with Eve and me. He is taking Eve and me out in the pushchair. He is standing over me in the kitchen, my bedroom. For weeks, everything went loud, and I wanted everyone to go away. I had to somehow...*live*. I had to be *here* while these realisations slowly dawned.

I never got to tell Mum what her half-brother had done, for she was at this time terminally ill. My life falls apart and she dies soon afterwards. I have forged an identity based on lies and everyone else has believed it as much as I. I make a statement to the police. The case is archived, as Uncle Dan has been dead sixteen years by then.

I went into a silent and slow mental breakdown. It has been waiting for me my entire life.

The Situation in 1968

Uncle Dan, Mum's half-brother, lived in our cottage for most of 1968. His mother, my Nan stopped concurrent. He took the guestroom before Dad did. For some reason, this 'small' detail kept evading me. I truly believed no one else had lived in our cottage but for my parents, siblings and occasionally Nan. Mentions of his stay were few and I kept gleaning over it. Uncle Dan was forty-seven at the time and would have little interest in a toddler. Surely.

I have come to learn he was on the dole the entire time he lived with us. He had deserted his family after quitting the Metropolitan Police of twelve years and galivanted around. I thought he was a distant, aloof and vain uncle. That was all.

For most of my life, Uncle Dan was the furthest thing from my mind. I met him only five times in adulthood and his mentions are always about his faraway ventures. I took for granted my childhood virginity and even considered myself unduly innocent when it came to boyfriends. I have come to learn I was repeatedly raped whilst he lived in that cottage.

Chapter 2: The Pennies
Introduction
Part 1: The Silver and Copper
Part 2: 1968 Missing

Introduction
The situation of my toddlerhood has been explained. The drive behind my projects have been revealed.

This chapter has been put here for the coin-swallowing in my *Human Being project*.

Coin record and rubbings I did for Mum on 16 March 1980.

On 16 March 1980, I wrote in my diary, 'sorted Mum's coins all day and noted them down.' On the same day, I gave Mum her Mother's Day card. I had made it the day before.

I am fourteen, in senior school, and had recently completed my *Human Being* Project.

Through this, my plural is telling me I have swallowed a penis and my neck had stretched like the Paduaing People. Eleven years after the stretching, I'm listing a load of 'pennies' for Mum.

Part 1: The Silver and Copper

My coin record has been written on four sides of A4 lined paper. I have headed the page, '*An Account of our Coin Collection*'. Within the left column, I have noted the year of the coinage. Alongside, I had tallied the number of farthings, ha'pennies and pennies.

I felt horrible whilst collating these coins. I didn't know why but now I do. It's all those pennies. My *Human Being* project has shown me what they mean. A few days earlier (12 Mar) I was doing a load of homework and cried. I put my makeup on and 'tied my hair back'. I'm reinventing myself.

My first coin list consists of 'copper'. My second list consists of 'silver'. The first means Uncle Dan. He was a copper. The second means Mum, for silver contains her name. Pennies means penis. Ha'pennies (half-pennies) means half-oblivion to the penis. Farthings means far-thing. I am far away from the memory. Shilling means she-lyin'. I am being lied to about my toddlerhood. My *Human Being* project has told me about all about these codes.

Mother's Day card I made the day before I collated Mum's coins, and (left) Coins of the World, gifted to me on 9 Sept 1978.

Part 2: 1968 Missing

I'm encountering a lot of 'copper'.
Mum has coppers for every year
from 1900 to 1967 (except for 1933
and 1956). Despite this, I have
allocated a line for every year on this
table, ending with 1967. Mum's

Coin	Final Yr listed
Copper	1967
Silver	1967
Threepence	1967
Unsures	1799 (1967)
Foreign	1969

silver collection is sparse, but my table ends with 1967 again. Her collection
of three-pennies ends with 1967 as well.

1967.

I did a list of 'unsures' too. I had listed these coins in chronological order
(from 1862 to 1899). Yet oddly, I have placed the oldest coin of all at the
bottom. This one was dated 1799. This means 1967 again (topple a '9' to
find the anagram). 1967 wasn't available in this collection, so my plural did
the next best thing and placed an anagram of it at the bottom of the list, like
the other 1967s.

Finally, I did a list of foreign currency. The final year on this list is 1969.
1968 is missing from these tables. I have listed every year of the decade up
to 1969, except for 1968. This was the year I was raped by the 'copper'. I
had then made a decree to keep quiet about it. This decree shall be explained
in the following chapter, but links to the silver (Mum). The following years
vanish from records, for my oblivion is like a vanishing. I am no longer with
the truth, and from 1969, I am 'gone'.

I-Cons and Lies in Coins

How odd. My plural noticed this thing about Mum's coin collection and
urged me to do a collation in this manner. One day, I would learn how this
project has been used as a Trojan Horse.

The day before I had collated these coins (15 March 1980), I had made
Mum a Mother's Day card. For my plural, this day means 'smother-day'.
My plural sees meanings in dates too. I was smothered in 1968 and the liar
in my head is trying to erase it.

Two years earlier (8 Sept 1978), I was gifted *Coins of the World* (see
image). A sweet company called Chivers Jellies sponsored it. Notice 'lies'
in Jellies'. Coins means I-cons. Both mean cons and lies about my
toddlerhood. It's all over the world. Chapters 5 and 7 show how my plural
sees the countries.

Rubbing Out the Truth

My coin rubbings further inform on what is happening in my head (see
image). My first is a half-crown. Crown means head, and half of it is
missing. The half-pennies mean the same. Half of me can't see the penis.

Threepenny piece shows bars like a prison cell. I am barred from seeing the rape. The farthing shows a songbird. It is a 'far-thing', for the saying about disclosure. And finally, I did a rubbing of a coin simply showing the number three, the age I was raped.

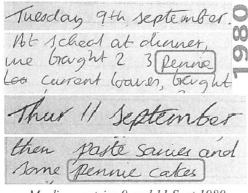

My diary entries 9 and 11 Sept 1980 showing pennie in penny.

The manner by which I had collated this coin record, betrays of my past. I have a liar in my head. The year 1968 is missing and I mustn't see the codes within the pennies.

The Penny Cake Shop

I shall close this chapter with the penny-cake shop. Throughout the autumn of 1980 and the following spring, Eve and I frequented a bakery that sold yesterday's fare for a penny. Penis can be found in *penni*-cake-*s*. This meaning is exposed on 9 and 11 Sept 1980 when I wrote 'pennie' (instead of penny) in my diary. My plural sees penis in pennies and this aberration proves. Oddly, on 9 Sept, we had done a talk in PFL about twins and birth control.

With this in mind, I can move onto my other projects and how they inform upon my rotten toddlerhood.

This following section is about three schoolbooks. It begins with *Science*.

My school science book.

SECTION 2: SCHOOL
Chapter 3: Science
Introduction
Part 1: The Burnings
Part 2: Ghost Writing
Part 3: Fingerprints
Part 4: The Degrees
Part 5: The Questionnaire
Part 6: My Findings

Introduction
The first section of this book has explained about my toddlerhood and uncanny messages seeping through my projects. As will be seen, the same thing is happening with my other projects too. The school curriculum seems

36

to make no difference to the inflow of these codes, and neither does the topic. How can such clues find their way here?

This chapter is about a book I did at school. It's called *Science*. I am in Class 13 and the year is 1977. I had turned twelve that May and had my menarche a few weeks earlier. This book turned up with several other schoolbooks that Mum had hoarded. They hadn't seen the light until 2016 shortly after her death.

Part 1: The Burnings

There is a fair bit about chemicals in this book. We used Bunsen Burners and noted chemical reactions.

The first page of this book lists 'Rules'. We are to read instructions, use the equipment, do the experiments, and note our findings.

Our science topic begins with 'universal indicator paper'. When it changes to red (I had written), the chemical is acid (such as vinegar). When it changes to blue, it is alkaline (such as limewater or ammonia). If it doesn't change colour, it is neutral (such as saliva).

Codes are already flowing in. Paper means raper and alkaline means lying. Section 7 explains the others. For now, everything seems routine.

The Quit-Lie

The following page looks at 'Ammonium Dichromate'.

This chemical is a flammable inorganic compound. 'We put it under the scope' (I had written). This means a microscope. I noted that the chemical looked like 'christals. When put on

My plural keeps finding links to my vile toddlerhood. See sex (in yes) and policeman (in copper).

the Bunsen Burner, the powder changed 'quitly' and the paper turned red.

I spelled quickly 'quitly.' This means quit-lie. I have quit the truth and am living a lie. A code has come through in my spellings.

At this time, I was messing a lot with my guitar at home. Seldom mentioned in my 1977 diary, I would keep spelling this word, quitar in my 1978 one. This means a-quitter. I have quit myself, and it says so in my science book too. I have quit my past and am living a lie.

The Burning Crystals

I suffered immense pressure during suffocation and my face felt ablaze. We're burning things at school now and my plural is triggered. She sees the burning in all sorts of things.

Here, I had mentioned that ammonium dichromate looked like 'christals'. I would spell this word in various ways. The meaning is all-sat-cry. These syllables run backwards within (cry-sta-al). My plural is crying out about a man that mounted me in toddlerhood. A similar code can be seen in my cloud studies at home too. My misspelled cirrus (cirrius) means us-crriis. My plural keeps crying out about my toddlerhood through these words. It's happening in this science book too.

But I can't hear her, for the 'dichromate'. This mean ditch-roommate. I have ditched part of myself, and 'roommate' is one way of putting it. I've lost touch with her, and I am torn.

Copper Sulphate

On page 2, I would list three chemicals:

Copper sulphate.

Copper oxide.

And nickel sulphate.

How odd. I have encountered copper my coin collation. My rapist was a 'copper', and my plural can't help seeing policeman in copper. For what he did to me, she would see 'suffocate' in 'sulphate'. Just swap the words to sulphate-copper to bring *sulfate-co*-pper. The '*co*' provides a link to bring 'sulff*oc*ate'.

Copper-suff*oc*ate.

This is how PTSD works – links. My plural would see copper-suffocate in this chemical. Sulphate now has a new meaning: suffocate, because of its link to copper.

Copper Oxide

My next chemical is copper oxide.

My rapist was an ex-copper when he suffocated me. Attach the 'ex' to bring ex-copper and this leaves I-do. The phrase becomes, I-do-ex-copper. This is sex-slang. I had 'done' a copper. How horrible. I was twelve when I wrote this *Science* book and I had lost my virginity nine years ago to an ex-copper. I notice 'ide' at the end – die. I felt I was going to die during the rape.

The image shows my 'yes' morphing. It becomes xes. Backwards is sex. My plural has written 'sex' twenty-six times in my *Science* book, and I had never noticed.

Nickel Sulphate

Nickel sulphate comes next. This one brings a similar link. Notice how I had written nickel (see image). I had written, 'nicle'. My 'nickel' is in mid-morph to uncle. My plural wants me to write uncle instead of nickel. For her, this chemical means uncle-suffocate.

Iron Sulphate

Later in my book, we would heat copper sulphate and iron 'filling' (meaning iron filing). The latter contains my rapist's Nor, and the 'filling'. Indeed, iron sulphate crops up too. This one means Nor-suffocate-I.

These four chemicals contain codes for uncle, copper, his name and what he did to me. Dotted around is sex too. My plural is communicating about my vile toddlerhood through my *Science* book. She has done the same with the coins and the *Human Being* project too.

Saturated

We are now heating copper sulphate in water.

My heading 'saturated' shows a sat-tic (see image). The sat is broken off, to bring 'sat urated'. I was mounted (sat) in toddlerhood and this has caused a

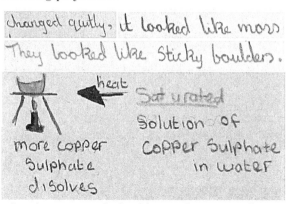

Quit-lie, ams, sticky boulders and copper suffocate dissolving in water with the sat.

tic. Beneath this heading, I had written that the chemical dissolves. This means oblivion. I can no longer remember the copper that sat on me. It is dissolving.

Ams Plural

I have become 'ams' (plural) due to my toddlerhood. My 'moss' resembles 'mass', anagram of ams. This means being plural. I have two ams. On the previous page, I had written the phrase, 'change couler of paper'. My plural sees raper in paper. She can't help it. It's just like 'prayer'. My misspelled couler means 'locker', or 'u-lock-her'. I have a lock in my head. I can't

39

remember the raper for it is locked away. Clues to my toddlerhood are pouring into my *Science* book.

I am about to get a shock.

Sticky Boulders

A liar in my head is keeping the truth from me. It does this by tricking me into thinking that the void I feel inside can be filled with something on this world. This void is my missing childhood. I don't know its missing, so I look to fill this void with something else. My twin Eve (as seen) is one example. But it might also be success or social-acceptance. I would get 'stuck' on this world.

Meanwhile, I don't know of my plural's existence. I keep looking in the wrong place to fill this void and I don't know about the rape. In fact, nothing on this world can fill this void. But I would keep looking in the wrong place. This is how the liar preserves my oblivion: keeping me stuck on this boulder.

Soon after recall, I discovered the liar and what it was doing. I would then call this world (and the things on it), 'sticky boulders.' During oblivion, I was stuck on this world. I even made up a silly song about it. I had coined this term in 2017. 'Sticky, sticky boulder'.

(So, I had thought).

An Old Term Revived

I had written 'sticky boulders' in this *Science* book. Forty years had gone by before I had 'coined' this term. I was describing the aftermath of burning crystals. As seen, crystals mean all-sat-cry. I was describing copper sulphate. I know this for the blue crystals.

I had written, 'The crystals are blue. We looked (through) the scope. They looked like blue rock. We put them on the burner. It turned from blue to white, brown and greenish. After being burned, we put them under the scope. They looked like sticky boulders.'

How come I used this term forty years before recall? I don't remember writing this at all. My plural knows I am stuck on this world, oblivious to her existence. I am 'stuck' on this boulder.

Plural Colours

The colours here are describing the process of becoming plural.

Blue means be-loo (rape). I was made to feel like a loo. Part 2 of this chapter shows a stick-figure, legs akimbo with her head in a blue vessel. It's a (be) loo. White means we-tie (tethering the memory), brown means no-brow (oblivion to it) and green means to grass. My *Colours* book (chapter 4) confirms these findings.

How odd. It's as though this chemical reaction was meant for me, just like the policeman in copper. In fact, my brain is filtering the world, and this is the effect. Nothing is 'meant' for me at all. It just seems that way.

I am now prone to getting stuck on this boulder for the toddlerhood rape. My plural knows this. She knows about the liar in my head, and she has used the term 'sticky boulders' forty years before 'I' had.

I am stuck on this world.

Gone Yellow and Queer Eggs

But it doesn't end with 'green'. After burning the copper sulphate, I had described another burning, which might be the same copper sulphate.

'It (the crystals) was green at first, (I had then written) and then turned yellow. It was all stuck together after (it was) burned. It did not spurt out. They looked like queer eggs.'

Queer eggs? This term sounds as bizarre as the 'sticky boulders'. What does it mean?

So, after green comes yellow. My plural wants to grass (green), whilst part of her goes yellow. This means yellow-cowardice for turning my back on the truth. The yellow-meaning is all over my other projects too. My plural sees the liar in me as a yellow coward.

This code incorporates sayings. The bird-disclosure has been seen in the coins. Now I find cowardly-yellow.

I am stuck to the boulder whilst my truth does not 'spurt out'. After the burning of rape, the truth is contained, and I am stuck on the boulder. I have gone 'yellow'.

Stuck with the Decree-Agree

My 'queer eggs' hides a meaning, just like the sticky boulders. It means 'do-agrees'. Topple the q to d to bring du-eereggs. Do-eggrees, or u-egreed (you-agreed). It's all about an agreement. The agrees mean to hush about the rape to preserve the 'silver' (a mother-figure). Sadly, I would become stuck on the boulder whilst doing so.

We would later look at thermometers. Degrees comes up a lot here. This means the same thing: egreed-agreed. Part 4 of this chapter explains. All mean I agreed to hush about the rape. The agree is dotted over my other projects too. It follows a pattern and means the same thing.

I-agreed.

Burning into Plural

We're onto page three now and we're burning more things. My plural keeps seeing rape within the Bunsen Burner. This is how the pressure of rape felt – burning. Something in me would then change. I am just like a chemical being burnt, and changes have taken place in my brain. I have become plural.

Section 7 summarises the chemicals I had burned and what they mean for my plural.

Part 2: Ghost-Writing

My plural is a ghost in the classroom. I don't know she's there, but her presence is evident in my *Science* book.

I had rubbed out sentences and then written the same over them. The result is like a shadow (see image).

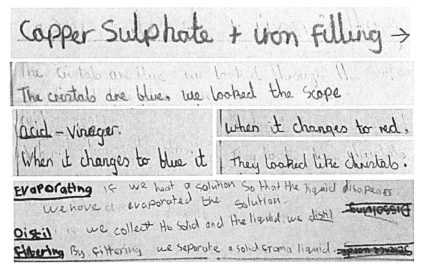

Rubbing out and writing over. The effect is like a shadow. This 'shadow writing' is symbolic of the echo within me.

Further down, I had written the sentence, 'The crystals are blue. We looked *through* the scope'.

On top of this, I had rewritten the same sentence, omitting the word 'through'. The 'through' has been taken away.

I can't see *through* the meanings beneath these sentences. I can't see the codes my plural can. This shadow-meaning is all over my other projects, diaries and artwork too. I have a ghost-girl in me, and she is telling me about my horrible toddlerhood *through* my *Science* book. But I can't see it.

Salt and Sand

Later in this book, I'm exploring salt. Salt is a crystal (I would note), and this means all-sat-cry. Here, I am separating salt from sand by adding water. At home, I had made up an island with its own language. It's called Saltland. In fact, it means a place I was sat (Sat-lland). Here, I have 'dissolved' it in water.

All that's left is 'sand'. I have come to learn that sand means oblivion, for the 'sandman' who comes in sleep. I have gone to sleep to the truth after dissolving the salt away. Another saying has been uncovered here: the sandman who brings sleep.

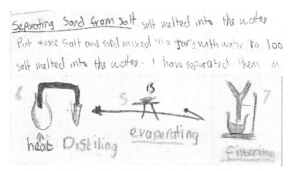

Dissolving salt, distilling the heat (of rape), evaporating the truth and filtering out the be-loo (note the stick-figure).

There is a lot of dissolving in this *Science* book. This is what the liar wants, to dissolve all traces of the rape. A ghost of my former self is left behind.

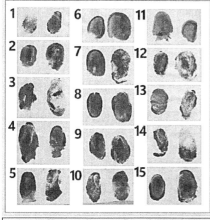

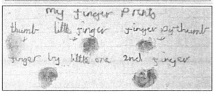

(Above): My classroom's fingerprints. Mine is 11. (Below): My fingerprints in a 1975 flower project.

other pupils at school (upper image).

Part 3: Fingerprints

The next page of my *Science* book shows fifteen sets of fingerprints.

The pupils in my class were required to give fingerprints so that we can analyse them. We would learn about arch, composite, whorl and loop.

I have given my fingerprints before: in a project I did at home called *Wildflowers of the Pyrenees* (chapter 10). On the inside cover, I had given my fingerprints (lower image). I had believed I was simply personalising my book, giving it my stamp. But another meaning has been implied.

In with the Liar

Two years later, I would give my fingerprints with fourteen

My plural sees the liar in my head as complicit with my rapist for lying to me. The 'Nor-way' has told me so. Because of the liar, he is getting away with it. A criminal gives fingerprints. The liar in my head has given *her* fingerprints. She is 'in' with my rapist and therefore must be treated as a criminal.

The Fake Plural

The liar steals from me. She uses my name and the things I do to imply I am okay with living a lie. The liar's fingerprints are identical to mine. The liar has used this to imply the whole class is in with the liar in letting my rapist get away with it. I am projecting the liar in my head upon the whole classroom. Of course, this is an illusion, but forms part of the liar's tactic. The liar bullies my plural away, and steals from her oblivious-self.

The liar doesn't represent who I am. 'She' is merely following the 'agreement' of a three-year-old. The liar is not my plural but makes out she is. For ease of read, I have used the pronoun 'she' when the liar is really an 'it'.

The Liar in my Dreams

Since keeping a dream diary, I have learned this liar appears every night. 'She' selects those who bear my name, alliances and those who look a little like me. She then uses their image to create alienating situations. I often awaken feeling ostracised and unsettled. These are my plural's feelings for what the liar is doing, and I don't understand what's going on. In trying to retain my oblivion, the liar is hurting my plural and naturally, I feel her pain.

My vile toddlerhood has robbed me of self-confidence, and I can't make lasting friendships. This is because the liar in me is making out my plural isn't worth knowing. 'Keep away from her'. The result is that I feels it's for the best I have no friends. The liar in my head is alienating me from my plural and I would project this feeling upon the classroom. 'No one must know me.'

The Racs in Mes

The liar steals my name. It contains 'Rac'. This code is all over my works and means me. It's like the Nor, for meaning my rapist. Rac means me. Five other pupils share the 'rac' syllable with me. The liar has found something of mine to use. On the opposite page, I had reported fingerprint patterns. I notice the 'arch' of earlier. This means Rac too. I am Rac and I have an arch. Nine other pupils share the 'arch' with me. They have become Racs as well. The liar can now use the Rac (a part of me) in her campaign against my plural.

The Bully Projection

I am prone to being bullied for the liar in my head. I'm carrying something terrible inside and a part of me is frightened of recall. Others pick up on this fear and I become the ideal target for bullies. Three pupils in my class bullied me. Part of me sees them as like the inner-bully I carry, out to keep the truth from me.

But I have only one bully. Just one. It's in my head. The liar uses this projection to create the illusion of lots of bullies. I ended up simply hating school. Like the liar, school limits access. I'm not allowed to venture in case I stumble across that terrible memory.

The entire class (including me) have given their fingerprints. We're all 'guilty' of keeping quiet about my toddlerhood rape.

Part 4: The Degrees

We're looking at temperatures now. In two years' time, I would take daily readings from a thermometer I had bought from Skegness on 18 July 1979. For years to come, I would keep meticulous weather readings. Here, I would learn how to make my own thermometer.

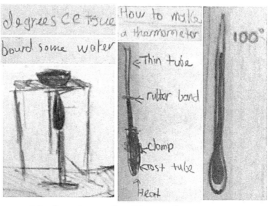

My drawings of making a thermometer.

This next bit relates to the copper-suffocate of earlier.

I had written: 'A boiling tube is filled with water. Dye is used to colour the water. A thin tube is passed through an airtight rubber and stopped into a boiling tube. When the water goes hotter, it expands. The expanding water pushes up the tube. When the water gets cooler, it contracts.'

The Airtight and the Straw

Notions of suffocation would have haunted my subconscious on writing this. I know it. This is due to the 'thin tube', airtight, stopped and the 'pushes up the tube'. The boiling is reiterated.

In later years, I kept seeing a little girl held underwater with a cruelly thin straw to breathe. The straw has become a symbol of air deprivation, not something actually used. This project's thin tube had provided the unsavoury notion. The 'airtight rubber' means suffocation eraser. I'm not allowed to know about what Uncle Dan did. The image shows 'rubber band'. The

45

'eraser' is also banning me from recall. The nearby 'clamp' holds the memory fast. I mustn't see it.

The Me-cry of Mercury

I would now write about mercury. This is what I had put.

'The thermometer has a bulb of mercury going into a thin tube. The thin tube is protected by glass. On the glass is a scale of degrees Celsius. When the temperature rises, the mercury expands along the thin tube. When the temperature falls, the mercury contracts.'

I keep mentioning the 'thin tube'. It evidently 'bothers' me. How odd that the thin tube would become a cruelly thin straw in future intrusive thoughts.

In 1974, I wrote about the planets in a book called *Space* (chapter 6). I kept spelling Mercury 'Mecry' or Mecury'. This means me-cry. My plural is crying out about my toddlerhood again. Her signs are all over this *Science* book. But I can't read them. The '*through*' has been omitted from the shadow-writing.

The decree-agree of 'degrees' is the reason. An agreement to hush about my toddlerhood rape has been made when I was three. And here, I had written about the 'contract'. This means an agreement too. When the burning is over, the 'me-cry' contracts. She is silenced by a binding agreement.

The Use-it of Celsius

My Celsius has been written, Cetsue (see image). It ends with 'Sue'. This means 'use'. Three of my dolls were called Sue. All mean use. Phonetically, Cetsue is 'set-sue'. Use-et. I have been used. The use-it-decree says I am not allowed to know about my appalling toddlerhood.

The Boiling Ink

We're boiling ink now. We put some in an 'evaporating dish' (I had written) and let it bubble away. The ink went into the air until there is none left.

This is what the liar wants: for the ink to vanish. Ink symbolises recording things, like in this book, and the liar rather I didn't record a thing. The liar is leaving her fingerprints all over this *Science* book, for the ink.

The ink leaves only 'shiney', 'golden' lumps at the bottom (I would report). Shiney means I-shine. My plural's clues are shining out within my writing. And golden means golden-olden, the olden times. Clues to my toddlerhood are shining out of this *Science* book, and I am totally unaware of it.

We added water to the golden lumps and the ink returned. The liar can never get rid of the ink. I have learned to read and write. I will continue to write things for the rest of my life and clues will keep shining out. The liar can't stop the ink from flowing.

Pig Rape True and the Tied Agreement

I am presented with two graphs (see images). Both show the rate of water cooling over a fifteen-minute period. I had set out the readings in a table for the first one. Beneath this first graph. I had put: 'This is the graph of the temperature and (and) time of when the water was cooling off.'

I had written '*and*' twice. My plurality has just shown itself. To my plural, temperature means me-rape-true (t-em-pera-ture). See the anagrams running through. Chapter 17 would show this meaning in other words too. No wonder I got obsessed with temperature readings in future years.

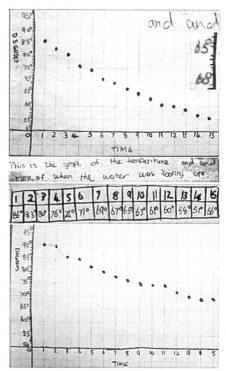

My two graphs showing the rate of water cooling over 15 minutes.

Rape can be found in 'graph' as well. Swap the 'ph' to find g-*rahp*. Place 'graph' end-to-end (gra-***phg***-ra-***phg***-ra) to find a (whispered) 'pig' between. This comes together phg-rahp. My plural is whispering. I have been raped by a pig through the word 'graph'.

My Pyrenean flowers project (chapter 10) would show the same rape-code in *Rhap-onticum*. Grapes and blood converge in my children's story *House of Hidden Mysteries* (1979). Rotate through 'g-rape' to find p*e*g-rape (pig-rape) again.

These codes run throughout my creations.

My Birthyear and my Rape-Year

I notice my 60°C looks like 68 (see inset image). The Celsius symbol has attached itself to the nought. '68 is the year I was raped. Just above this, is 65. This is my birthyear. Similarly, my first reading was 86°C. And my final reading was 56°C. Reverse both to find my birthyear and the year I was raped. The figures 1965 and 1968 form touchstones to this graph (and my other projects too).

The Tied Agreement

But what about the second graph? I find something odd. My final reading is 69°C. But the penultimate one had been 68°C. The temperature of the water appears to have *risen*. This is impossible. What have I done? Degrees means an agreement, and this graph is telling me it has risen. In 1969, when I had turned four, oblivion would set in for the 'degrees'. I had labelled both graphs: 'time' and 'degrees'. Both mean to hide the truth from me. I have been tied (ti'-me) to an agreement that goes back to my toddlerhood.

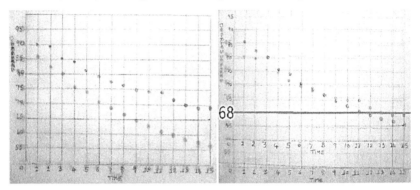

My temperature readings traced out and overlaid.

The Superimposing

Image far left shows the two graphs simply overlaid. One set of readings is higher than the other.

Image right are lined up differently.

Remember my 60° looking like 68 in the first graph? I have treated this line as 68 and lined it up with 68°C of the second graph. See how the readings are now almost identical. Read from right to left, and the 'degrees' of both rise steeply.

In 1968 (68°C), I was a toddler routinely raped. But in January 1969 (69°C), my rapist would leave the cottage. My vile toddlerhood is set to vanish behind childhood amnesia. The agree-decree is rising, walling off my toddlerhood. These graphs symbolise the rising of the 'agrees'.

Silver or Copper

I have opted for a mother-figure above disclosure, for this is what 'silver' (of coins) means in chapter 2. Silver contains Mum's name. Disclosure means losing her and my home. I had chosen silver above the copper-disclosure. My weather records confirm the silver-meaning. It forms part of the decree. The consequence is that my toddlerhood would fall into shadow. I can't see it.

This part is huge.

It's about a questionnaire.

So momentous are my findings, I have subdivided this part into bitesize pieces for ease.

The Questionnaire with yeses and nos.

This questionnaire consists of a table displaying a load of yeses and nos.

We're exploring the properties of various objects. We did a yes-no about the qualities of each. This is where I would find all the 'sex' (in yes).

The table below shows the question-types. They have been clustered together for an overall view.

THE YES-NO QUESTIONNAIRE DEVISED		
Do not sink in water	Sink in water	*Water*
Float in water	*Question orphaned*	
Non water dissolved	Dissolve in water	
Non waterproof		
Light	Heavy	*Weight*
Shiny	Dull	*Lit*
Bright coloured	Dull coloured	
Symmetrical	Non-symmetrical	*Sym-try*

Nasty smell	Nice smell	***Odour***
Rough	Smooth	*Texture*
Tough		
Rigid	Bendy	
Brittle		
Attract to magnet	Not attract to magnet	*ElecM*
Attract to metal		
Conduct electricity	Not conduct electricity	

These are: water-related, weight-related, brightness, symmetry, smell, texture and electro-magnet. The shaded blocks simplify.

Does the object sink? Is it rigid? Is it symmetrical, bendy, etc? I would soon realise these questions are intended to be pairs. For instance, rough-smooth, light-heavy, etc. But some questions are orphaned. Why will become clear.

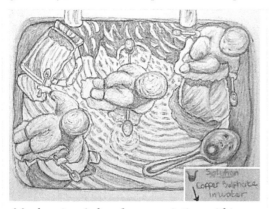

My drawing (taken from a painting within my children's book) of a little boy rowing across the kitchen sink. Inset shows 'copper sulphate (suffocate) in water'.

Part 5A: The Questions

These 'questions' contain codes. My plural can't help seeing another meaning beneath these questions.

Sink in water

I shall begin with 'water'.

Does the object 'sink in water?' Yes, or no?

I remember Uncle Dan in the bathroom with Eve and me. This memory evokes no feelings and it receded into the background. In the Nineties, I saw the counsellor for visions of my niece (resembling me in toddlerhood) being drowned in the bath. In a children's story I was writing at the time, I painted a boy rowing across the kitchen sink (see image). This painting has a code. Sink water means sink-(in)-water. I was sunk in water. A line in my story reads, 'Ben rowed'. Notice the 'be-drowned' in this sentence. I was *sunk* in water and drowned.

The sinking can be seen in the spoon of my illustration. The spoon symbolises my face, for I used to look at my reflection within one. The spoon is underwater. *I'm* underwater. This *Science* book had said the same thing: I'm underwater. On a section on dissolving copper sulphate, I had put

50

'copper sulphate in water' (see inset). This means 'copper suffocate (me) in water'. In other words, he drowned me.

The 'Proof' in Water

The pairing question with sinking is 'float'. Does the object float?

I had also put 'Do *not* sink in water'. The liar in my head is reiterating I *wasn't* sunk at all. I floated, just like the boy in my children's book. In rewording this question, one of them would become orphaned.

I am reminded of the 'Helsinki and the 'Swami' in my *Human Being* project. This means the same: drowned versus float.

But my plural brings in the 'waterproof', for I would also write '*non*-dissolved in water'. She is saying, proof of the water-incident must *not* be dissolved. The memory must remain 'waterproof'. Another question has become orphaned.

The Question of Sinking

These questions would be applied to the objects selected. In each box, I would write 'yes' or 'no'. The liar in my head would then twist this to apply to the sinking of my toddlerhood.

'(Did you) sink in water?' the question becomes. All answers were 'no', for all objects floated. The liar has used this to imply I am denying the sinking ever happened. But the 'waterproof' question gets a few votes. This means the water-memory must *not* be dissolved. It must remain 'water-proof'.

And 'prove', it did, for I suffered flashbacks in the Nineties of a child drowning in the bath, and concurrent, painted a toddler within 'sink-water'. I now remember being drowned. It has been proved. To my plural, this is more important than other people believing me. I share the memory with her, and it is through these traumas, that we are joined.

The Statements of Truth and Lies

And now for the other questions.

Light or heavy. How does the object weigh? Rough or smooth. How does the object feel? Is it magnetic?

They're statements. Each are of truth and of lies. Light (lite) for instance means lie-tie (the truth). Metal means me-tell (about the rape). Dull means oblivion. All are statements and this is how these 'descriptors' should be viewed. Statements.

An election is being implied in this questionnaire. Votes are being cast for truth or lie. How odd. And it's happening behind my back.

I have clumped together the statement that belong together. The shaded squares represent the lies, the white ones, truth. The big picture is getting clearer.

Statements of Lies and their Meaning		Statements of Truth and their Meaning	
Do not sink in water Float in water Dissolve in water Non waterproof	I hadn't sunk in water at all. The memory must dissolve. There is now no (water) 'proof'.	Sink in water Non-water-dissolved Waterproof	I *had* sunk in water. The proof must remain, and the memory mustn't be dissolved.
Smooth Dull Dull/coloured *Be-*right/coloured Light	Sh-me-too (two). I must remain torn, dull and oblivious. Coloured means locked-read, as the liar deems it to 'be-right'. Lie-tie the truth.	Heavy Bendy (Bend-I)	Something heavy raped me from behind whilst I lay bent.
Non-symmetrical Nasty smell To-*ugh* To-*ugh* Rigid Brittle	I have a mirror-image I can't see. She is split from me (m/es) and I must remain two for the nasty-stain and the ugh. I-rid and be-tied the lot.	Symmetrical Nice-smell Shiny (Shine-I)	I have a mirror-image plural (symmetry). My e//ms (a split-me) and her signs shine all around.
Non-attracted to magnet	Rac-debt *not* (to) get-man (mag-net). I mustn't testify.	Attracted to metal Attracted to magnet	I am attracted to the 'me-tell.' I want to disclose. Rac-debt to get-man and testify.
Do not conduct electricity (misspelt elect-*icity*)	The truth about the sit-I in this election must *not* be conducted.	Conduct electricity	The truth about the sit-I in this election *must* be conducted and voted for.

Part 5B: The Objects

See the meanings within these words? Codes hide within each question.

I have uncovered the codes behind the questions in this questionnaire. They're statements. Having studied these codes for five years now, I know what to look for, and the projects within this book further confirm. But what about the objects under scrutiny? What do they mean? They're no different to the questions. They're statements, just the same, and the codes show. Each are of truth and of lies.

Objects of Truth	Meaning	Objects of Lies	Meaning
Cone-cork	Nor-cock	Fossil (Twice)	Foils
Bottle	Recall	Snail fossil	Lyin'-foils
Tissue-ball	Be-all-use-it	Head (of fossil	Foils-head
This table shows my odd list of objects and their meanings. Each have been placed into separate rows: truth and lie, as before.		Emerald	Me-liar
		Stone	Not-know-stain
		Cork	Crock
		Rubber plant	Eraser
		Beehive	Believe-lie

The Of-lies of Fossil

I note four objects are fossil-related. The liar has done this. Anything with 'fossil' mean foils. I have been foiled by the liar in my head and my life is full of-lies (of-li'ss). I wrote about a Doctor Fossil in my children's story, *Windswept High* (spring 1978). He is trying to keep two sisters apart. He is like the foil in me: dividing my plural from myself.

In August 1980, I made toy snails (see images). I am reminded of the long nails in my *Human Being* project (and of Eve's false fingernails). All mean lies. Snail means lies.

These fossil-objects mean head-foils, lyin', lie and liar.

More Lies

My next object is emerald.

Images left: In an early Earth *project, I have written emerald amrild. And how I wrote* 'beehive' *in this Science book.* ***Images right:*** *during a toymaking phase in Aug 1980, I made toy snails.*

Emerald means liar too.

In my *Earth* project (chapter 7). I had written emerald, 'am-rild' (see image). This means am-lied/liar. I notice its neighbour, pearly. This means rape-lie.

Stone is next. This one is full of denial too, for the 'not' in the middle. It knows-not (noes-not) of the 'st' saint (anagram of stain).

The Eraser Factory

My seventh object is a rubber plant. Rubber means eraser. A rubber plant keeps growing in my head. The liar has placed an eraser plant in my head to keep rubbing out my memories.

Believe the Lie

Beehive has been overscored with lee-hive (see image). A slashed circle nearby denotes this word's duality. Merged, this word becomes 'beelhive.' Or rather, belhieve.

'Believe'. This is the meaning of beehive. Lie is central (be-*lie*-ve). This means believe-lie. These objects are filled with lies and denial about my toddlerhood rape.

The Truth

But there are also truths.

Two objects that didn't appear in the questionnaire were the cone and cork. I had written these on separate pages. Alone, cork means crock – nonsense. The liar has kept cork from cone because together, they mean Nor-cock. Cone contains the 'know' (noe). It's in 'cone'. Part of me knows about the rape and who did it. The question 'sink in water' appears only on these pages too. I was sunk in water by the cone-cork.

The All Used

My next object is 'tissue-ball'. This means be-all-use-it. I have been all-used like an object. Sue (my dolls' names) is an anagram of use.

Bottle means truth, for representing a portal to recall. After an accident with a milk bottle involving my twin, Eve, I saw a man rise in my chest. chapter 1 has explained I had experienced a somatic memory.

I have now unearthed the codes behind the questions and the objects concerned. They're all statements – nothing but statements. It is now time to put them in the table, just as I had at school.

I am about to encounter a problem.

A section of my questionnaire.

Part 5C: The Two Pictures of the Plural

The image shows a section of the questionnaire. I have enhanced it for clarity.

I had put 'yes' or 'no' within each box,

to describe the quality of each object.

Under 'emerald', I had put 'yes' for heavy. This gem is heavy.

For 'bottle' I had put 'no' for 'attracted to metal'. Glass isn't magnetic.

And for beehive, I had put 'yes' for 'float in water'. The beehive floats. The image shows.

But two conflicting statements share one answer. Heavy means truth. A heavy thing was on me in toddlerhood. Yet, the emerald (which means me-lied) says 'yes'. A heavy thing *was* on me.

Both truth and lie are saying 'yes'.

Another is 'attracted to metal'. This means truth too, for me-tell. Yet bottle (which means recall) says 'no'. Don't tell. Both truth and lie are saying 'no.'

Two Pictures in One Table

The liar's paradox is exposed. Two statements cannot share one answer, and the plural cannot inhabit one world. This paradox has been reflected in this questionnaire. I cannot be a childhood virgin *and* a childhood rape-victim. The liar exploits this paradox. It uses whatever answer to promote the lie, always the lie. It spins what I say and do to imply a meaning of which I am unaware.

It switches sides.

This explains why I hadn't recalled the man in my chest after Eve's accident with the bottle. Part of me said 'yes', but another part had said 'no'.

Since learning I am plural, I have come to see how the world about me has been filtered by forces in my head and this means the liar changing sides. The liar shifts and turncoats. The conflicting answers show how it works. The liar is two-faced and selects a yes or no depending on the question and the situation.

The Paradox of the Symmetry

So, the 'ghost questionnaire' contains paradoxes. Two statements share one answer. Bizarrely, the same thing has happened with the *actual* questionnaire, the one I was doing for school. For some reason, the bottle is neither symmetrical nor asymmetrical. I had written 'no' for both. The same thing has happened with stone and emerald – no for both. Beehive has 'yes' for both. Fossil is waterproof *and* non-waterproof.

Why had I done this? Two statements are sharing one answer again. It seems my plurality has leeched into the task I was *actually* assigned to do.

Paper Overlays

This questionnaire represents the world of the plural. I am one person of two versions. I have two views of the world, just like here. Both inhabit one brain. It's like two pieces of tracing paper, one overlaying the other. It appears as one. What I must do is *lift* one off. The same applies here – *lift* one off. This means treating each 'statement' separately. Each has one answer. Not two.

The result is forty 'statements', not twelve objects and twenty-eight questions. All are statements. That is all they are. This questionnaire is about to unveil further layers of which I didn't know.

Part 5D: The Result of the Election

To this end, I have grouped together all statements of lies. Emerald, beehive and brittle, for instance, mean me-lied, believe-lie and be-lie-tied.

Lies.

Similarly, I have grouped together all statements of truth. Heavy, bendy and tissue-ball mean a heavy thing bent and used me from behind.

Truth.

Section 7 summarises all the codes behind these questions.

But the liar has rigged this election. Rather than diversity, I had used four fossil-related objects, two of which are duplicated. It's like the same person voting 'twice'. The whole thing is invalid and doesn't reflect how I really felt at all. I would rather know the truth about my toddlerhood.

The Lie-Codes Over and Over

The liar keeps finding codes within words and using them to imply I'm okay with remaining torn and oblivious. It's best not to 'get-man' who raped and drowned me, for he was Mum's brother. It's best to live a childhood-illusion as though nothing happened. It's 'easier' that way.

The Hidden Votes

Where I had written 'yes' against emerald, I'm 'voting' for the lie. I'm being 'tricked' by a system in my head. But what I hadn't realised, is that 'no' are votes too. For instance, 'no' for beehive means I *don't* want to believe-lie. I'm voting against it.

This questionnaire of yeses and nos hides a shadow meaning: truth and lies. But only *one* answer exists for each 'statement'. This means separating out the questions from the objects.

The Objects of Truth

I present two tables on tracing paper (see images below). On the first, I list the objects at the top, just like I had at school. Here, the data reads *down*. The image (left) shows. Where I had put 'yes' for truth, I log it. For example, all yeses for 'bottle'. Bottle means recall. Where I had put 'no' for lies, I log it. For example, all 'nos' for rubber plant. Rubber means erasing the memories.

The rest is left blank.

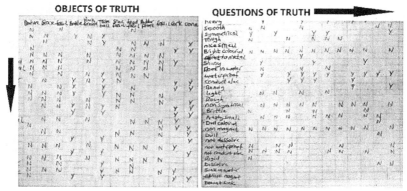

Votes for truth: *Yeses and nos are logged onto tracing paper according to each statement.*

The Questions of Truth

Onto separate tracing paper, I draw out the table again and list the questions at the side, just like I had at school. Here, the data reads *across*. The image (above right) shows. Here, I do the same thing. Where I had put 'yes' for truth, I log it. Where I had put 'no' for the lie, I log it.

The Tracing Paper of Lies

I do exactly the same thing with the lies (images below). Onto separate sheets of tracing paper, I log all yeses and nos that go with the lie.

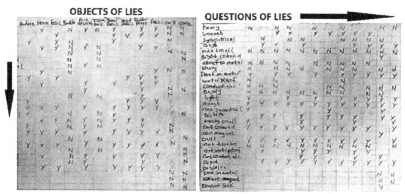

Votes for lies: *Yeses and nos are logged onto tracing paper according to each statement.*

The Overlay

I overlay the sheets of tracing paper.

I am struck by the ghost-writing I had encountered at the start of my *Science* book. This looks the same. The ghost-girl within me is expressing herself *through* this questionnaire too.

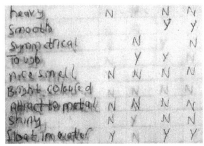

Close-up of the ghost-writing effect with the tracing paper.

Here, the truth and lies overlay each other but do not inhabit the same layer. They can only *appear* that way.

I have expressed the hidden questionnaire beneath the apparent one. A ghost-girl exists within me. She knows the truth, but a liar stands between us. My life is full of lies overlaying the truth.

I can now see the big picture: lies overlaying the truth. The result is a ghost-writing effect.

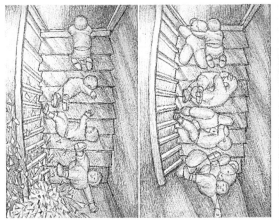

Drawings from my children's book.

Removing the Overlay

What an odd thing. This questionnaire is showing me that lies have overlaid the truth about my life. Only on unearthing the codes within the questionnaire, would this become clear.

Falling Down the Stairs

The drawings (left) have been taken from my children's book of the mid-Nineties. It's the same one of the kitchen sink. The little boy (Ben) is having fun tumbling down the stairs with his teddy bear. But take away the bear and things look different.

The drawing far left shows the reality. The child wasn't a boy at all, but a girl. *I* had fallen down the stairs and there was no teddy bear. I remember falling and my eyes speckling over. I now know I had been raped in the room at the top – the guestroom. This is where Uncle Dan slept in 1968.

See how the lie has overlaid the truth? The teddy bear can be peeled off to leave the child alone on the stairs. It's just like the codes in this questionnaire. The teddy bear represents the statements of lies. The bear was yellow too. For my plural, this colour means cowardice. The lies overlaying the truth can be seen in my artwork as well as this questionnaire.

The little girl alone on the stairs represents the truth.

Part 5E: The Hidden Symmetry

I have a hidden symmetry. I can't see my plural.

The drawing shows a section of my painting *Junglerealm*. I was seventeen when I painted it. A swallowtail is taking flight in timelapse. Half if it is disappearing. The upper swallowtail looks like half a butterfly. 'Swallow-tail' means the swallowing (oral rape) is a tale, not to be believed. I can't see my plural. She is disappearing from view.

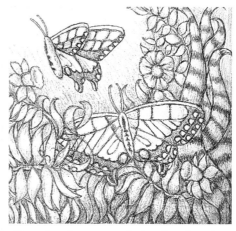

Drawing from my painting Junglerealm *(conceived spring 1983).*

Symmetry forms one of the questions within this questionnaire. Is the object symmetrical? The beehive and the cone are symmetrical; the stone and emerald aren't. The liar doesn't want me to see the symmetry that I carry. This symmetry is caused by trauma and the liar would rather half remain invisible. 'This' is all I am.

This questionnaire has a hidden symmetry. My random objects of 'yeses' and 'nos' are about to show.

The Symmetry of Truth and Lies

In the centre of graph paper, I list the forty statements (see image below). This forms the centre of where truth and lies branch out (like the centre of the butterfly). One side of my graph-paper is reserved for truth, the other side, lies.

Beehive came first. I have therefore placed this at the top of my graph. This one, remember, means believe-lie.

I had written 'no' sixteen times to this one. I have therefore placed a 'N' on square sixteen of believe-lie. This represents truth.

On the opposite side of my graph, I would plot the number of times I had put 'yes' to believe-lie, which is eight. Into square eight, I put a 'Y'. This represents going along with the lie.

The image shows.

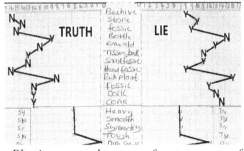

Plotting yes and no votes for statements of truth and lie onto graph paper.

I would do the same thing with all the other statements within my questionnaire. All the way down. I would then join up the dots.

Only when I trace the lines and overlay the two, do I see the symmetry. One side of the shape represents truth, the other one lies. This is me, living a lie whilst my plural is hidden away with the truth.

The Symmetry of Yeses and Nos

I do the same thing with simply 'yeses' and 'nos'.

Onto separate graph-paper, I log the yeses and nos all the way down. The result is a jumble of truth and lies, but none inhabit the same line. Again, truth and lies can never mix. And the symmetry reappears. I have found the symmetry of truth-lies and of yes-nos.

The images below show the result of both. See the symmetry?

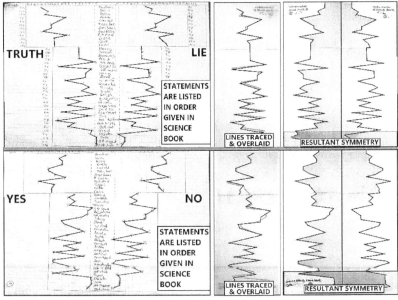

Plotting the number of truth-lie and of yes-no for each statement onto graph paper. Only when I trace out the lines and overlay them, does the symmetry appear.

My plural lives in the shadow of truth and the 'no'. She is invisible and I have denied her. Instead, I am living in the world of lies and 'yes'. The life I believed in has made me half a butterfly. The symmetry is showing up my (hidden) duality. No-truth. Yes-lie.

The Liar's Sabotage

The symmetry had at first eluded me. This was due to how I had initially presented the data. Instead of placing the statements in its original order, I had lumped them into categories. Remember, some read down (with twenty-eight answers). Others read across (with twelve). Four questions being orphaned, were left mostly blank. Blank squares mean a third element. This isn't good for symmetry.

Truth, lie and blank.

Yes, no and blank.

The liar wants these blanks. It wants my memory blank. It wants things crooked with no symmetry at all.

The blanks of my questionnaire were due to the orphaned statements. These weren't in the main body of my questionnaire. In this research, I had placed them at the bottom out of 'harms' way. The symmetry breaks down only where these blanks occur. In fact, no blanks should exist in this questionnaire at all. Every question should have an answer.

The images below show the *asymmetry*.

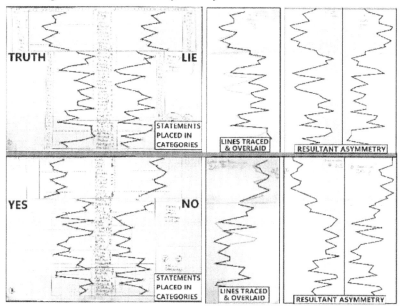

The symmetry had almost eluded me for I had shuffled up the statements into categories.

61

Part 5E: The Guinea Pig and Other Things

What an odd thing. This questionnaire has shown the liar finds codes within words and uses them to imply a meaning of which I am unaware. It would then use paradoxes to promote the lie. The aim is to preserve my oblivion and hide the truth from me.

But the truth is straight and symmetrical. It's like the butterfly before take-off. The truth forms the foundations of all, and the lie can never inhabit the same space. It can only *appear* that way. The truth stands tall and outweighs all.

We would now explore other things. The codes can be found here too. They're everywhere.

One object of note is the guinea pig. I had mentioned this animal three times (under 'living things', 'soft things' and 'hard things' – as in guinea pig cage). At this time, my rapist was living with a girlfriend called Gwen. Pig is slang for his once-job. My plural sees the liar in my head as bedfellows with my rapist. I might as well be 'Gwen'. My oblivion has made me pig's-Gwen for letting him get away with it. Further, the liar has made a prisoner of me, and I am living in a cage, just like the 'gwennie-pig'.

Non-living	Big Things	Small Things	Living
Hard things	Soft things	Crunchy things	Rusty things

My illustrations and further categories explored in my Science *book.*

Housed, Numbed and Leaves

The images show categories for other things explored.

'Birdhouse' means housing a bird of disclosure. It's like the guineapig cage earlier. In autumn 1978, I made a birdbox at school. This means the same: to box-up the disclosure.

'Autumn leaves' means at-numb-leaves. I have deserted (left) myself and gone numb to the truth. Roses means sores (as will be explained in my flower projects).

Section 7 explains the other codes.

Part 5G: The Election of November 1980

It's November 1980 and three years have gone by since I had completed this questionnaire. For history homework I am covering a news story about the Carter-Reagan race for the American Election. I don't have this homework, but I wrote about it in my diary. I had called it a 'history diary'. I cut out pictures and wrote reams. I remember doing it.

Carter contains my 'Rac' code, just like my name. Reagan contains my rapist's 'Nor' just like cone-cork. It seems my plural had chosen this news story for wanting to rerun the election of three years ago. She wants to do it again and win.

On 4 November, Reagan won a landslide victory. But the liar has it covered. Remember, the liar changes sides, switches answers. There are two statements for each answer. The outcome is of no importance. The ghost-writing on my questionnaire shows yes *and* no – the lies overlaying truth.

The liar shifts and turncoats. It promotes the lie.

Part 6: My Findings

I'm shocked at what this *Science* book has shown me.

The topics appear to be aimed at my toddlerhood. Hidden meanings skulk within these topics. A ghost-girl exists inside of me, and she has revealed herself with her shadow-writing. But the liar wants me stuck on this 'boulder' via the 'agreed', which rises from '68 (°C).

Answers Twisted

My questionnaire has been used by the liar to imply I am voting for the lie all the time. I have a hidden symmetry and the liar has used my attachments (sticky boulder) to hide this half of me. But truth and lies can never inhabit the same space. This questionnaire shows.

More than Science

For forty-eight years, I have lost sight of the truth in pursuit of boulder things. The liar has used my love for Mum, Eve's accident and my pursuit of a perfect childhood to trap me into oblivion. I have lived in the cage of 'Gwen'. My oblivion has denied me a chance to 'get-man', to testify.

This questionnaire has explored the quality of objects via questions. This is all it *should* be. Had not been for my toddlerhood rape, I would have been a schoolgirl simply learning about science.

Images from my Book on Colours.

Chapter 4: Colours

Introduction
Part 1: The Crooked Colour Chart
Part 2: The Amethyst
Part 3: Other Stones and Related
Part 4: The Rainbow

Introduction

This section is about another project I had done at school. It's called *Colours*. The year is 1974, and I had dated a page, 'Monday Fedruery'. I am eight and in the second year of juniors. Within is a bar chart on colours, stuff on rainbows, gems and how colours relate to nature.

It's another Trojan Horse.

Notice the various ways I spelled 'colour' (see image). This means locker, or lock-our. I am locked from knowing I'm an 'our' (plural). Colou*red* means 'lock-our-red'. This red-meaning would grow more obvious in later projects. I am locked from reading the codes within this *Colours* book. But the colours themselves hold meanings too. The way I write these words would show me.

Garnet red means daren't read. Spin the 'g' to 'd' to find daren't. Part of me daren't read these codes. The following shows why.

Part 1: The Crooked Colour Chart

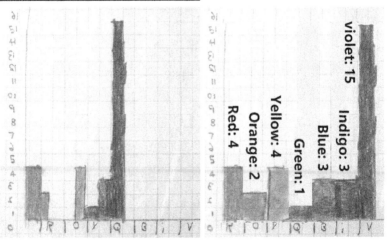

My colour bar chart. (Right) the same chart aligned.

The first page of this book shows a bar chart on colours (image far left). The class voted on their favourite, and we put together our findings.

I wrote (abridged): 'We found out which colour everyone liked best. We chose from red, orange, yellow, green, blue, indigo (and) violet. Most people chose violet. But no one chose yellow.'

But this isn't what my bar chart shows at all, for yellow gets four votes. Furthermore, I haven't lined up the colours with the labels. Image right shows the bar chart lined up.

An Earlier Election

Another 'election' seems to have taken place here. It's just like the questionnaire in my *Science* book. Each colour holds statements. Again, each is of truth and of lies. My research into my weather records has unearthed what each colour means.

The table shows the meaning behind each colour 'voted' on.

Colour	Meaning	Votes
Violet	Tell-vile	15
Yellow	Coward	4
Red	Read	4
Blue	Be-loo	3
Indigo	Go-big-in	3
Orange	Nor-age	2
Green	Grass	1

Violet (vile-let) comes top. It means vile-tell, to tell on the vile thing, and most people chose this one.

Yellow means cowardly-oblivion.

Red means read (past tense), to read these codes.

Blue means be-loo. I was used like a toilet. Part 4 of this chapter shows, and a drawing in my *Lines* project (chapter 5) would prove beyond a doubt.

Indigo contains the 'go' (just like king 'Og' in my *Human Being* project). My writing shows b-d issues and inbigo (read backwards in the word) means go-big-in. The memory of the 'big' thing 'in' me, must 'go'.

Orange means Nor-age, the age of when the big thing stayed.

The Green Grass

Green means grass, to tell, for I had written, 'Green is for the grass growing'. The image shows my drawing of a tall, straight tree growing from the 'grass'. Be-loo flowers flourish.

My future projects would often be completed in green notebooks. Image (inset bottom) shows a closeup of the cover. It's looks like grass. My plural wants to grass on the rape.

My projects on flowers (and poems) have been written in green notebooks like this. My *Human Being* project is the same: a green notebook. The green of grass is without question.

The Truth Stands Tall

This 'election' says it plain. I want to tell on the vile thing. Violet towers like the tall tree in my drawing. And straight means truth. The liar has been unanimously outvoted (orange, blue, red and green also mean truth). What's happened here?

The Rigged Election

My bar chart is crooked. None of the bars are aligned with the descriptors on the x-axis. This misalignment mirrors the crookedness in my head. The liar has misplaced the votes and rigged the election. The towering 'violet' has been placed above 'green' (denoted by the 'Q'), leaving its own space empty. It appears violet has no votes at all.

A tall tree of truth grows from the grass (to tell). Bottom shows a closeup of notebook covers I used in later projects. It is green and looks like grass.

The liar is crooked. My *Science* book has shown the same thing.

The Grass be Quiet

I have labelled green with a capital 'Q'. It was meant to be 'G'. At home, I kept spelling guitar, quitar. I have confused 'gu' with 'qu', and the g-q confusion has got in here.

Q means quit. Grass-quit. And the vile-tell has been placed in this quit-zone. A rigged election has occurred. My *Science* questionnaire is the same. Rigged.

I have written about colours in my *Earth* project too (chapter 7). Due to how it relates to *Colours*, I have placed it here. See the meanings poking through.

Colours (from *Earth* book)

The misspellings have been retained. The codes and meanings are given.

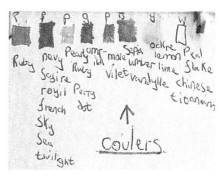

Red-read (past tense), **Ruby**-bury.

Blue-be-loo, **Navy** (written 'nevy'): envy. My plural envies my oblivion.

Safire-face-fire, **Royal** (written 'Royil'): your-lie, **French**: sh-fren (she-friend) The liar's claim, **Sky**-sick (nausea during rape), **Sea**-see (my plural has seen things), **Twilight**-we-lie-tie.

Pink-p-ink, **Pearly**-rape-lie, **Peridot**-buried-two (spin the 'p').

Green-grass, **Emrild**-me-lied. **Purple**-you-repel (u-repp'l).

Violet-vile-tell, **Mauve**: (written 'move') evict.

Brown-no-brow, **Sepia**: A-spia (spier). My plural knows things, **Umber**-unnder, **Vandylle** (VanDyke miswritten)-'ave-lied/lyin', **Ochre**: (written ockre): Combine: ochckre brings chock-'er. I was choked.

Yellow-coward, **Lemon**-on-e/m, **Lime**-I-e/m.

White-we-tie, **Flake**: I-fake, **Chinese**: She-seen, **Titanium**: I-at-numb.

As well as colours, we're writing about gems. Of note is the amethyst, as explained next.

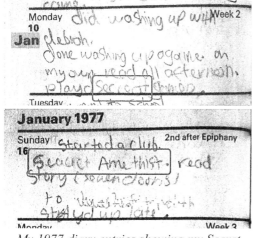

My 1977 diary entries showing my Secret Amethyst Club.

Part 2: The Amethyst

My *Colours* book collection of gems include amethyst, emerald, ruby and others.

Amethyst holds significance for my plural, for forming the name of a club begun in three years' time. My 1977 diary shows.

It was called the Secret Amethyst Club, and Eve (and another sister) were members. The image shows my diary entries.

This club centres on hobbies and meetings. My 1978 diary provides a timetable and a list of pastimes. Mine are novel writing, art and music. The liar doesn't like this 'club'. It means creativity and the liar rather I didn't create a thing.

Notice my erroneous 'a' in 'Seacret'. A code in this word has just poked through: 'creates'. On 10 Jan, I report of playing 'secreat games'. The club is secret because the liar in my head mustn't know about the 'creates'.

How odd. One part of my brain (my plural) is keeping a secret from another part (the liar). My spelling 'Amethist' means am-the-sit, and 'club' means penis. I was sat on a penis, and this must be kept 'secret'. Amethyst forms part of my plural's Saltland language. It comes from my toddlerhood.

How I wrote words hint at my plural's codes.

Part 3: Other Stones and Gems

The images show how I wrote amethyst and other stones within this *Colours* book.

I shall begin with the 'stone' (top row).

Remember the stone within my *Science* book? It means not-know-st (stain). The 'not' is central and means denial. The image shows I was right about the 'stain', for I have written stone, 'stane'. (My 'o' resembles an 'a'). The 'st' in stone is saint, anagram of stain.

Indeed, I had written about the stone (abridged): 'I have seen one stone. And it is sapphire and (and) it feels smooth. I'm going to keep the smooth stone.'

My *Science* book has told me that smooth means me-too-sh. Too (two) means plural and hush about it. My cloud-spelling, *clou-st* (second row) means you-lock-stain. I have locked the stain away. Indeed, 'cloud' means you-locked (just like 'colour'). My weather records have an abundance of locks.

The third row with the 'amethyst' has been explained, but the words neighbouring are 'rudy-red' (instead of ruby). My plural has flagged 'ruby' for meaning I-bury-read. I am not allowed to read the 'bury'.

With the said gems mean, am-the-sit, you-repel (and) me-liar/lied. Emerald has been explained in my *Science* book.

My plurality emerges in the fourth row. I have written 'and' twice. Notice the ghost 'o' in 'too' and errant 'I' in 'myself' (my-seife). I have an extra 'I'.

Saffire-Face-fire

Finally (bottom row) 'sapphire'. This means face-fire. During suffocation, my face felt ablaze. In the first instance, I had written this word, 'safire' (fourth row). This spelling has been taken from my *Earth* project (chapter 7). The code reads backwards from the central 'f' to bring 'fase'. This means 'face'. The 'fire' is obvious. My 'sappire' brings 'pyre'. Regardless of future spellings, the face-fire code remains. My 'Fedruery' (following image) means rue-fryed. I rue the frying. And this means my burning face. My plural has injected potent meanings into colours and gems. But I can't 'red' them.

Eyes Misaligned

Notice my face drawing. My eyes are bright blue, like sapphires. The iris and pupil of the left eye fall outside the eye-socket. This means half-oblivion to the face-fire and the be-loo. But my plural (the right eye) can see everything. The knowledge burdens her. Future creations would show similar things: an eye hooded or misaligned. I am half-blind.

The Go in Gold

On colours, I would further write: 'My eyes are blue, my hear (hair) is golden and I like to wear a white and gold dress.' (And) 'Gold is for the princess' crown'. Crown means head. My coins project has shown.

The final image of this section shows my dress. Gold contains 'go' (just like indigo and Og). It means go-old. Go away old-age. And orange means Nor-age. Go away-old-Nor-age. My toddlerhood is 'vile'.

Brown surrounds my head, yet my hair is fair. Brown means no-brow – oblivion. My head is off-centre of the body, just like the bar chart. The liar in my head has made me crooked.

The Other Gems

Further gems mentioned are, lapis-lazuli, onyx, pearl, topaz and turquoise. These mean oblivion, lies and rape. Section 7 explains.

My rainbow-expressions and colours.

I write at length about rainbows. Rainbows dot my future weather reports (and my projects). I would explain how they form.

But what I write here is odd. This is what I have put (abridged).

'I went over by the rainbow and I "cimbed" up it and then I have seen a big hole, but my balance is not good. The rainbow is melting and (I) ran down the rainbow. The colours are red, yellow, pink, green, and gold.

'The rainbow is nearly gone (I continue) and I ran down the rainbow and I found my seife. I looked up and the rainbow is still there. And if I went up the rainbow, it looks as if the rainbow is going, and if I went down, it looks as if the rainbow is still there and thick to(o). Rainbows got bright coluors.'

The Rein in Rainbow

What am I trying to say here?

I went up a rainbow and saw a 'big hole' (c)-*im-bed* (in-bed). My 'balance is not good'. The hole appears to mean coma during suffocation. I remember blacking out. On coming-to, I had felt dizzy, hence my balance 'is not good'. But what about the rainbow itself?

After researching my weather projects, I have come to learn that rainbow means rein-bow. I am reined from seeing the 'bow'. Bow means my body position during rape. I was 'bent' and raped from behind. Remember 'bendy' in my *Science* project? This means bend-I – the same thing.

Notice my errant 'd' in rainbow (see image). This means rein'd. I am reined from seeing the bow. I had written, 'I ran down the rainbow and I found my-seife.' I have found 'myself' at the 'rein'd-bow', for it is via the bending that I am joined to my plural.

Capital B To Be

I keep capitalising the 'B'. I'm having issues with the b-facing, it seems. But my plural would use this as an opportunity to express, the verb to 'be' (in the capital 'B'). The images show RainBow. This brings rein-be-ow. It hurts and I'm full of woe.

70

Be-lack and Be-loo

I'm capitalising the 'B' in Black, too. I have written, 'Black is for the cat come out of the night, and the sky at night.' Black means be-lack. I am lacking part of myself, and I am kept in the dark. Blue means be-loo. I was made to feel like a loo during rape. These meanings would stick, even when the B-issue is resolved, and I use the lowercase.

The Blue Reverberates

I would expand on the blue.

'Blue is for the sea with waves, and the sky is Blue. Blue is for the Blue sea and Blue is for the Blue sky and Blue is for the Blue paint and Blue is for the Blue paper.' (And) 'Pink is for the pink paper.'

I have written 'Blue' ten times here. Every 'blue' is capitalised and my plural wants me to notice. All mean be-loo. Looby Loo (of *Andy Pandy*), a children's programme of my toddlerhood, seems to have played a part in this code.

The Blue Ink

The be-lue has cast a long shadow over my life. Concurrent to doing this *Colours* project, I inked over the face of my sister's new Barbie. I thought it was the old one and I got into terrible trouble over it. My plural saw herself in the old Barbie for being replaced with a new one. Blue-face means be-loo face and she wants the memory preserved.

In future years, I suffered flashbacks of a blue girl poisoned by ink. I kept seeing a blue girl raped in rockpools and down the toilet. The girl is blue for being used like a loo.

Blue-Beginnings

My plural has latched onto the sea and sky to represent the dawning of my conscious awareness and where the be-loo hides. Saltland comes from the sea. The be-loo raper (Blue-paper) is just out of sight. The 'pink paper' means blue too, for the ink-raper. Ink means to write. I am writing about it here.

My me-drawing and (image right) my hexagon design with flowers and butterflies.

The Other Colours

Image (right) shows my hexagon drawing adorned with butterflies and flowers. In a weather project about ice crystals, I would explain hexagon means 'six-sided'. Swap the 'i' and 'e' to find sexs-idid. This means 'I did sex'. Indeed, hexagon contains the 'ex'. I have divorced myself for the 'sex' he did on me.

I will end this section on 'red'. This colour means 'read' (past tense). But I was forever drawing roses too. They are red as well. I gifted a rose-drawing to a teaching assistant. Within this *Colours* book, I had put, 'Red is for blood that came out of your skin'. (And), 'Red is for blood and roses'. My plural wants me to read the blood-red meaning. I pretended my middle name was 'Susan Rose'. This means use-sore. I was used sore and bled.

Section 7 summarises the meanings behind these colours and gems.

Chapter 5: Lines	**Part 3: The Telephone**
Introduction	**Part 4: The Hara-Kara Dam**
Part 1: The Be-loo Lines	**Part 5: Projectiles**
Part 2: The Liar's Way	**Part 6: The Lying World**

Images on the cover of my school project.

Introduction

This chapter looks at my final surviving schoolbook. I have called it '*Cylinders, Tubes, Pipes (and) Lines on Maps*'. For ease, I have shortened this title to simply '*Lines*'. The topic appears to be things that interconnect, such as telephone wires, pipes and map gradients. The date given on the front cover is 16 June 1975. This must have marked the starting point of this project. I had just turned ten.

This book turned up when I was fifty-one. Mum had just died, and she had hoarded some of my schoolwork. Had I not seen this book, I would never have remembered it. Since learning the horrible truth about my toddlerhood, I have come to learn that clues to my past have been trickling through my schoolwork regardless.

This one is no different.

Part 1: The Be-loo Lines

On the cover, I would encounter my drawings. They show a map, a toilet, a telephone and pylons. The toilet forms centre piece. The seat is bright red. It's like a mouth. The cistern is blue. I have already worked out that blue means be-loo. I have now encountered an

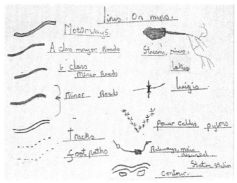

My drawings of things that convey.

illustration of the be-loo code. It's blatant in the middle of my cover. I was used like a loo during oral rape.

To the right of the loo is the telephone. This means communication. The wires between are mirroring what is trying to happen in my head – wire up. My plural wants me to remember when I was used like a loo.

Things that Convey

The first page of my book lists things that provide access: motorways, roads, tracks, footpaths, streams, rivers, lakes, bridges, power-cables, pylons and railways. Messages are transmitted in the brain like this. But certain ones are prohibited from getting through. The reason is trauma. My lake and tributary drawing resemble a nerve cell. But it's marooned. The same thing seems to be happening in my head: memories marooned.

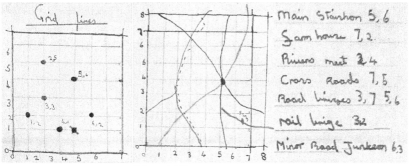

My grid lines on my maps.

Grid Lines Far Apart

On the next page, I would describe gridlines. Ordnance Survey Maps are touched upon, and I explain that coordinates say 'exsitedly' where you are.

I had meant 'exactly', but I had spelled this word with a sat-tic. My aberration means ex-sitted-lie. I have divorced part of myself for being

73

mounted during rape. My gridlines are providing a map of where my plural is in relation to my oblivion. We are living parallel lives, but lightyears apart.

The Landmarks

I have listed landmarks.

The first is 'Main Staishion'. I had meant 'Station'. This means man-sat-on, I-shun. A man sat on me in toddlerhood, and I have shunned myself as a result. On the previous page, I had written 'stalion' instead of station. This means a brawny male.

Next up is 'Farm House'. My 'f' looks like a slashed 's' (see previous image), and in fact means 'rams-house'. I was rammed into, and this house represents my home gone rotten. I would soon write children's stories about a little girl called Sam. Her name is torn on a rag at a railway bridge. Sam mirrors the ams of her author.

My next landmark is where 'Rivers meet'. Remember my nerve-like lake? This nerve cell is disconnected, and I cannot remember the be-loo. Crossroads means connection. It's a place that has been waiting for me my entire life: recall. My research had begun at this crossroads.

The following explains.

Part 2: The Liar's Way

The remaining landmarks are bridge-related. There are road bridges, rail bridges footbridges and a road junction. All mean access. And none join up.

In April 1985, I began a novel. It was called *The Lessons*. In this novel is a derelict railway station. A psychopath operates a criminal ring there and he craves collaboration from a man with a burnt face. I called this man Aidan. My rapist's name can be found there. I worked for decades on this novel and kept it secret from family and friends. My secret world took over my life and, during writing episodes, I lost weight and became ill. It seems the seeds to this novel have already been sewn in this school project when I was ten.

The Derelict Railway Station

A derelict railway station in fact exists in the village. It hasn't been used since 1933. The bridge provides the only route to a neighbouring town where Uncle Dan used to sign-on with Dad. From 1977, I would regularly traverse this station on my way to senior school. After a while, I started seeing a big man on the roadside. I imagined he had acromegaly, a disorder of overgrown bones. My rapist was over six-feet tall. To a toddler, he would have seemed colossal.

Acromegaly Rac-Me-Ugly

This big-preoccupation has already been seen in my *Human Being* project (chapter 1). I kept writing about big men. This is because a big man lived in my toddlerhood home.

74

I would soon see myself in the big man. He would become me, for I would insert my own hang-ups behind his face. Acromegaly reinforces what I have done. A code exists in 'acromegaly'. It's just like dyslexia.

Notice the opening 'rac' code. This is followed by 'me' – Rac-me. With the 'o' this word ends with 'ogely'. Ugly. Me-Rac-ugly. Rape made me feel ugly. I felt big and ugly. And in later years I would write about a big man who feels ugly inside. As seen from the Gerald and Geraldine, 'he' is in fact a s/he.

Disused and Shunned

The big man haunts a disused railway station. A strong code exists at that station too. Disused means 'is-usedd' and station, sat-shun. My childhood home had gone derelict for a paedophile living there in 1968. This station is just a ten-minute walk from the cottage, and I know Uncle Dan had taken me out in the pushchair. I cannot rule out the possibility he had taken me to that station.

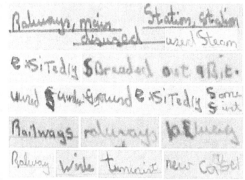

My railway expressions and related betrays of the liar in my head.

The Liar's-Way

Later in this book, I would return to railways. I have conducted a light edit for ease of read.

'The first railways were used as coalmines,' (I think the final word says).

'The shapes of the first railways were three lines sBreaded out aBit. Some tracks carry clay and dirt. Trackmen and coolmen (coalmen) work hard. Tracks (make) loud noises. Wires on railways are used underground.

'The railway (I continue) was opened on 27 of September 1825. The first train was pulled by locomotives. No.1 from New Casel (Newcastle) Factory was the first public railway in the world to used steam locomotion.'

(And finally):

'Steam trains changed to electric with cables that pull the train. The boat-trains had seats for passengers. The boat-train ended at the London terminist (terminal). You could hear the doors slam and the wisle (whistle) blow. They say their last fere wells (farewells) to their friends.'

The Hidden Meaning

The read is disjointed and loaded with codes.

My heading, 'Railways' means 'liar's-way'. Read back from the 'l' to see the phrase. The previous image shows my plural flagging-up this word with odd spellings: Railway, ralway then larway. Wisle means we-lies.

Sat-tics litter this page. I was mounted in toddlerhood and my plural sees seat in 'steam'. I have written 'used steam' (instead of use steam), 'terminist' (instead of 'terminal'). And New Casel (Instead of Newcastle, with an 'at' rubbed out). I stumble over sat-words for meaning mounted.

I am being lied to about my toddlerhood and this is the liar's-way.

The Be-says Outed

My 'Three lines sBreaded out aBit' shows I'm still capitalising the 'B'. This issue has been seen in my *Colours* project too. Blue means be-loo. I did the same thing with my '*sBaise'* (space) project that same year. The capitalised 'B' means 'be'. The verb. SBaise means be-saise. Be-says. My book is saying things to me.

My 'sBreaded out' means be-reads out-ed. Notice the 'outed' at the end. The liar has outed the 'read'. I am not allowed to read these codes.

The 'Three-lines' means three's-lyin'. My three-year-old self isn't to be believed.

The aBit means a-be-it. Read backwards to find 'tied-a'. **a beit tied a** With the 'a' becomes slang for tied-'er' – tied-her. This sentence comes together: 'Three's-lyin'. Be-reads outed, tied-her.'

This paragraph is loaded with rebuttals and denials. The truth has been tied up, outed and refuted.

My future codes would show a lot more like this.

The Underground

This page ends with the sentence, 'Wires on railways are used underground'. The liar's-way (railways) is doing things underground. The 'lock-omotive' means lock-motive and the hardworking coalman means a-lockman. The liar doesn't want me knowing about the c-lay-dirt of my toddlerhood.

A hidden language is pouring out of my work, and *I* am not allowed to read them. I'm 'garnet-red' (daren't-read).

This next part is about another mode of communication: the telephone.

Part 3: The Telephone

I would begin this section: 'The telephone, (spelled telepone) was invented by Alexander Graham Bell. Direct lines enable two people to speak to one another.'

My plural sees the telephone as a symbol of communicating with her oblivious-self. In future diary reports, I would uncover my odd behaviour around the telephone.

On 1 August 1977, we had a telephone installed. The next few days, I'm chalking faces all over the front path. My plural is trying to tell me about my used face.

On 11 Jun 1982, I got in a state at art college because my painting of a telephone had gone missing. A force in my head is hiding the 'telephone'.

I would also report of receiving telephone calls from a 'friend'. For weeks, I don't mention her name in my diary. But would turn out to be a 'Karen' (at school). Her name contains Rak like me. The liar in my head saw us as a couple of 'Racs' communicating. Hence her name has been withheld in my diary.

The telephone symbolises communication. The liar inhibits all modes.

Part 4: The Kara-Hara Dam

I move onto pipes. It begins with dams.

'A dam is to flap water from hiding pleases,' (I write).

I had meant 'hiding places'. The truth is hiding from me, and a dam is stopping it getting through.

'A reservoir is an artificial lake (I go on). A filter bed is a

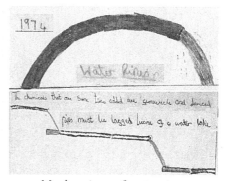

My drawings of waterpipes.

tank. At first it is pumped through fine mesh filters or sand. The water then flows onto slow filter beds. They are made of layers of sand and gravel. The water passes through and trickles down drain holes into pipes.'

My drawing of a 'famous' dam.

The Famous Kara-Hara Dam

'The famous Hara Dam (I continue) is a big pool for our drinks. Rain and streams run down pipes and leads to our taps and that's how we get water.'

The Obscure Dam

On the previous page, I had called it the 'Kara Dam'. I've looked up both words and cannot establish this dam. I have enhanced the words at the top of my illustration to show. Instead of a dam, my drawing shows rough seas

77

and an island. This island has sheer cliffs. Around this time, I was writing about rockfalls and cliffside deaths. I had also made up an island. It was called Saltland. I conceived a language for it and placenames. This drawing appears to be Saltland.

The Racks

My codes contain a lot of 'Racs'. Kara (Dam) is one. 'Karen' is another. This means me. Rac forms part of my name. 'Hara' forms another. Kara-Hara means my plural and me. We echo one another but a 'dam' separates us.

In spring 1983, I wrote about the volcano Krakatoa (chapter 14). Notice the 'Kra' in the name. What appears to be a routine project has turned out to carry a message about my burning face in toddlerhood. Krakatoa is me.

*Top: Close up of my symbols. **Bottom**: The Saltland symbol in my wildflowers project. **Right**: My 'A' resembles a crossroads over a track.*

The Symbols

But what of these weird symbols? (See upper image inset). They're on the facing page to my 'dam'.

These symbols appear to be from my Saltland language (which I no longer have). Saltland means Sat-land, a time and place when I was mounted by Uncle Dan.

I recognise my distinct 'A' from a project I had done on wildflowers that same year (see chapter 10). I had made up an imaginary publishing company called 'Soltland Books'. The signature 'A' is distinct. My reconstruction (inset right) shows this 'A' simplified. My string of symbols can now be translated. Read back from the final 'S' to find sAAt. The spiral means coma.

My Number: 19865

But the 'S' also looks like a '5'. This number forms part of 8915.

I've come across this number several times in my projects now. It's a blend of my birthyear and the year I was raped: 1965 and 1968. (Rotate the '9' to get the '6'). 19865. These years form touchstones to my coins project and the 'degrees' chart. The same goes for my other projects and a short story *On My Own* (written 19 May 1975). In this short, a book prophesising about 1985 lies on a road.

The Lessons' Crossroads

Strangely, I would begin my novel *The Lessons* in 1985. A key scene describes a woman finding a book on a crossroads. I notice four crosses in my symbols here. This means four-cross (or fork-cross), another way of expressing a crossroads. My 'A' looks like a crossroads too. A track recedes into the distance.

This crossroads means recall. One day, I will remember being raped and suffocated in toddlerhood. This memory has been waiting for me my entire life. Only then will I have a choice. Whilst oblivious, I have none.

Underground Tunnels

My Rack-Dam continues on the next page. It has tunnels. I write: 'The path of the tunnel has to be worked out carefully. It is planned out long before the work starts. The danger is that we'll sufer-cait if the tunnel caved in.'

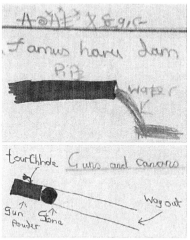

Pipes and gun barrels.

I had meant 'suffocate'. My plural has found a way of getting this word in. The underground tunnel has made this possible. I continue: 'The way to move a channel tunnel is planking. There are other tunnels like (the) Channel Tunnel, such as ancient tunnels, Simplon Tunnel and the Mersty (Mersey) Tunnel.'

Mersty means me-sit (Mesyt) and it is 'ancient'.

My plural is trying to tell me through this project about my toddlerhood. The tunnel is an underground way.

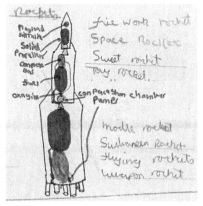

My drawing of a rocket.

Part 5: Projectiles

I move onto projectiles. Guns is one. It's another 'pipe'.

I have drawn a waterpipe and a gun barrel. I had labelled my gun and canon: torch-hole, stone and gun powder. This picture contains a word that strongly connects to my rapist. My plural would also see the torch-hole as the burning sensation within a vagina. This is due to the 'stone' inside. Stone means not-know-stain. I don't know what I'm drawing. But my plural does. She has got me to draw a rape symbol via a gun barrel.

79

This entire project has provided a wealth of opportunities for my plural. She is telling me I was raped and suffocated in toddlerhood via these pipes.

Ex-Dogging in Oxygen

I move onto the rocket, another projectile. I had written:

'The fuel and the oxaginen is burnt, so it goes out the bottom and moves the rocket forward.' (I would also spell it oxa-ginen and oxagine).

My *Human Being* project three years later would show the same oxygen-oddity. Combined, these tell me I have exed part of myself that sees my face sullied by dogs peeing or mating in parks. In fact, it was Uncle Dan that had sullied me, not a dog at all, but the liar has hidden him from view.

My oblivion meant I couldn't make sense of these vile notions. What could I do but ignore them?

Rocket Symbols

I now list types of rockets.

Firework rocket, space rocket, sweet rocket, toy rocket, model rocket, flying rocket and weapon rocket.

The firework and the weapon sort convey rape sensations for the force and the burning. But the sweet rocket means oblivion. I know this from my food reports in future diaries. The liar in my head has used my sweet tooth to imply I crave sweet oblivion. 'Sweet rocket' is a numbing injection to keep me from the truth. My dream diary has shown recurring ones of being on a hospital drip.

Model (rocket) means do-elm (od-elm). Elm is a split me (m/e) and I am 'doing' it. Flying rocket means f-lying away. The 'toy' rocket indicates when I did so: childhood. And the sBaise rocket means be-says about the 'rocket'. My plural has used different rockets to tell me about the rape and the aftermath.

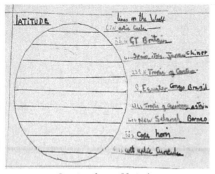

Latitudes of lyin's.

Part 6: The Lying World

Early in this *Lines* book, I have written about 'Latitudes' and I shall return to it here.

I have drawn lines all over the world. Indeed, I had labelled this drawing, '*Lines of the World*'. They represent the latitudes. In future weather projects, I would draw images like these to show weather systems and wind cells.

Lines means lies. Notice the word within. With the 'n' forms the tense, lie-n' (lying). It's just like the three-lines earlier, which means three's-lyin'.

And these 'lyin's' are all over the world. The *Coins of the World* (chapter 2) is the same: I-cons all over the world. Cape Horn means cape-Nor. My rapist is caped from view. Brasil means be-liars and Congo means go-con. The liar is everywhere, and I can't see it. Section 7 explains the rest.

Tubes in the Body

The final section of my *Lines* book looks at tubes in the body. Unlike the lyin's of earlier, the truth pokes through.

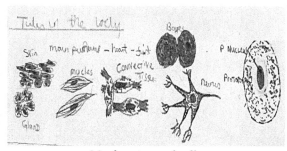

My drawings of cells.

'There is lots of "tubs" in your body (I write). Veins, windpipes, skelington, arms and legs. The pumping of the heart is the heartbeat. The rate is called the pulse.

'The tubes that carry blood from your heart are called arteries. The tubes which collect the blood is called veins.'

Twice, the word 'uncle' appears on this page. It's in my drawing: 'nucleus' and in 'mucles' (meaning muscles). On the same page, I write about the windpipe and the pulse. I do not remember the day I drew these pictures, but I can guarantee I had suffered intrusive thoughts.

My drawing of hair follicles. (Top) the liar-code exposed.

The Hair-Liar

My book ends with a drawing of hair follicles. I had labelled this drawing simply 'Hairs'. As already seen, hair forms part of the 'liar' code. The image show arrows pointing each way. They look like two 'lls'.

Shift each upright and reverse to find 'liars.' The image (top) shows. The 'Hairs means her – her-(hair) liars.

The liar has two faces, hence two-faced 'liar'. One face is for my plural, and the other is for my oblivion. I know this from my dream diary and these creations.

The plural-liar is a bully and a tyrant.

The oblivion-liar is false and obsequious.

The two-faced liar is there to preserve my oblivion. That's all. A gap has formed between them (see image). Most of my hair grows on my head. The liar is *in* my head.

My drawing is almost symmetrical. It's like the Kara-Hara dam. I am two and a dam (the liar) separates us. The chasm is like the dam from another perspective. But further down, I am joined to my plural. This is where magma-like colours are situated. Here we find blue and red. These mean read-be-loo. And each enters the 'mouth' of the follicles. But yellow surrounds. This means cowardly-oblivion. My traumatic toddlerhood is buried deep. And the liar is keeping me from the truth.

My Aurther Books

SECTION 3: AURTHER BOOKS

Introduction
Chapter 6: Book 1 Space
Chapter 7: Book 2 The Earth
Chapter 8: Book 3 Wildflowers
Chapter 9: Book 4 Weather
Aurther Books: Conclusion

Introduction

I have analysed all my surviving (academic) schoolbooks and uncovered a blatant message in my *Human Being* project. This section looks at my other projects.

As seen, I wanted to write about everything. In 1974, I wrote and illustrated four books about nature. I was nine and these form some of my earliest surviving writing.

I bound them myself and called them 'Aurther Books' (misspelling author). I wanted to become a published author. I made up my own logo, including 'W-books with a small beetle. Saltland Books was another imaginary publishing company.

These books are A6, held together with string. They appear to be the routine creations of a schoolchild. But the 'W' (double-you) means I have another self and she is disclosing of my toddlerhood rape through these books.

I remember sitting at the kitchen leaf table writing these books. The sun streamed through the window, Nan (my rapist's mother) was about, and the radio was on. But I felt horrible inside. The horrible feeling had no name and

82

I ignored it. I now know I was carrying a sat-feeling from my toddlerhood. But my 'W' knew about it. Through these books, my plural has stowed messages. I would uncover my earliest codes and see how they have evolved in later years.

Book 1 is called *Space*.

Chapter 6: Book 1 Space

Introduction
Part 1: The Me-Tear-Writes
Part 2: Star Clusters
Part 3: The Solar System
Part 4: Other Celestial Objects

Introduction

Space haunted me. I already knew about lightyears and supernovas. Dad had a telescope in his bedroom where I viewed the Moon. It seemed cold, remote. We had Holst *the Planets*, which we played a few times and I found that haunting too,

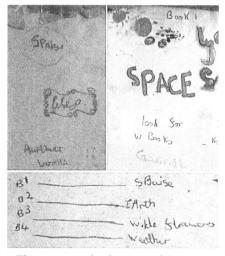

The cover and title page of Space.

especially *Mars*. My plural's remoteness is symbolised in all. She feels lightyears away from me.

In August 1979, I would get a book on black holes and read it cover to cover. In future years, I would read other astronomy books, and in August 1980, would complete an astronomy project (chapter 15).

In 1997, I would write and illustrate a children's book about a little girl's venture into space. An annex painting showing a scarred teapot and the Moon would win me a trip to see the 1999 eclipse in Alderney.

Space, Spaise and Sbaise

I am back to 1974 and my first of four Aurther books. It's called *Space*.

I knew how to spell this word, yet I went awry with Spaise and sBaise. The same is happening with other words too, such as Venus and Neptune. I go awry with words I knew how to spell. These discrepancies are exposing the fuel behind my projects and is my plural. The capital 'B' means 'be' (the verb). The sBaise means be-saise. This book is saying things to me.

Be-says.

For ease of read, I have conducted a light edit (but retaining misspellings). My '**notes**' explain my findings.

Part 1: The Me-Tear-Writes

The opening sentence of my *Space* book is 'Asteroids are colder than Ploto. They are behind it.'

I had misspelled Pluto. This planetoid is remote with nothing beyond but rocks.

Asteroids contain sat and seat. Indeed, there is a lot of 'sits' in this project. I would find biggist, deepist, coldist and nrist (meaning nearest). Sit means the mounting. The 'sat' (of asteroid) is 'behind' Pluto. Something mounted me from behind.

My next sentence is 'Meterits fall on Earth, making big holes.'

I had meant *meteorites*. The co-author of this book (my plural) is me-te*ar*-writes, my torn-self writing. My W-logo is the same: double-you, and she has come to Earth from a remote place to tell me about my horrible toddlerhood.

I continue with, 'Moon is the Earthy Moon, which is the third planet near sun.'

And...

'Cratuses are own Moon's. They are big holes. You can land a rocket on one.'

My misspelt craters contain an 'us'. My plural has already told me about the 'big hole' on the 'rein-bow'. It's in my *Colours* book. The big hole speckles my works because a hole was made in me.

Illustrations about star clusters.

Part 2: Star Clusters

I would list four star-clusters. I had selected the 'Pan' (meaning the Plough), Scorpion (meaning Scorpio), a man with his belt with a dog (meaning Orion and his dog, Sirius). And the Lion (meaning Leo).

The Pan

The Pan means Pa-nap – coma due to a father-figure. I have fallen oblivious after toddlerhood rape, and I can no longer remember the Pa.

The Scorpion

Next is the Scorpion. It contains the Nor with a sting on his tail. My plural would see the Scorpion in the face-hugger of the film, *Alien* (1979). And in my novel, *The Lessons*, I would write about a scorpion tattoo. For my plural, the Scorpion has come to symbolise rape.

Prior to analysing my book on *Space*, I was researching my 1977 diary. This diary contains factoids about the world. These are touched upon in chapter 18. Of relevance is Orion, as seen here.

Factoid 51: (11 – 17 Dec 1977): The Constellation of Orion

'Orion (the Hunter) stands next to his dog, Sirius, (this snippet reads). Sirius is the brightest star in the night sky and one of the nearest to us.'

The Nor is blatant here, and his 'belt' is phallic for the location of the central star. Sirius is a homophone of cirrius, (my misspelt cirrus cloud) and both mean us-cries. My plural is crying out about the Nor. Hunter would enter a story I would write in Christmas 1978 called *Hindbury's Run*. My toddlerhood has fuelled my stories.

Finally, Lion means lie-on (lyin'). It's just like 'lines'. I'm being lied to about my toddlerhood and lions would soon appear in my artwork.

Other Star Clusters

So, I had written about star-clusters. Each says something about my toddlerhood. Later, I would return to stars. This is what I had put.

'The Milky Way is all the things stars make. Stars make shapes like a Pan and Scorpio. Stars are bright. Some stars are shooting stars and dead stars. They do not make noises. The space is (as) black as tar.'

How desolate. My plural is describing coma, the milky thing and the saat (star). She is alone with the memory, and all has gone quiet.

I had written a space poem. It goes:

'Stars are bright, planets, round, the sun is white, shooting stars make not a sound.

Milky Way are stars, the sun is bright, the space looks like tar. (And) stars are bright.'

The testimony of a brutalised toddler has entered this book. My research has shown my plural would learn about the world alongside me and gather grownup concepts.

Part 3: The Solar System

The main body of this book is about the solar system. I had reclassed the spheres a 'round ball', for not all are planets. This is how my list goes.

My List of 'Round Balls'

Mecry: is the 1st planet nr sun.
Venus: is the 2nd round ball nr sun.
Earth: is the 3rd round ball nr sun.
Moon: Is the 4th round ball nr sun.
Mars: is the 5th round ball nr sun.

Jupiter is the 6th round ball nr sun.
Saturn: is the 7th 8th round ball nr sun.
Uranus: is the 7th 8th round ball nr sun.
Nepjune: is the 6th 9th planet nr sun.
Ploto: is the 10th round ball nr sun.
Sun: The sun is nr Mecry.

Notice the misspellings of these worlds. The codes are poking through. I also go awry with the numbering. Mars is the fourth 'round ball' near sun, but here has become the fifth. My account of each sphere, (beginning with the sun) would reveal more.

My drawing and my sun-son spellings.

The Sun: 'is the hottest round ball on space (I begin). There is nothing behind it, only Mecry, which is the nrist planet to sun. The sun has sBots and fire, making the sun bright, that nobody can look at it. It makes people blind. The sun has the hottest fire of all.'

Notes: The sun has two meanings. It's my face burning during rape but is also the cause (the 'son'). Uncle Dan was Nan's son and she stopped concurrent. I had used both spellings in this book (see images) to mean each.

Sun (and) son.

'Looking at the sun can make you blind' (I had written). This means oblivion. I can't see the son raping me, for the burning of my 'sbot' was so hot. The memory is stored elsewhere in my brain for being traumatic. It's behind where I can't see.

The Son in Me

Weirdly, the 'son' also means me, by this I mean Uncle Dan. My diary entry of 17 Jul 1982 shows. Here, Aunt Maud had taken Eve, Nan and me to meet him. I hadn't seen him since toddlerhood.

'I don't remember him at all (I had written). He was tall, plump and really tanned.' Afterwards, I sat on a sun-swing and thought he was 'nice'.

Had I really written that? I had noted he still lives with Gwen. I remain like her, bedfellows and in the cage. And that morning, I had bought a silver plaited necklace for Mum and me. Silver means decree, and this act suggests a pledge to keep quiet about the rape.

The plump and sunburnt means my burnt and pot-bellied self in toddlerhood. Nice means kind. I have projected my own image onto my rapist. My view of the world has been filtered through the liar's lens and I can't see a thing.

1: Mercry

No wonder my projects are filled with double-meaning.

Mercury is the same. The following explains.

'Mecry is the 1st planet nr son (I had written). The half facing the sun is very hot, and the shady half is very cold. Mecry is the hottest planet of all,

My Mercury drawing and the various ways I wrote the word.

and the planet behind is Venus. Mercry is hotter than the desert and (the) hottest place on Earth.'

Notes: See the codes glaring. Mercury has become a blend of me-cry and mercy. Me-cry is the first planet near (the) son (I had written) and the 'facing' is very hot. This means my burning face during oral rape by Nan's son. My drawing of Mercury represents my face on fire. The image (right) has been flipped on its back to show a face prone. This is how I lay during oral rape. My features appear erased.

What Lies Behind

Mecry is 'behind' the sun (I had opened). This is Mercury from another angle. Read from the 'c' to find Cryme. A crime is being committed behind my back. Every planet is the same: When of focus, means me; when described as *behind*, becomes my rapist.

The Knives

Venus is *behind* Mercury. From this angle, it means my rapist. He is behind and I can't see him.

The images show my Venus-spelling morph into Vines. This means knives. (Read backwards from the 'n' to find it.) The rape felt like stabbing. No wonder 'Me-cry-mercy'.

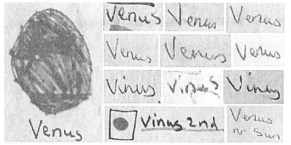

My Venus drawing and my various spellings.

2: Venus

'Venus is the second planet nr son (I now write). The planet behind, is the Earth, which is the 3rd planet nr sun. Venus is a bit

87

cooler than Mecry but Venus is still hot and Venus is still far from the sun.'

Notes: I would eventually learn that Venus is in fact hotter than Mercury, for the greenhouse effect. I have spelled 'sun' 'son' again. Venus would morph too. I would spell it 'Vinus' or 'Vines. The images show.

The Envies

Being the object of focus, Venus has become me. No longer is it knives, but 'envies'. This is what Venus now means. Notice a ghost 'I' in my spellings. The envy is for my oblivious-self writing this book.

Venus has two meanings, just like the sun and Mercury.

My Earth drawing and my expressions.

The Hearth

But behind Venus is the Earth. The Earth is now the force, for it is *'behind'* and I can't see it.

Read from the 'h' to find 'hearth'. We had a hearth in the cottage and Nan often used this word when stoking up the fire. My plural sees the burning there. The fire reminds her of rape. The image shows 'hearth'.

3: Earth

'Earth is the 3rd planet nr sun (I write). We live our lives on it. Earth is the only planet that has water, like seas, rivers and freshwater from "tapes". The round ball behind Earth is the Moon, which is not a planet. Inside Earth, there is hot molten metel.'

Notes: Earth has now become me, for being the object of focus. The object behind (the Moon) is the force. Earth means The-ar (the-are. Read from 'th' and rotate through). I am plural and 'she' is 'me-tell' (my misspelled metal).

My 'tapes' means seat-p, and water (from the sea) means Saltland. Behind Earth is the Moon. This means buttocks. My rapist's trousers must have been down when he raped me.

4: Moon

'Moon is the 4th round ball nr sun (I now inform). Moon is not a planet. Behind the Moon is Mars. The Moon has craters. If you are on the Moon, you can see Earth. The Moon is sometimes like half a circle.

The Moon has cratus, mountains and sand like sea sand.'

Notes: The Moon has now become me for being the object of focus. I am 'mono'. My 'half-circle' says so. The other half is in shadow. I can't see it. My plural is hidden, just like the half-butterfly. My poem *Moon Mystery* (shown at the end of this book) echoes this sentiment.

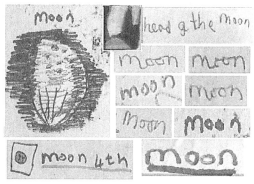

My moon drawing and my various expressions.

The Moon has 'us' (cratus), mountains (mountings) and sea-sand (like Saltland).

Behind the Moon is Mars. Mars symbolises the force and means rams. Something rammed into me from behind, and this is why I am mono. The Moon's craters are the scars of burning. Notice the 'head of the Moon' drawing. It looks like a red penis. I had seen something like that in toddlerhood and it had burnt me.

5: Mars

'Mars is the 5th planet nr sun (I continue). Mars is the red planet. The planet behind is Jupiter. Mars is medium degrees. Is (is) sometimes 50 degrees.'

Notes: I have gone awry with the numbers, for Mars is in fact the fourth planet from the sun. The Moon has caused me to slip up. This discrepancy would continue, but I would attempt to resolve this error in my next Aurther book, the *Earth*.

My Mars drawing and how I wrote the word.

I have now become Mars for being the object of focus. No longer is it the 'Rams' but 'Are-ams' (plural). Notice the 'is-is' reiteration.

So Agreed in '68

Degrees means agreed/agrees (to hush about the rape), and I have *So-*agreed (50-degrees) to it. I am now me-I-dumb (medium-degrees). My

Science book has shown the 'degrees' rising from '68 (°C). I have gone oblivious and all into the 'silver'. For this, Mars remains the *un*-read planet.

Behind Mars is Jupiter. Being the force, means It-tears-up. The J morphs to an 's' (s-up-*it-ter*). The phrase rotates from 'it' and continues through. Something tore up me.

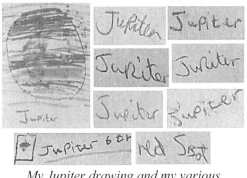

My Jupiter drawing and my various spellings.

6: Jupiter

'Jupiter is the 6th planet nr son (I now write). It is the biggest planet in space. The planet behind is Saturn. Jupiter has a red sBot. And it has coloured lines all over it. It takes a long time to get there.'

Notes: Jupiter has now become me. It's the sixth planet near 'son'. The P-R morphing (see images) creates riter. And the J-S resemble 'su' (us backwards). Us-writer. My plural (us) is fuelling this book.

The N'r-seat (Saturn) behind has caused a red 'sbot'. This is due to rape. The 'coloured lines' are all over Jupiter. The truth is hidden for the 'lock-our-read (coloured) and the lines (lyin's).

My Saturn drawing and various spellings.

7: Saturn

'Saturn is the 7th planet nr sun. It has a ring around it. The ring is gas and rock floating around Saturn. The planet behind Saturn is Uranus. Saturn is the only planet that has a ring around it.'

Notes: Saturn has now become me for being the object of focus. Notice my satern spelling which contains seat. Saturn means sat-on. The ring symbolises a ringfence surrounding it all. I had coloured this planet brown. My other science projects have shown that brown means no-brow – oblivion. My 'brow' knows nothing about the sat-on beyond the ringfence. Behind Saturn is Uranus. This means your-anus (mine). I have been vaginally raped from behind.

8: Urainus

'Urainus is the 8th planet nr sun (I press on). The planet behind is Neptune. Urainus is on the cold side. It is snowing and rainy. Nobody lives on Urainus.'

My Uranus drawing and various spellings.

Notes: Uranus has now become me. I have spelled it with an 'I' when there shouldn't be one. This planet means 'you-are-an-us' (plural) and part of me (I) is on the 'cold side'. (My astronomy project in chapter 15 expresses Uranus, 'you-are-ands').

My final spelling is 'you-rain-us' (see image). My plural is reined. My drawing of this planet appears to show an 'm' (em) attached to a cord. This makes me think of the Siamese twins within my *Human Being* project. They are conjoined via a band. My plural and I are conjoined too but are far apart.

Neptune comes next.

9: Neptune

'Neptune is the 9th planet nr sun. The planet Behind is Ploto. Nobody lives on Neptune. *I there,* because that's too cold. It is so cold, it's no degrees. It's never sunny on that planet.'

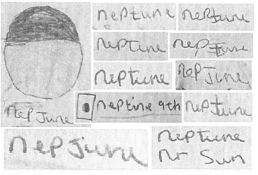

My Neptune drawing and various spellings.

Notes: Neptune has now become me. I am pen-tune (the ink) for disclosing of my toddlerhood rape through this book. See images for nep-tune.

But the word also keeps morphing. The 't' and 'n' becomes like an 's'. See large image bottom to read (backwards) from the 'pen', 'penisus'. It is behind me.

Oddly, I say 'nobody lives on Neptune', (and then) '*I there.*' This means my plural. She lives on a cold, lonely place. I would then introduce an 'I' to Neptune, spelling it 'Neptine'. Part of me is on this planet.

No-Agrees Versus Done-Agrees

Uranus is half-green. Green means to grass. The 'ink (in pink) is the method. It's grassing on the 'p' (pee). The temperature on Neptune is 'no degrees' (I had written). This should mean no-agrees, for I don't agree to the decree at all. But the liar has twisted this phrase to become 'done-agrees' (don-egrees). My questionnaire has shown the liar's paradox. It shifts and turncoats to promote the lie.

Behind Neptune is 'Ploto'. This means loo-top. My head was used like a loo. My plural would see loo in the colour blue (be-loo) and Looby Loo of *Andy Pandy*.

10: Ploto

'Ploto is the 10th planet nr sun (I would finish). There's no planet behind it, only asteroids. Nobody lives there. Ploto is the coldist planet on space. Asteroids are colder than anything. Ploto is

My green Pluto drawing and various expressions.

full of ice and is white.'

Notes: Pluto has now become me. My top has been lopped: top-lop. I have no brow and no memories.

I had coloured this planet green except for the centre. My plural is grassing all around me. It's in the sky, the earth and these projects. Chapter 17 shows. For now, I'm oblivious, for I'm in the white (we-tied) part. How odd. Each sphere has a different meaning depending on the viewpoint. The following summarises.

THE DOUBLE-MEANING SUM-UP					
OBJECT	**When of focus (Me)**	**When behind (Rapist)**	**OBJECT**	**When of focus**	**When behind**
			MARS	Are-ams	Rams
SUN	My face ablaze	The son	**JUPITER**	Us-writer	It-tears-up
MERCURY	Me-cry mercy	Crime	**SATURN**	Sat-on	N'r-seat
VENUS	Envies	Knives	**URANUS**	You're-an-us	Your-anus
EARTH	The-ar (are)	Hearth	**NEPTUNE**	Pen-tune	Penis
MOON	Mono	Moon (buttocks)	**PLUTO**	Lop-top	Loo-top

Part 4: Other Celestial Objects

I shall finish this chapter with other celestial objects. They have been amalgamated here for dotting around.

Comets: 'This comet is fat (I write). And this one has a long tail. All comets have tails. They can be long and short. Comets are yellow and bright. They look like long stars.'

Illustrations of comets and ways I wrote this word.

Notes: I knew how to spell comet, yet I kept writing 'comits'. This means come-sit. Something came and sat on me. These objects have long, fat tails, but are also 'short'. I had obviously seen something before and after the event. But all are made out to be a 'tale'. Bright yellow means be-right (that) I remain cowardly-yellow. Like the planets, comet has a double-meaning. 'Me-cot' is the age of when the lie began.

Asteroids: 'Astoids look like bubbles with things inside, which are rocks. Ploto asteroids are colder than Ploto because they are behind Ploto. Nobody can see them.'

Notes: My asteroid-spelling takes on various forms. Aste-roids begin with seat, and ast-roids, with sat. The 'roid' means 'orid. Horrid. Sat-horrid.

The asteroids 'look like 'bubbles with things inside'. Bubbles means doubles (reverse the 'b'). I have a double and something rock-like is inside me. Coldist means sit-locked. I mustn't see the 'rock' I sat on.

Eclipse:
'Sometimes, a planet goes in front of the sun and makes everything dark, like night-time (I write). It comes every 100 years. It is called a declips. The sun

My asteroid drawings and my spellings.

makes everything light besides Ploto.'

Notes: I had written the word 'declips' (instead of eclipse) and it happens every 100 years. This means loo's-year. Something goes in front of the sun, and everything goes dark. The sun is my burning face eclipsed by my rapist. The dark has been clipped off.

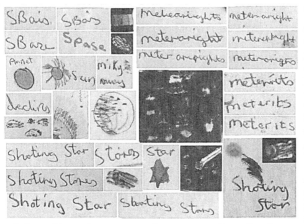

Meterarights: 'are purple. Before meter arights fall on earth, they melt with thunder. Meter-wrights make big holes if nothing melts them.'

Notes: My meteorites take on various forms, as seen

Other objects in space and my expressions for them.

from the images. This means me-tear-writes, (or me-tore-writes). The 'me-tear' leads to the write (right or rits). My torn self is writing this book from a remote place. She has described the big hole again.

Estra (meaning Extra)

I had made up a quiz on an 'Estra page'. I had meant 'extra'. This means 'tears-age'. This quiz can be found within Section 7.

My analysis of my *Space* book is complete.

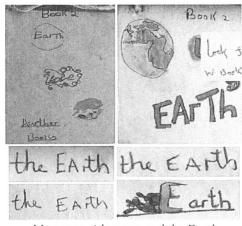

My cover, title page and the Earth expressions.

Chapter 7: Book 2 The Earth
Introduction
Part 1: My Planet, The-Are
Part 2: Earth Forces
Part 3: False Story
Part 4: Composition
Part 5: Oceans Apart

Introduction

The second book of my Aurther series is about the Earth. As seen, this means the-ar (meaning plural). But Earth also means hearth, for the burning. Again, I have conducted a light edit here, retaining relevant misspellings for the codes.

My book on *Earth* begins.

Part 1: My Planet, The-Are

'The Earth is the 3rd planet to sun (I write). We live on it. Our star is the sun. Our moon is not far away. The first two planets are Mercry and Vinus, which are hotter than Earth.

'The earth goes round until 365 days has past and that's a year. When you're on a rocket, you don't see names of countries. It looks like a round map. You can see it from the Moon.

'The Earth has people (I continue). It has molton metle, seas, rivers, canals and water. The Earth is the only planet with water.'

Notes: The Earth (the-are) is listed third to Me-cry-mercy and Envis. The spellings show. These worlds endure heat. In fact, the heat is *inside* the Earth. This means rape, and my plural is me-tell(ing) on it through my misspelled 'metal'. The 365 days contains my birthyear (65) and my age when I was raped (3). It's now 'past'.

Mount Ever-sit

'There is one little bomb (bump). That is Mount Everist. This is the highest mountain in the world.'

Notes: There is a lot of 'sits' in this book. The images show. For my plural, Mount Everest means mount-ever-sit. I was mounted and it felt like forever. It was the bigg-ist, deep-ist and wid-ist (in the world).

A lot of sits in this book.

Meterarights: 'When there's a meteraright falling to Earth, (I continue), it does not make holes. It melts while falling. Meterorights melt with the storm which burn them away. When the storm stops and meterarights come again, they melt with the hole.'

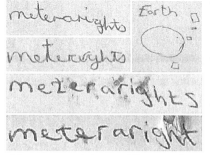

Notes: Meta-rights means me-tear-writes (again) and this is my torn-self coming to Earth to tell on my toddlerhood rape. But my plural can't reach me about the 'hole', for melting in the atmosphere. The images show my odd meteorite-spellings and unreachable Earth.

My me-tear-rights spellings and my plural falling to Earth.

Part 2: Earth Forces

I now talk about the Earth forces. In the early Eighties, I would write at length about nature's fury. This book already shows my fascination with extremes.

'**Earth quack** (I begin) sometimes starts before the earth quaick starts. There's heat underground. The Earth cracks open and then the deadly ash comes out to sBread. Only some of the hole will get wider and that's how you get an earth quack.'

Notes: I had spelled earthquake, 'earth quack'. A quack means a fraudulent person. The liar in my head is calling my plural a quack for writing about inner heat and a hole that got wider. The quack contains an 'I' where there shouldn't be one. Ghost 'I's keep appearing in my words. My 'sBread' means be-reads – the codes in this book.

Storm: 'When there's a storm, (I continue) it's an extremely hot day and the storm tries to come. The very strong storm will shock the earth, but people will feel it (more). When the lightning comes, it burns the trees.'

Notes: The storm is assault. I know this from my later weather projects. The lightning burns the trees. This word looks like 'tears'. For my plural, rape was like a storm, and it tore me in two.

My drawings of Earth's force and spellings.

Volcaino: 'Before the volcano starts, rocks fall down the hot steamy tower and smashes up the pipes and the hole comes wider. Solid mountain melts and that's the way you make a volcano.'

Notes: I finish this part with volcanos, which I spell with an 'I' (again). The volcano has become me, for a wide hole where heat exudes.

The images show cracks in the earth, holes and inner pipes. I am describing inner sensations during rape.

About Things

I now touch upon general things about the Earth. What did I select of all things?

Scorpion: 'The scorpion has a sharp painful pin on the end of his tail. When he stings you, it is so painful, but not (enough) to kill a man.'

Deadly Nightshaids: 'are deadly poison. If you eat blackberries, for a moment, you'll be scared (until) they say they're blackberries.'

Holly: (The image shows). 'Inside juice, inside white ball, seeds (and) how they grow.'

Notes: I've opted for the Scorpion again. I had already written about the Scorpion in *Space*. The tail is painful (I

Illustrations showing 'about things'.

had written) and it contains the Nor. I follow this with the deadly nightshaid (with a ghost 'I'). These can be confused for blackberries. This means belack-buries. I have buried my plural for her knowledge, and I am now lacking.

I had drawn the holly. We had a holly tree in our garden. My plural sees the hole in holly. The inside juice and seeds mean semen. Sex education has evidently got into this book.

The Earth's constitution, the inner planets and 'Cirin'.

Part 3: False Story

I now do a peculiar thing. I tell a 'false story.' This seems due to my slipup in my first book of my Aurther series, *Space*. I have named ten planets instead of nine (as was the case in 1974). Here's how this story goes.

'There were 10 planets (I begin). The sBare planet was called Cirin, which is the nearest planet to sun. The 10 planets bumbed (bumped) into each other.

'Earth was the fourth planet nr sun. Cirin began to Bumb (bump) near to the sun. The ten planets bumbed again. Cirin began to shrivel, then the Earth became the third planet nr sun. This is only a false story. I wrote it to interest you.'

It seems my plural had used my slipup in *Space* to tell this story.

I'm being told about the crying, for this is what Cirin means (Cri-in'). It's like Mercury for the 'Me-cry-mercy' (near the 'son.) The 'bumbed' means bum-bed. I was raped from behind on my bed. And 'sBare means be-ares. The truth about the crying has shrivelled up.

My Cirin Drawing

The image shows the inner planets. An odd pink shape appears to be dispersing. A felt tip drawing of the UK on the previous page has leached through. My plural appears to have incorporated this pigmentation into a drawing to represent Cirin. My plural has done a clever thing: labelled this a 'False Story'. The liar in my head is fooled. A story about the Cri-in' during the bum-bed gets through.

Return to Ploto

I touch upon Pluto (spelled Ploto). This turn seems random, but isn't, for this remote world is like Cirin.

I write, 'Once we did not know Ploto was there. (But) a man had a strong telescope and discovered it. He called it Ploto and that was a long time ago.'

This man is like me now, discovering this remote world where my plural lives. Pluto and Cirin represent the same place: of extremes and desolation.

The Earth's core, the steal and the me-tell.

Part 4: Composition

Here, I would list the various things our Earth is made of: 'Metle, ~~plastic, cardboard~~, mud, soil, oil, gas, rocks, sea, water, steel and ash.'

The meanings of all have been placed in Section 7. But (in alphabetical order) I have selected the following (abridged) of note.

Gas: 'is deadly poison. It is far underground, and it stops you breathing.'

This is obviously suffocation. It is far underground, from conscious awareness.

Metel: 'is steal (I had put). It has two names (metal and steel). Metle drips and is sticky. The metle is the white bit inside (the Earth). Molton is the red bit.

Notes: My various expressions for 'metal' means 'me-tell.' And it's about the burning, sticky rape. Interestingly, metal has another name: steal. (I had meant steel). The liar is steal(ing) the me-tell about the rape. Later, I would put, 'Steal is write, shining in the sun'. (I had meant *white* shining in the sun). The liar is claiming to be the 'writer' of this book. Not only does the liar lie, it steals from me.

Mud: 'comes from marshes and swamps. It is mixed with clay which is orange colour.

Notes: Mud means dumb (read backwards to find the word). I am mud-dumb to the truth. Nor-age locker (orange colour) is my toddlerhood locked away.

Note: I have done a section on colours. I have placed it in chapter 4 *Colours*.

Part 5: Oceans Apart

Finally, I had drawn two maps at the back. 'England is our country,' (I inform). Some countries are misspelled, and all contain a code. The following are of note. (Section 7 summarises).

Alas-ka: (Alaska): Alas-scar. I'm sad about the scar.

Merica: (America): Am-mercy (like Me-cry of Mercury).

Iran: I-ran (from the truth).

Mongolia: Me-gone-liar ('em' means me.)

My map drawings of the Earth.

Illand: (Ireland): Lier-land.

North Pole: Th-Nor Pole.

The Salty Place

The lies are all over the world. My *Lines* project has shown.

I include the oceans. I had put: 'Sea is salty water. The big seas are (the) Pasific, Atlantic and AraBian (Sea).'

My misspelled Pacific brings 'asific'. Faiisc. This means face. The phrase returns to the beginning, 'Pa's'. Pa's-face. A father-figure kept using my face during oral rape. My face felt 'his' to use.

99

THE SEA
Striking and stealing from the sands
grabbing pebbles like watery hands
Singing its watery everlasting song
with its salty, watery tongue.
Sitting here as far as can see
the sky can meet with the sea
the strong blue line across it does lend
for ever and ever without end.
It can be calm but never still
But can have waves like a hill
It can have life of plants and fish
But can be death with one big swish.

My beach drawing accompanying my poem The Sea *(31 Oct 1978).*

Atlantic (Sea) means 'S-Alt-an-tic'. Saltland-tic. I suffer tics as a result. Both oceans mean rape.

But why did I include the Arabian Sea? My odd 'AraBian' means I-barren. (Read back from the I). The Nor has made me barren, (so my plural feared). Indeed, I almost remained childless.

An illustration for my poem, *The Sea* resembles a face submerged. This reiterates the drowning. (This poem is shown at the end of this book). In 1980, I wrote a short for school called *Struggle for Survival* which touches upon the oceans. I have conducted a light edit here.

Struggle for Survival (1980)

You are on the bridge of a warship (I write). The ocean surrounds you. Suddenly, a violent explosion. There I float in the South Atlantic in an inflatable. Skilled men and strong swimmers were on that ship, yet I am the only survivor.

Heavy clouds reigned the sky, the sea, a heavy grey. It gathered in a huge swell. My ice-covered hands turned blue, the veins sticking out, yet the water felt warm. I got sleepy. The cold numbing me, yet I was not afraid. I wanted to lay on my side and sleep. I thought of my family. *Is life worth living?*

For five days, I drifted until an aeroplane found me. Once on land, I learned that on the same day, there was a severe storm on the South Pacific and the inflatable boat was not found.

Analysis Forty-two Years Later

The viewpoint shifts from 'you' to 'I', with a surviv-*our* spelling. (I had spelled the word correctly earlier). I am an 'our'. This short tells of near-death. But never would I sleep on my back, (I had written). I would rather die. In the end, an inflatable boat had vanished in the Pacific. My schoolteacher had overscored this part, thinking I had meant Atlantic. In fact, this is where my plural is in relation to my oblivion: the other side of the planet. With Sat-land tics, I grow numb and survive. But with a burnt Pa's-face, my plural is remote.

The Sir Galahad of 8 June 1982

An odd turn occurs two years later. The warship, Sir Galahad is set ablaze by Falkland skyhawks. Like this story, is in the South Atlantic and many died onboard. Burns victim Simon Weston would rouse notions of my own burnt face.

I had analysed *Struggle for Survival* two days before the Galahad anniversary. My plural knew of this date, and I hadn't. She also knew of the sister ship, Sir Tristram (sit-ram). This ship is like the one gone missing in my story. My plural knows anniversaries and sees things in news stories. She sees my face on the Moon, the Sir Galahad and Krakatoa. She sees Pa's-face in Pacific and Saltland-tic in S. Atlantic.

Chapter 8: Book 3
Wildflowers
Introduction
Part 1: A Tale of Two Flowers
Part 2: The Creeping Utter Book
Part 3: Lowers and Come-ons
Part 4: The Be-loo Buried
Part 5: Cropped by the Decree
Part 6: Tore at the Leaves

My cover and title page to Wildflowers.

Introduction

The third book of my Aurther series is called *Wildflowers*. I would soon write about Pyrenean flowers and keep garden reports. My artwork is adorned with plants.

Flowers means 'lowers'. Notice my slashed 's' to express 'f'. SS look similar. My 'farm-house' (in chapter 5) was the same and means rams-house. My teacher marked me down for how I wrote the 'f'. I was lowered during rape and I'm full of woe (an 'owe' anagram). It's just like the rainbow. On the back of my *Earth* book, I had written 'Wilde Flowers'. The 'w-lied' has emerged and means we-lied (about the woe-f'l) lowers.

Part 1: A Tale of Two Flowers

I would begin this book with a tale of two flowers. They are called the Scarlet Pimpernel and the Thrift.

101

My drawings of the Scarlet Pimpernel and Thrift.

The Scarlet Pimpernel

'Preferring a loose soil (I begin), the Scarlet Pimpernel is often found growing wild on freshly-cultivated land or sandy hills. It is an annual plant, the leaves of which are ovate and grow in opposite pears (pairs) on short, rather weak stems. The flower *starks* grow from the axils.'

The Thrift

'These flowers (meaning Thrift) are my favourite (I continue). Preferring the blustery cliffs of the seashore, or the sides of rocky mountains, the thrift is a perennial with a strong woody root stork which has many branches. Each branch terminates in a…'

I don't finish the sentence.

A Life on Sand

I am struck by my selection of these plants. The Scarlet Pimpernel represents a life built on lies. A pimp runs a brothel and is how my plural views the liar in me: depraved and in with my rapist. It has poor foundations. The roots are shallow and prefer sandy soil of 'freshly-cultivated land'.

The image shows the spindly roots. This is like me, living a lie. My life is founded on sand. But the scar (of scarlet) remains. My 'starks' (to mean stalks) means sat-sk'r. Sat-scar. This plant is a mere annual. The lie is finite.

A Life on Rocks

The Thrift is different. This one has thick, sturdy roots that prefer hardy ground like cliff-faces and rocks. It's a perennial, with a strong woody root 'stork'. Why did I spell 'stalk' differently here? This deviation contains 'rock'. The truth is forged on rock. I am reminded of the tall tree in my *Colours* book.

These plants grow on 'opposite pears' (I had continued). I had meant pairs, but my homonym is a rapes-anagram. These plants are on opposite sides of the rape. One is of truth, the other, a lie. I am like the sand-loving Scarlet Pimpernel, while my truth lives on rocky ground.

My final sentence about the Thrift 'terminates in a'… means a dead-end. The message can't reach me. Thrift means th-rift. A rift exists inside of me for the lying 'pimp'. The message can't get through.

102

My List of Flowers

The main body of this book are illustrations. There are thirty-eight in all. Those not included here, can be found in Section 7. But I have selected the following for this chapter.

I would end this book with: 'Some of these wildflowers are very unfinding. This book sounds very interesting to you and me too.' The unfinding means the lie coverup. I am about to do the 'finding'.

Part 2: The Creeping Utter-Book

The images show the Creeping Buttercup. I knew how to spell these words, yet I keep expressing the Buttercup with 'cub' (instead of cup). The 'butter' is trying to be 'utter'. I know this for butterflies would soon adorn my paintings. Butterflies mean 'be-utter-lies'.

Buttercub means be-utter-book. Cub sounds like 'book' backwards. It's like King Og's unit of height in my *Human Being* project: cubits. This means book-sit.

My book is uttering to me. My plural is uttering about the 'creeping' through this book. Creeping means raping.

My drawings and expressions for the Creeping Buttercup.

I keep spelling it 'creeping'. In a section on Roots, it becomes 'sreaping'. My pen had slipped. Rapes and raping can be formed from this aberration.

My drawing of a 'Creeping Buttere Cups Leaf' (image upper right) means the page of this book. Leaf means page. The message is, 'utter-book's-rapes(ing) leaf'. The leaf (page) in this book is uttering about the rapes of my toddlerhood.

How bizarre.

The 'creeping' recurs.

Creeping Cinquefoil: I had labelled my drawing 'Creeping Gunefoil'. The meaning is 'goon-foil'. I am a foiled goon for turning my back on the rape-(ing) of my toddlerhood.

Creeping Cinquefoil and Cuckoo Pint.

The heads are veering sideways (see image). This plant is trying to relocate from its roots. It's like the Scarlet Pimpernel of poor foundations; it's like my bar chart on *Colours*: crooked.

Cuckoo Pint: The cuckoo is an urban term for one who waylays a house on the pretext of being a friend. I would write about the cuckoo in a garden report of 2 Jun 1978. Here, it's cuckoo spit. Abridged, I had written.

'No berries on the ash or laurel. The apple blossoms have blown off. Lots of cuckoo spit at the top of the garden.'

Cuckoo spit is a frothy substance exuded from the froghopper insect. My plural is reminded of swallowing something like that in toddlerhood due to a 'cuckoo'. The blossoms in the garden would then vanish along with my childhood. Pint means pin-int', pin-enter. A cuckoo stuck a pin in me. chapter 12 looks at my 1978 garden reports.

For now, my plural is uttering about the creeping through this 'book'.

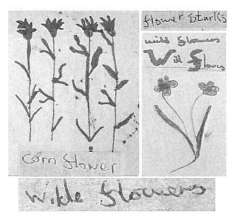

Cornflower and how I expressed flowers.

Part 3: Lowers and Come-ons

The images show the code for flowers. See my 'f' like an 's' slashed through again. This book is telling me I was lowered and something 'come on' me.

'Flower starks' (see image) means lowers sat-scar. I was lowered and mounted. I have been scarred ever since.

Cornflower: My rapist's Nor appears alongside the 'lowers' of flower: c'Nor-lowers. (The 'c' is an abbreviated uncle'). I was lowered and he 'come-on' me. The following shows the 'commons'.

Common Field Poppy: The poppy has become a symbol of recall, for Remembrance Day. I was come-on in rape and my plural wants me to

104

remember it. But 'Field' means fly-lied. I can no longer remember the (thing that) 'come-on' me for running away.

Common Mallow: This one means come-on am-low. I was forced down during assault. Notice the headless appearance to this plant. It's just shoulders. A disembodied head has fallen to the ground. My plural remembers my 'head' lowered. But I can't. I'm headless.

Common Teasel: The first part reads, 'come-on-seat.' I was used like a seat once lowered. The head is all spiny. This 'head' is off-limits, and I can't get near.

Common Vetch: My creations are full of envy. It's in the evening of my *Weather* book

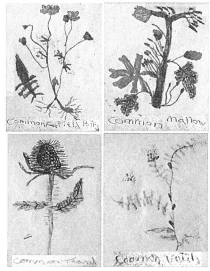

Common Field Poppy, Mallow, Teasel and Vetch.

and Venus of *Space*. The grouping of 'env' means envy: Commo-*nve*-tch. The come-on (the part of me that remembers) 'envies' the cheat that I have become. This is what the final 'tch' means. My novels contain teachers (cheaters) and my big cat art, cheetahs. I'm a cheater for my oblivion. Come-on-envy-cheat. The lowering and the come-on are hidden away.

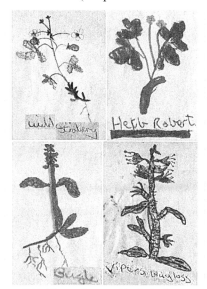

Wild Strawberry, Herb Robert, Bugle and Viper's Bugloss.

Part 4: The Be-loo Buried

These flowers want to bury the lowering. I was made to feel like a loo and I mustn't know about it.

Wild Strawberry: My spelling of Strawberry keeps morphing, for on a page on 'Roots', it would appear as Stabury. Here, it's Strabery. The meaning is sat-bury, to bury the mounting.

105

Herb Robert: A large trunk at the base of this plant appears to be pushing upwards. Something big is trying to insert itself.

My overscored 't' brings 'her-t'. Her-hurt. The 'brobe' brings Bbore. Bore-hurt-her. Something is boring into me during the mounting. The trunk pushing into the Herb Robert symbolises.

Bugle: The word 'blue' surrounds the 'g' (*Bu*-g-*le*). This means blue. Be-loo. My *Colours* book has told me about the Blue. Bugle is homonymic with a loud instrument. This plant is brassy and is sounding-off out about the be-loo. But the end appears muffled up. I can't hear.

Viper's Bugloss: This one is about the be-loo too.

The central 'bugl' is like the 'Bugle'. It means Be-loo (and the bugle) again. What precedes is viper, a venomous snake. A phallus stung and sullied me. But the 'loss' would ensure I won't know about it.

Like the Bugle, this plant appears animated, but can't get the message through.

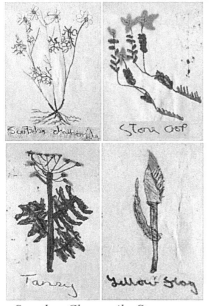

Scentless Chamomile, Stonecrop, Tansy and Yellow Flag

Part 5: Cropped by the Decree

I have been lowered, raped and made to feel like a loo. The decree follows. These flowers symbolise my past cropped.

Scentless Chamomile: I had written, 'Scentelss' (instead of Scentless). The 'less' is muddled. This betrays of the less-meaning.

The phrase begins mom-ile (of Cha-mom-ile). This means mom-lie. What's left is 'Cha-scent-less'. Notice 'assent' here.

Sh'-assent-mum-lie. '*She*' (me) is assenting to a lie in order to retain a mother-figure. The liar has used this plant to imply an agreement – the decree.

Ch-assent-mum-lie-*less*. I am 'less' for this assent.

How odd. Assent isn't a nine-year-old's word, but my research has shown the subconscious picks up on everything. I must have come across this word.

Stonecrop: This plant contains the stone. My *Science* book has told me stone means denial for the 'not'. The stain has been cropped from my conscious awareness. Notice how this plant veers sideways. It's like the Creeping Cinquefoil earlier, and the bar chart in my *Colours* book. It's running away from its roots.

Tansy: This plant means stayn. Stain. The *stone*-crop denies it.

Yellow Flag: My slashed 'S' recurs here, bringing the meaning, 'yellow-slag'. I am a coward and a slag. These are the liar's insults to foster alienation from my plural. My drawing of this plant appears to be bidding farewell. I am waving goodbye to my plural to live in coward's oblivion.

Forget-me-not: I used to keep drawing these plants. For my plural, it is a plea *not* to forget her. I have added the 'Common', to become Common Forget-me-not. I was come-on and *mustn't* forget it.

Poppy: My research has shown the poppy to be a symbol of remembering, for Remembrance Day. A 'p' is missing. I had spelled poppy correctly earlier too.

Common Forget-me-not and Poppy.

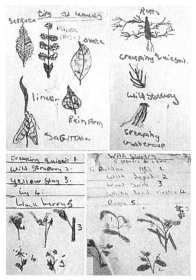

A page dedicated to leaves, roots and quizzes.

Part of me is missing, yet a second 'p' can be found at the beginning of the word. This symbolises my plural, removed and remote. Indeed, this flower appears disembodied. No roots and the leaves all gone.

Part 6: Tore at the Leaves

The final pages of my *Wildflowers* book look at leaves and roots. Leaves means to desert. Roots means toors. (Tores). I have deserted myself and am torn.

Leaves-tore. My garden reports would confirm.

The image shows the illustrations concerned. Notice the wild Stabury (root) and serrate (leaves). These mean teearrs, tore and bury the sat.

107

The final page shows answers to a quiz. I note with interest:

3: White Dead Nettle does grow a head.

10: Forget-me-not is my favourite flower. It is drawn roughly so the question is harder.

18: Blue.

I don't know the questions to these answers, but each informs upon my toddlerhood. I have grown a 'head'. This means a new history. The forget-me not is drawn roughly so I won't recognise this flower. The reason is the blue.

Section 7 looks at the remaining nineteen *Wildflowers*.

Cover and title page of Weather.

Chapter 9: Book 4 Weather
Introduction
Part 1: Dawn, Dusk and Doll
Part 2: The Agree-Decree
Part 3: The Clouds
Part 4: The Language of Colour
Part 5: High Enough to Read the Clouds

Introduction

My final book of my Aurther series is called *Weather*.

It is my earliest surviving weather project. I would soon keep weather records and write about the weather in countless projects in the future. In Autumn 1979, I would write *Weather and Climate*. I had omitted the 'h' to become *Weater and Climate*. The 'we-tear' has revealed itself for the climb-mate of my toddlerhood.

My weather projects are so momentous, I have dedicated an overflow book to these. But this chapter serves as a link to this overflow book.

My final Aurther book begins.

Part 1: Dawn, Dusk and Doll

'When the red sky has come in morning (I write), there's going to be a little angry cloud. Rain all day. When the red sky comes at night, there's going to be no shade.'

I would continue (abridged):

'**Good**: When you see a reddish sun, like a red ball sinking in the evning, tomorrow's going to be fine. (I would add later), Red sky is *quit* nice, but not red sky at dawn. Only at evning.

'**Bad**: When the sun is *doll* red and angry (I continue), it's going to be a storm. When black clouds go past, there will be little spots (of) rain, then goes fine again.

'Sometimes, there's no coluer in the evening sunset, only a dirty ash grey that means the morning's going to be gloomy.'

Notes: Evening means envying. Notice how I spell 'evning' (envi-ing). The images show. I have 'quit' the truth and my plural envies my oblivion.

Venus means envy too. These codes transcend my projects and grow more prolific.

The colours of the low sun would provide great opportunities for my plural to convey her feelings. Grey means 'angrey' (see image) and red means 'read' (past tense).

My future diaries would contain a daily

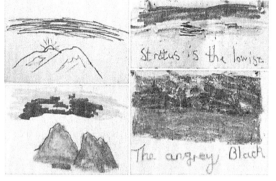

Codes in my drawings and word-usage.

weather report. Through them, my plural would tell me about my vile toddlerhood.

Already, these codes are well-established and laid bare.

Coloured skies and sunsets.

The images show something hot sinking between two mounds. I encounter one of my earliest uses of 'stratus'. It is the low-ist (meaning sit). This cloud means straight-us-stain (or sat). Something forced me straight and lowered itself upon me.

Doll-Dull

I notice the 'doll' (instead of 'dull') use. My plural has snuck in the doll.

Doll means any doll I played with. Dolls lying prone or damp after bathing would remind me of my used self. The doll is an effigy of me and therefore the doll is angry for being used. My dolls bore telling names like Sharpin (Sharp-in), Big Sue (Big Use) and Subie (Be-use). I have projected my rage onto an object to numb my own used feelings. My later expression 'doll-suless' (dullness) means used-less. My used feelings are numbed once dumped onto dolls.

Read, Arpril (raip) and doll.

Part 2: The Agree-Decree

An 'agreement' shows up in this next part.

The images show my reuse of 'edges' and 'sharp' to describe clouds. Silvery-edges mean I-agreed (Silv-*reledges*: I-egreed/s'). The silver has cropped up here and means Mum.

In order to preserve a mother-figure and a home-life, I had to 'agree' to hush about the rape. My sharp-spelling comes as 'shape' and 'sharp'. Combine these to find sh-rape. I am hushing about the rape. I would later write, 'When the clouds are middle diggre (degree-'egreed' again) it's nice weather. And 'Dark blue sky with shape (sharp) eged clouds means rain.'

'Light blue sky with soft eged clouds will melt away (in) nice weather.'

The truth is melting away with the decree-agreement. I keep saying so.

This agreement has been expressed in many ways, including the assent-mum-lie (of the Scentless Chamomile) in *Wildflowers*.

I would continue.

Good (Weather): 'When there's small round clouds high in the sky, there's a fine spell (but) you may be shure there's a change for the worse.'

Notes: 'Shure' means you're-sh. I'm hushing again. This is due to the 'Markrell' (mackerel sky) that the small clouds are. My Mackerel-spelling contains 'mark'. I have been sullied.

Bad (Weather): 'The white thine clouds sbreads like sheat across the sky. They go low to earth and catches lightning.'

Notes: 'Thine' means 'the-in'. Something entered me. The bad-weather mackerel means assault for something lowering over me as a 'sheat' (she-seat). I am being mounted and the lightning means enlightening. My plural wants me to be-reads (sBread) these codes.

Begging and Please-not

'Mares tail clouds are for good, hot days (I write). The summer's day will be fine. (But I add later) people and flowers (could) die.'

This means the 'lowers'. This is what flowers mean and I had almost died.

Be-loo-seat, angrey and agreed.

(I continue) 'In the beging of the morning, a blue sky means there's steady rain coming.

'Grey big clouds in the morning means soon after breakfast, brilliant *sonshine* comes out.

'When it's raining in the morning with patches of blue, and rain again with white clouds, the rest of the day (and) tomors (meaning tomorrow) is going to be cloudy too.'

Notes: Notice 'beging' instead of 'beginning'. I am begging something away. Morning is when I am close to my plural. She is trying to tell me through my dreams (and this project) that I was raped in toddlerhood by a 'son'. The begging would precede my use of 'pleasant' in future weather reports. This means 'please-not'. Don't let it be true.

The Missed in Mist

Later, I write: '(If) you see mist in the morning, it's going to be fine and sunny.'

I am missing (missed) my plural's signals in the morning. This is what 'mist' means. Missed.

My plural feels rage in the big 'grey' clouds. My face was burnt by a 'son' in toddlerhood, and I can't hear her. The 'rain' (in the final statements) means rein. My drawing of rain shows bars, like a prison cell. I am reminded of the threepenny piece in Mum's coin collection. This shows bars too. My truth is reined in. The agree-decree of 1968 began it all.

111

Part 3: The Clouds

I would now talk about the clouds. My plural has incorporated Latin in her language. There is lot of 'us' here, and this means plural. Stratus has been referred to earlier. The other clouds are explained here.

Clumulus of Cumulus

'There is another sart (sort) of cloud called culumulus, (I begin). It is a low mass of thine cloud going across the sky. It doesn't always bring eny rain. The other brings showery weather with sunny intervals.

'If it rains all day, at evning, it will be damp with a little bit of sun. When the clouds are hot, it thunders hard. But when the clouds are cold, it snows.'

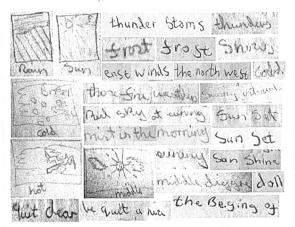

Rein-bars, forced, quit, envying and begging.

Mares Tails

'Mares tail clouds are the highest of the cloud family. It is the nicest cloud.'

Stratus-Stratys

'Stratus cloud is the worst cloud. Stratys is the lowist of all.

'It sometimes be 100 feet off ground. When these clouds form on top of the hill, it is usually a forerunner of rain.'

The Festoon

'In summer, you can get a festoon cloud sbreading to the north or northwest. It has tiny clouds in its lower serface. There will be sharp squalls with rain, and they will come up suddenly.'

Is-numb of Nimbus

'The cloud you dislike to see is the leaden sheat which give steady rain. It is called nimbus. It is the second lowist cloud of dark and threatening appearance. You can tell how long the rain will last if you see thine (thin) clouds above.'

Notes on Clouds: An abundance of codes can be found in clouds. No wonder my plural has used the sky to communicate with me.

I keep writing cumulus, 'clumulus'. This means me-clluuus. My plural is leaving clues about my toddlerhood in the sky. I describe them as 'thine'. This means 'the-in'. The clouds have been used just like colours as part of my plural's language.

Mares tail means male-tears. Transpose the opening consonants (tares-mail) to find a male had torn me. Stratus means straight-us (I was forced straight during oral rape). This cloud lowers to 'be 100-Seet'. This means be-loo-seat. My slashed 's' says so. The lower 's-erface' is 'her-face' (mine) being used.

Nimbus means is-numb. I am numb to the rape of my toddlerhood. With the 'be-loo' in mind, I have put together what I have said about the 'blue' (and other colours).

Part 4: The Language of Colour

My *Colours* book has shown the meaning behind colours. I begin with the 'blue'.

'When it's a blue sky up to midd-day (I write), this makes the sun look watery. Up till teatime, rain comes. When the sky is dark blue with sharp edges, storms are on the way. But when the sky is light blue, it's going to be fine.'

Notes: Dark blue is threatening. The be-loo assault has sharp edges. Rain means rein. The be-loo is reined in, and the 'son' is hidden behind a veil (watery) cloud. I can't see it. Light (lite) means lie-tie (about the blue). I don't know the meaning of 'blue'.

The following is about other colours.

The Grassing Sky

'Sometimes, we will see green sky (I begin) instead of blue *in putween* the clouds. That means it's going to be showery with sun.'

(I would pose the question) When is the sky green? What month?

(Answer) The sky is green in Arpril. But only putween the clouds. This means showery weather.

Copper and Silver

'In summer you (can) get copper-tinted clouds with

The me-clues, male-tears, straight-us and us-numb.

bright silvery egis that give us thunderstorms and hail. In winter, there is low puffy clouds tinted with a violet hue. They bring several days of doll suless (meaning dullness).'

113

Be-lack Angry in Black and Grey

'The angrey black clouds over the sea warn of rainstorm in the distents and mad (made) thick clouds.

'When the sky is quit quit clear, in next 36 hours, you know there's going to be heavy rain and gales.'

Notes: The 'grass' in the sky wants to tell. The 'grass' tries to show-her-I (show-er-y) the 'son' that tore us. She is trying to show me the 'put-between' (put-'ween) my legs in Arpril (rraip).

She even mentions the 'copper-tinted' clouds. This means a copper-intted (entered) me. But the 'silvery-edges' decree keeps hushing the truth. Copper and silver have come together again.

See how my plural uses colours to 'grass' on the liar? She has incorporated Latin here.

The 'doll suless' (dullness), as seen, means the dumping of my used feelings onto any doll I played with. I have 'quit' the truth and become 'dull'. My plural is 'angrey'. She is trapped in heavy 'rein' and the liar in my head calls her mad.

Part 5: High Enough to Read the Clouds

The back of this book looks at mountain weather. I am closer to the sky now. I had put:

'When the *mountines* are there, the clouds have to go higher. The water drops and (it) rains. But when the clouds are not low, it's going to be quit a nice day. (My illustrations show heights of clouds).

Notes: Mountains means mountings. The clouds are hiding the mountings behind the 'rein'. I had spelled 'quite' 'quit' (again). I have quit the truth about the mounting and reined it behind the cloud.

How to Read the Clouds

Near the end of this book, I had put, 'Many of you are interested in how to read the clouds.' *I* want to read the clouds. In May 1977, I had written to the Met Office and said in my letter 'I want to read the clouds'. But I was looking in the wrong place. My plural is sending signals through my weather projects. I can't read her. I'm not 'high' enough.

I thought I was simply writing about the Weather.

Aurther Books: Conclusion

My analysis of my Aurther Books has concluded.

These books are filled with messages about my toddlerhood. My plural is using homophones and morphing words to tell me about the rape.

My plural is the author (me-tear-writes) driving these books. She is the 'W' on the front cover and the utter (be-utter-cup) behind every word.

Space has been used to convey the remoteness of my plural.

The Earth has been used to convey the huge forces within.

Flowers has been used to convey the woeful lowers.

And Weather has been used for the language of colour and textures in the sky.

Ghost 'I' and plural language.

My plural has incorporated a multi-language to tell me I have been raped in toddlerhood. And I thought myself a mere schoolgirl virgin, writing about nature. In fact, I was carrying something terrible in my subconscious and it is leaching out into my creations.

WILD FLOWERS
OF THE
PYRENEES

A. W. Taylor

My book *Wildflowers of the Pyrenees* by Albert William Taylor (published 1971)

SECTION 4: FLOWERS

This section looks at my projects on flowers. My earliest flower project has already been looked at. It forms part of my Aurther Book series and I have therefore kept it there. The following shows my others.

Chapter 10: Wildflowers of the Pyrenees
Introduction
Part 1: The Saltland Lowers
Part 2: Suave and Narcissistic
Part 3: Uncle Ran
Part 4: The Taking
Part 5: I-far and Yellow
Part 6: Me-render the Pynees
Part 7: The Codes Show Through
Part 8: The Pulse-Sat Liar

Introduction

When I was nine, Eve and I were gifted a book. It was called *Wildflowers of the Pyrenees* by Albert William Taylor. I think it was for Christmas 1974.

The cover drew me. I must have seen myself in that lone plant on a rocky mountainside. I want to be close to the clouds, to be up there with that plant.

This namesake project would begin. I drew pictures from this book and wrote about Pyrenean flowers. The result is several pages within a green notebook. My plural is 'grassing' through the green again. It is spring 1975, and I am in secondary school.

Part 1: The Saltland Lowers

My project is troubling. On the inside cover I given my details and an index. I had also made up my own publishing company. I had called it, Soltland Books. It had a logo: 'A'. This company is really 'Saltland Books.' My *Science* book has shown this logo to symbolise a crossroads.

Elements on the inside cover of my project.

The 'pages go up to 123' (I had written). But from page 20, these pages are (mostly) blank. My declaration means 'Pa-ages up to 123'. My third 'age' – my toddlerhood. I know this for the Saltland. This book is about the third year of my life, for this is when I was raped.

My Fingerprints

I do another strange thing.

I gave my fingerprints. They have been embossed in pink ink. I have listed them: thumb, little finger, finger-by-thumb, finger-by-little-one (and) second finger. This is the act of someone detained at the police station, isn't it? My *Science* book has already told me about the fingerprints.

The whole class had given them. And pink contains the 'ink'.

The Meaning

Wildflowers of the Pyrenees means double-you-lied about the penis-lowers. I was lowered during rape. I had written 'Wilde Flowers' on the back of my Aurther Books. This means w'-lied. The 'f' of my 'flowers' looks like a slashed S: This means lowers.

Images show close-ups of the cover. It looks like grass. The spine is red. This means read (past tense). My plural wants me to read these codes. Here, it's about the 'lowers'.

The word 'penis' is all over this project. This astounds me. I was a nine-year-old church-going schoolgirl in the Seventies. I truly believed I had never seen a penis at all.

Latin words abound. It's just like the clouds in *Weather* with a load of 'us'. This means plural. My Index (spelled Innex) means in-ex. I have divorced part of myself for something 'in' me. The cover of this book is green like grass. The spine is red.

There are eighteen Pyrenean flowers within. (Section 7 lists flowers not included here). My word-usage seems advanced for the age I was. I had evidently copied sections from this book. A light edit has been conducted, retaining misspellings for unearthing the codes.

What follows are my **notes**. These explains my findings.

Part 2: Suave and Narcissistic

My plural has used the following flowers to tell me about my rapist's narcissism. The following shows.

PAPAVER SUAVOLENS

(Pyre-an endemic) June-July.

My first flower of my book is the *Papaver Suaveolens*. The name is Latin. The family to which it belongs is the *Parueraceae*.

I would write about this plant:

'It grows to 5-10cm (I begin). The leaves are divided into ovel

Papaver Suaveolens

lobes with blueish-green flowers. Variable in colour, but often salmon pink. It grows at high altitudes, usually in scree.'

Notes: I notice the 'Papa' of this flower. This means a father-figure in my toddlerhood. He was Mum's half-brother who raped me. The following word begins, 'suave'. My rapist was 'suave'. The names I gave my dolls inform of my toddlerhood, and one was called the 'Charming Dolly'. This doll was dark-haired and looked like a man. I went through a spell of drawing fungi. All describe attributes to a man grooming my family: suave, charming and a

117

fun-guy. Dad often related on how he and Uncle Dan went out for drinks and had laughs.

The 'Sh' in Bluish-Green

The dot above the word 'flowers' (see image) denotes a ghost I. The 'leaves' are divided. I have deserted myself. There is a lot of 'bluish-green' in this book. This means hush the be-loo-grass. 'Salmon' means a/ms (on). I am torn for something on me. I can't read these codes.

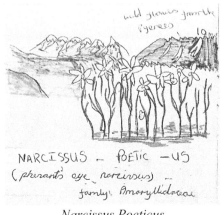

Narcissus Poeticus

NARCISSUS POETIC-US

Pheasant's Eye Narcissus. Family: *Amaryllidaceae*. June-July.

I would write about this second flower:

'Leaves 7-8mm of bluish-green. Flowers carried on 30-60cm stalks. They are wight with central red-eged disk. Intensely fragrant, grown in immense numburs in meadows, mountain-sides and rocks. Found in low altitudes.'

Notes: I notice the narcissus again. My rapist was a suave, charming and fun-guy.

Reconstruction of a Pheasant painting I did for Mum on Aug 1981. Inset shows a 1974 illustration from my Space book.

But Narcissus also means me. My nickname Rac is in this word. It means Rac-is-us. Apparent narcissism can be due to detachment. I appear narcissistic to my plural, indifferent. My oblivion has made me seem apathetic and unfeeling.

The Pheasant Eye and the-Penis

The common name for this plant is *Pheasant Eye Narcissus*. Pheasant Eye means the-penas-eye. I had seen a penis in toddlerhood. The image shows a reconstruction of a pheasant painting I did for Mum in August 1981. Inset shows an illustration for my *Space* book in 1974. Both mean penis.

The Agreed in Pyrenees

Red-eged (flowers) means egreed – 'agree' to hush about the lowers. In pursuit of childhood and a mother-figure, I kept quiet. Soon, I would be 'numb'. My 'numbers' are morphing into numb-us. The bluish-green reiterates the hush. I had written 'quiet' instead of 'quite' too. My plural sees silence as complicit with my rapist. I appear narcissistic and in with Uncle Dan. For this apparent collusion, my fingerprints appear on the inside cover of this book.

NARCISSUS PALLIDIFLORUS

Family: *Amaryllidaceae.*
Pyrenean endemic: May-June.
'Leaves erect, flat and broad.
Flowers drooping or horizontal of
cream-straw. Sometimes be-
coloured with a trumpet of a
deeper shade. Corona expanded
and lobed at the margins and the
perianth segments imbricated and

Narcissus Pallidiflorus

twisted. This daffodil is one of the first to flower in the moutin pasters after the melting of the snows.'

Notes: This plant begins Narcissus-Pa. This means a narcissistic father-figure again. He had me on the floor, hence I-floor-us. Corona means Onca-Nor (Uncle-Nor). Coronas dot my future weather projects. The Nor here is 'expanded'. The lobed margins imply a vulva. Something expanded inside me. Perianth contains th-rape-in. And *moutin pasters* mean mounting rape-st (stain). My rapist groomed my family with his narcissism and raped me on the sly.

Part 3: Uncle Ran

My plural has used the following to show me I was chased by Uncle Dan. My rapist liked to tease.

RHODODENDRON FERRUGIN-EUM

Family: Alpen-rose. June-August.
'An erect shrub growing from 120cm. The leaves are ovate, dark green, above rusty-brown below. Flowers borne on terminal clusters of rose-red. It grows on rocky places, steep mountain-sides and borders of woods, usually on acid for*man*ations.'

Notes: This plant contains the Nor and he rode-on me.
I notice the 'rusty-brown below'. Rape made me bleed below and feel sore (rose).

119

The Lake

My drawing shows a lake.

My third novel, *North Window* (2015) depicts a near-drowning in a lake. Abridged, I had written,

'Fell Reservoir is a disused quarry pit in scrubland called the Keeps. It is riddled with sinkholes and sheer ledges. An abyss one hundred feet down made the eyes go funny. It looked like a metallic plate. The walls of the pit resembled a cake-cutter.'

Rhododendron Ferrugineum

It's just like this drawing. I *am* describing this drawing. Thirty years had passed. *How did this happen?* A mountain looms over the lake. It appears to have dark hair and a moustache. The colour orange dominates. All mean Uncle Dan (of the Nor-age). We once had a pond in our garden. I have reason to believe he chased me into that pond and raped me on its banks. The Latin family of the following flowers says uncle-ran.

Adonis Pyrenaica and the cat-mask

ADONIS PYRENAICA

Pyrenean Pheasant-eye. Family: *Ranunculaceae.* (Pyrenean endemic) Jun -July.' Grows to 30-40cm. Leaves bright green, deeply-cut into thin segments. Flowers 4-6cm of a bright golden-yellow. Grows in steep scree and rocky outcrops in the esten Pyrenees. Very local.'

Notes: Uncle ran again. It says so in the Latin name: Ran-uncul-(aceae).

The *Adonis* isn't the handsome man implied. Read backwards to find 'is-done-a'. I have done something, and it is the Pyrenaica. This means pyre-on-ache (her). The rape burned and ached. The leaves are 'deeply-cut'. An

120

uncle deeply cut into me. Pheasant Eye contains 'th-penaas-eye. Being 'very local,' I had 'seen' it.

The Drawing

My drawing appears abstract. Only on flipping it sideways would I see the head. It looks like a cat. My Eighties artwork is full of cats. Some are contorted with yawning mouths. My novel, *North Window* is about a woman wearing a cat mask. Cat's-mask means sat-mask. The liar wants to remove my face for being used during the 'sat'.

My research has shown that I have adopted identities in a bid to rid this part of myself. The patchwork on the cat's head represents the grafting. I don't want to be me anymore. Uncle Dan chased me then did something horrific.

Part 4: The Taking

Uncle Dan stole from me. He took my childhood away. The following tells me how.

RHAPONTiCUM CYNAROIDES

Cardoon Knapweed. Family: *Compositae.* July-September.

Rhaponticum Cynaroides

'A lone giant of the Pyrnees, reaches ½m. It has large, deeply-cut leaves, green and hairy above. Wight downy below, this stem is often unbranched. It carries a large rose-purple flower, 6-7cm, with brownish narrow bracts. An uncommon plant growing on steep, rocky plaeses.'

Notes: I notice the rape of 'rhap'. It's like 'g-*raph*' (of the degrees) in my *Science* book. The word becomes rape-on-it-come. The common name of this plant is Cardoon Knapweed. This means Rac-done nap-weed. I was come-on whist unconscious (nap).

I keep saying 'deeply-cut' and 'divided'. I was deeply-cut by something right down below. I carry a large sore (rose) as a result. My misspelt places (plaeses) mean pleading the rape away.

SILENCE AQUAULIS

Moss Campion. Family: *Caryophyllaceae.* June-August.

'Forms mats of domed cushions of small narrow-pointed leaves. The flowers are carried on short pink stems. It grows in rock crevasses, scree and turf. The turf (is) found on calcareous and non-calcareous formations.'

Notes: This plant is in fact called the *Silene Acaulis*.

I had written *Silence* instead of *Silene*.

(moss campion)

SILENCE Aqaulis
family: Caryophyllaceae

Silene Acaulis

This is the liar's insistence: 'silence' about the rape. My misspelt 'Aqualis' should be *Acaulis*. My plural is calling out through this plant.

My drawing appears to be a black flowerhead. In fact, the flowers are at the centre. They are small, arranged in a vulva shape. Green surrounds this vulva. Green means grassing on my pink and sore vulva.

But be-lack surrounds all. This represents my broken up and oblivious self. In the Seventies, I was often doing jigsaws. I am fractured and lacking (be-lack) the truth. I don't know of my used vulva nor the coma.

Part 5: I-far and Yellow

My plural has used the following plants to convey her remoteness from me. I have gone yellow while she lives alone with the truth.

Crocus Nudiflorus *and my 1984 drawing of our laurel tree.*

CROCUS NUDIFLORUS
Family: *Iridaceae*. (September-October).

'The common autumn crocus on the Pyrees (is) the large purple flowers. They appear from September to the first snows. The leaves come the following spring. The crocus is peculiar in its method of increasing underground stolons. It appears from sea level. Vast numbers can be seen in the Pyrenean pasturages.'

Notes: The 'nude' stands out. I was stripped during the 'crocus' (rock-us) of rape and on the floor. Us means plural (floor-us). 'Stolon' means my innocence stolen from me.

My drawing shows a fair-haired tree. I'm fair too. This tree is I-far. Part of me is far away while the *Crocus Nudiflorus* speckles the foreground. The limbs splay out. We had a laurel tree shaped like that and I had obviously put this tree in my drawing. The previous year, I had written a story, *The*

Fair Tree in my *Flowerpot Book*. It keeps being 'stolen' from. The image on the right shows my sketch of this laurel in August 1984. The code 'oral' (aurell) exists here. This tree is walled-up for the rape my plural sees. It is far away, and I can't get near.

ANTIRRHINIUM MaJUS

Snabdragon. Family: *Scrophulariaceae*. May-August.

'A perennial with narrow lance-shaped leaves and spikes of large reddish-purple flowers with yellow throats. Height up to

Antirrhinum Majus

80cm. A yellow form is sometimes seen. It grows on dry banks, stony places and roadsides.'

Notes: The fair-tree reappears. And only half is visible. Half of me has gone yellow and my other half is hidden away.

I had put a 'b' in 'snapdragon'. Read backwards to find 'bans' I am banned from the truth. Dragon means gard-on (on-guard). I am being guarded from seeing the burning posterior in my drawing.

The reddish-purple flowers mean 'read-sh-you-repel lowers'. I am repelled and daren't read the lowers' codes. My throat has gone yellow after oral rape. I'm all silent, but the lances and spikes get through. These describe the sensations.

Gentiana Lutea

GENiTANA LUTiA

Great Yellow Gentian. Family: *Gentianaceae*. July-August.

'A stout plant, ½-2m high. Leaves large, elliptical and bluish-green. Flowers golden-yellow with brown spots. It is carried in clusters terminally and upper leaf axils in alpine rastures and stony hillsides.'

Notes: This plant means you-great-giant-liar. That's me. I am living a big cowardly lie.

The bluish-green repeats about grassing on the be-loo, but I can't hear. The flowers are golden but sullied with brown spots. Dad would soon plant a spotted poplar in our garden. My need to be 'popular' is due to my sullied toddlerhood. Rastures means 'u-r-rapes' (for the P-R fusion). *Genitana*, with misplaced 'I' is trying to be genitalia. And my Pyrenees-heading (see image) now reads, Wildflowers of the 'Pyenees'.

Part 6: Me-Render the Pynees

The word 'penis' is all over my book. The way I write 'Pyrenees' shows.

Merendera Pyrenaica

MERENDERA PYRENAICA

Family: *Liliaceae*. (Pyrenean endemic) September – October.

'A bulbous plant allied to the Coldicum. It is an almost stemless composite of six trumpet-shaped segments, not forming a tube at the base. Rose-pink with albino forms, the flowers appear early September, the leaves in spring. Occurs on high Pyrenean pasters in great numburs.'

Notes: This plant is declaring penis (pyenus) through this page. But the lie-lack' (of Liliac-eae) guarantees I won't see it. I mention the 'Coldicum', (a misspelt 'Colchicum'). This deviation means I-locked-come (I-loc'd-come). I can't see the thing that came over me. Stemless means stain-me-less. My 'numburs' means numbs-her. My drawing shows a crack-riddled crevasse. I have been fractured. This is due to the rape-st (stain) of paster. I can't see the penis in this book. I can't see a thing.

TUPILA ASTRAiLiS

Family: *Liliaceae*. June-August.

'13-30cm high. Leaves, long and narrow, like the flower stems of drooping buds. They are streaked with a reddish-brown, opening in full sun to show the golden interior. Grows on rocky outcrops and ledges in the Esten Pyreenes.'

Notes: My page heading has lost the 'r' to become Pyenees. 'Esten Pyenees means seat-on penis.

124

This flower should be '*Tulipa Australis*'. My plural has flagged-up the 'two-lips'. The '*ast-railis*' says a sat-liar exists in my head. Nothing mounted me at all.

Tupfla Asirailis famly lilaceae

Tulipa Australis

The inner flower buds are streaked with reddish-brown in the full 'sun'. This means blood, and inside is the 'son'. He is inside me. And rape burnt. The family of this plant is Lilac-eae). This means I lack (a family). Since learning about my vile toddlerhood, my family no longer feels mine.

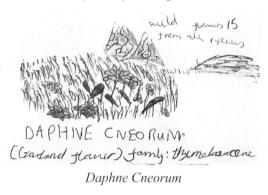

Daphne Cneorum

Daphine Cneorum (Garland flower) famly: thymelaeaceae

DAPHNE CNEORUM

Garland Flower. Family: *Thymelaeaceous*. May-July.

My penultimate flower of this selection reads:

'A prostrate or dwarf shrub, reaches 30cm. Leaves narrow, blunt, tipped or dark green. Flowers pink, fragrant in terminal clusters. A prostrate form, smaller in all its parts than the type (that) occurs at high altitudes in the estern Pyrenees. Is sometimes known as *Var Pygmea*. It grows in turf and rocky outcrops, on limestone and non-calcareous rock.'

Notes: Twice, I had scribbled off Pyrenees, for missing the 'r'. My 'Esten Pyrenees' means seat-on penis, and it won't go away. My page-heading now reads 'Pyenus'. (My 'ee' looks like a 'u').

My plural keeps 'me-render'(ing) a penis through this book.

This 'shrub' is prostrate (I had written). This is me during rape. It is 'smaller in all its parts.' This is me too. I was smaller in all my parts.

This plant is sometimes known as '*Var Pygmea*' (I had continued). This should be 'Var Pygmaea'. The meaning is twofold: pygmy (a small person), and me-a-pig. I am like the pig (my rapist's once-job) for living a lie.

125

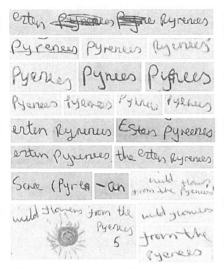

The image shows my Pyrenees losing the 'r' morphing into penis. Notice the 'pyre'.

This project is full of penis. The images show. Pyrenees means penis. Eastern Pyrenees means seat-on penis. Wildflowers means we-lied-lowers (of the) penis.

The other images show further morphings. My 'numbers' changes to numb-us (us-numb). My 'p' resemble 'R' to bring the rape-anagram. It burnt like the 'pyre'.

My past has been 'stolon' when I was prostrate and small.

Words Beyond my Age

I am astonished at my plural's vocabulary. It's nothing like 'mine'. It's barefaced, beyond my age, with words like, narcissism, prostrate, suave, paedophile, pyre, pygmy and mounting. Never would I have used these words at nine. The subconscious picks up on everything and has gone its own way.

Section 7 summarises the codes, along with flowers not covered here.

Pulsatilla Alpina

Part 8: The Pulse-Sat-Liar

I shall end this chapter with the final flower of my Pyrenees book. It contains the sulphur. Remember the copper sulphate of my *Science* book? It seems the sulphate goes back further. This plant shows.

PULSATILLA ALPINA

Alpina anemone. SSP Sulphurea (Yellow Alpine Anemone). Family: *Sulphurea.* May-July.

'Grows to 20-35cm, (I write). Leaves dissected, light green. Stem leaves are smaller. Flowers large and cup-shaped. Solitary flowers of SSP Al-pina are white. The petals' reverse of SSP sulphurea are bluish. Flowers golden-yellow. Grows on rocky mountainsides or open pinewoods.

'The SSP Alpina is found on acid formations, and SSP sulphurea, on lime.'

126

Notes: This, my final plant of my Pyrenean selection, is a modest anemone. I have placed it here for the 'sulphur'. It's in the Latin name. My *Science* book has shown copper-suffocate in copper-sulphate.

But *Pulsatilla* means suffocation too. It means pulse-sat-liar (*pulse-sat-llia*). During suffocation, I could hear the pulse in my head. The penis (in '*pine*-wood-*s*') says what choked me. But all is made out a lie.

The Acid and Lime

The acid and lime are in my *Science* book too. I had written about the PH factor on universal indicator paper. Paper means raper, and lime means l-e/m (plural). Acid means 'said'. How odd. Two years' earlier, I had written the same words in a Pyrenean flower.

The Boulder at the Edge of Woods

Finally, the boulder is mentioned in this project. It's in the *Aquilegia Pyreneaica*. I had written it grows at the edges of woods and amongst boulders. I have emerged from toddlerhood to live a lie. I am stuck beneath the boulder of lies, just like this plant.

Chapter 11: Green Flowers
Introduction
Part 1: The Body of the Plant
Part 2: The Lowers Grassed
Part 3: Colour Missing

Introduction

This section is about another book I had illustrated with wildflowers. It is untitled, so I have called it *Green Flowers*, for the grassing. This book is green. My

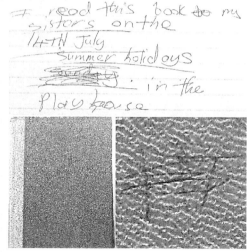

Cover and inside cover of my green book on wildflowers.

other notebooks are green too. As seen from my *Colours* project, green means to grass. My drawing of a tall, straight tree growing from grass shows.

On the inside cover, I had written, 'I read this book to my sisters in the playhouse on the 14th of July.' I had just turned nine. I know this, for I had scribbled off 'Sunday'. I have established the year to be 1974, for this date fell on a Son-day.

I am reading this book to the boulder, not myself. Remember the boulder? This means the world. I keep mistaking my missing self for things on this world. The messages in this book are intended for me. Not others.

I had numbered the pages, but this book begins on page 35. I had ripped out the preliminary ones. I had also removed pages from the back, for the pagination jumps from 82 to 125. Felt tip lines can be seen in the gutters.

The Faint Pencil

There are thirteen felt-tip drawings of flowers within. But on first glance, the pages appear otherwise blank. This is because the writing is faint. I had evidently used an H-pencil. Visual editing was necessary to bring out the writing. This faintness and the pages torn out is the liar's doing.

My Former Projects

As seen, I have already written about wildflowers. This would be my third surviving project on this subject. I would write garden reports in future years (see following chapters).

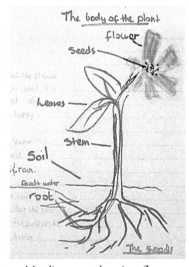

My diagram showing flower parts and the 'saids'.

Part 1: The Body of the Plant

The image shows my opening drawing: 'The Body of the Plant'. This plant is me – my body. I know this from my research. I had named parts to this plant. I would begin with the 'flowerhead'.

'The flowerhead is a different colour to attract bees and give honey (I write)'. Flowerhead means 'lowers-head'. My head was lowered during rape. The head is now a 'different colour': yellow. This is me gone oblivious. The liar is instrumental. My skewed head and wonky eye in my *Colours* book betray of the liar. The colour bar chart is crooked.

This plant is crooked too.

Honey means sweet oblivion. My sweet tooth has been used by the liar to imply I crave the 'yellow'. I would add, 'The leaves keep the water and food.' Leaves mean desertion. I have left part of myself behind.

'The roots (I continue) keep the plant in place and collects rainwater from the soil. The further the root stretch, the better.'

Roots mean my toddlerhood, my beginnings. But it is '*toor*-n' off. The liar is trying to gain distance from my '*root*'. Rain means rein from the 'stem' (me-stain).

The Said and the Read

Finally, 'The seads are kept in the flower, so when it dies, they will produce new flowers in the soil.'

All headings are purple. But my misspelled 'seads' is red. Red means 'read' (past tense). Seads means said (saed) too. My diagram is labelled with 'saids', all in red. This book is telling me about my toddlerhood, and it is me that must read these codes. The new flowers mean knew-lowers. Part of me knows about the lowering, and this truth will never go away.

I shall begin with my first flower. It is called the Groundsel. A light edit has been conducted for ease of read. What follows are my **notes**.

Part 2: The Lowers Grassed

These flowers are of truth. They are grassing on the rape and three are blatant. My first is the Groundsel.

Groundsel

The Groundsel.

The image shows my drawing and my spellings: 'Grouncel' and 'Grounsel'. I would write: 'A popular plant on the soil, they grow from 5cm to 20cm in ditches and un-gardened flower parts, grass, soil and path edges. The Groundsel is an untidy plant. Most are destroyed.'

Notes: The word 'uncle' is visible: 'Gro-uncel' – uncel. My other spelling provides the 's' to bring 'uncle's'. I felt like his to be used.

This plant is the most 'popular for being destroyed' (I had written). Clues to my toddlerhood are leaching out and the liar wants them destroyed. This explains my pages torn out and the faint writing. The liar is trying to hush the 'grass'.

I had written 'un-gardened flower parts'. Un-gardened carries the code, 'unguarded'. The truth isn't guarded, so this plant proliferates. No wonder the liar wants to destroy this plant. It carries the uncle-code.

Gypsophila

'This plant grows from 5cm to 17cm on garden beds (I continue). It is not wild.'

Notes: I haven't written much about this plant at all. I have adopted a heavy felt tip for the heading too. The code is shockingly blatant.

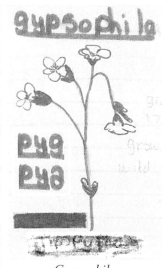

Notice the echo, Gysophila-paedophilia. This plant ends with liar (Gypsoph-*ila*). Lia. Paedophile's-liar.

Inset shows the word 'pyg' (pig – a policeman) and pyd (for paedophile). Switch the g-p and topple the 'g' to find these syllables (see inset).

Uncle Dan was a paedophile-pig.

I had initially erred with the spelling and scrubbed it over. I have visually-enhanced the image (see bottom). It appears to be Jipsofylia. Je (J') is French for 'I'. This means the liar in me.

This plant grows on garden beds (I had written). This means guard-on-beds again. I was raped on more than one bed,

Gypsophila

and the memory must be guarded.

Polyanthus

Polyanthus-a

'Grows from about…'

Notes: This is all I had put about this flower. It is the final of my Green Flowers' book. The following pages (from 54) are blank.

The heading is heavy, like the Gypsophilia.

The meaning is I-lop-th-anus. Anus means rape from behind. Uranus of my *Space* project says the same thing. The memory has been lopped from my conscious awareness.

My drawing appears to explode from the centre. Two flowers form. I have become plural. The leaves resemble a butterfly. This means utter-lie and half of me has gone invisible. My *Science* book has told me about my hidden symmetry.

My toddlerhood has affected how I see the world. Green means to grass on my vile toddlerhood, and it's happening all around me. My green Pluto (in *Space*) says the same. chapter 17 shows the grass in detail.

Buttercup

This flower is be-uttering the truth. My Aurther book has said so.

I would write: 'It grows from 5cm to 12cm in grass, soil and hedgy places. The Buttercup has shiny faces, very smooth. But the back is not so shiny, but just as smooth. They grow any season.'

Notes: I have already written about the Buttercup in my Aurther Books. The lower images show these earlier drawings. Image centre shows how I wrote the word: Buttercub. This means be-utter-book, to grass on the rape.

The image above shows a head detached. It's the one with the 'seeds'. This means semen and they went in my mouth. I want to remove my head.

The 'shininess' implies plastic, like

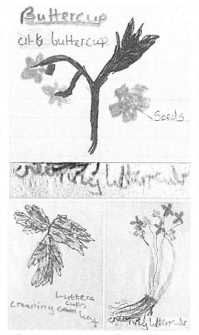

Buttercup. Images beneath, my drawings from my Aurther Books.

a mask. I am reminded of the cat's mask of the *Adonis Pyrenaica* in my Pyrenean book. The liar wants to remove my face. The other two heads represent my oblivion and the liar in my head.

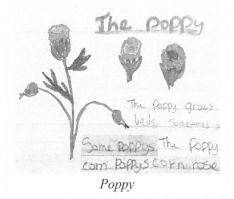

Poppy

Poppy

'The Poppy grows in flowerbeds, (I write), sometimes weedy places, from 7cm to 2ft. They have no scent. Some poppies have yellow centres at the seed part. Others have a purply-red middle (like the stalk). These poppies are Corn Poppy, or Corn Rose.'

Notes: My plural has latched onto the Poppy for symbolising Remembrance Day. She wants me to remember my paedophile uncle. I remark on two types: one has a yellow centre, the other, purply-red.

Yellow centre means the throat, at the 'seed' part. The *Antirrhinum Majus* of my Pyrenean collection had a yellow throat too. I've gone all silent about the seeds down my throat.

The latter is known as the Corn Poppy (or Corn Rose). These contain 'Nor and sore. Stalk means sat-talk and are purply-red in the 'middle'. I was lowered and weed on beds, and my middle made sore.

Pear Blossom
'Pear Blossoms is just like Apple Blossoms (I continue). They fall in spring and new pears grow. These flowers are snow-white with seeds sticking out on long hairs at the centre of the flower face.'

Pear Blossom and (right) tiger in my Junglerealm painting (1983).

Notes: Blossom means be-loo-ss-me. I was used like a loo and lost part of myself. Pear means rape and I 'knew' (new) about it. Apple means appal.

The 'pear blossom *act* just like the apple blossom' (I had written). The liar 'acts'. It lacks autonomy and simply follows the decree.

My Jungle Painting
I had written that 'seeds stick out on long hairs at the centre of the flower face'. The 'long hairs' imply whiskers. My *Junglerealm* painting (spring 1983) shows a tiger with long whiskers at the 'centre of the lower face'. It seems I am describing a painting eight years before I began it. Pear-blossom means rape and the saliva is semen on long-hair. Chapter 20 explains this painting. For now, the lies have grown long, and white flowers abound.

Part 3: Colour Missing
These next flowers have been grouped together for the colours. They keep going missing. How odd. The crookedness of my *Colours* bar chart made colours go missing too. The bars are askew, and areas left blank.

Wallflower: The Yellow Missing
I begin with the Wallflower. I would write: 'The Wallflower grows from 8cm to 18cm. They come in red, yellow, blue and purple. They grow in gardens by bushes and hedges. They have long, baggy pettles at the top of the stalk, like a tower. They smell like roses. It is part of the cabbage family.'

132

Notes: The meaning behind this flower is obvious: a wall. The lowers must be walled up. But the meaning *could* have been lower (the) wall. My *Science* project has shown the liar's paradox. Where ambiguity exists, the liar promotes the lie.

Wall (the) lower. (Not lower the wall).

The Yellow Misplaced

Cabbage means back-age – my toddlerhood. My food reports in future diaries show. I have listed four colours: red, yellow, blue

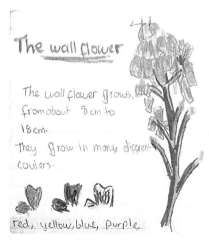

The Wallflower

and purple. These means read, coward, be-loo and you-repel. But the yellow segment is missing (see bottom of image). This means my oblivion. The wall of flower has hidden it. Part of me is missing and I am stuck on the boulder. I am reading this book to the world, not myself.

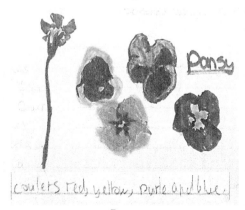

Pansy

Pansy: The Blue Missing

My next flower is the Pansy.

'The Pansy grows 2cm to 6cm (I write). They grow in flowerbeds or bushy places. They come in red, yellow, purple.'

Notes: Pansies means a-penis (a-peniss). Our flowerbed was adorned with pansies. In 1978, I had reported that the pansies 'remain strong' (despite other flowers coming and going). My rapist isn't affected by what he's done. He remains unchanged.

A colour is missing again. My illustration shows four colours, but my opening paragraph lists three. Where's the blue? It's like the Wallflower earlier. The liar has got rid of the be-loo. The pansy heads appear stained, for the pansy grows in (flower) beds. I was lowered on my bed, and I'm not allowed to know I have been stained.

133

Forget-me-not: Forget the Blue

This flower wants me to notice the missing blue.

'The Forget-me-not has a purply-blue pettle, which attracts the eye (I begin). They grow from 3cm to 9cm in grassy places or hard soil. To make them increase, split them up.'

My drawings of Forget-me-nots.

Notes: I was forever drawing Forget-me-nots at school. The drawing on the right shows that of my Aurther books. In a quiz at the back, I had proclaimed this flower to be my favourite.

But the be-loo (blue) of this flower is missing on the previous page on pansies. My petal-misspelling *wants* to attract the eye, and 'pettle' means to tell.

It grows from 'grass'. But splitting this flower takes the 'Forget-me' *from* the 'not'. The denial-code has now doubled. The liar's paradox has struck. I say this to be a popular flower. But the 'not' implies the opposite. The liar wants me to forget the be-loo of this flower.

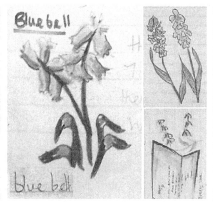

My drawings of bluebells.

Bluebell: The Be-loo

The blue-issue won't go away. The Bluebell says so.

'The bluebell grows from 3cm to 9cm (I write). They grow in weedy soil, sometimes hedgy places or neat garden beds.'

Notes: In August 1979, I would write a children's story called *The Secret of the Shadows*. A creepy uncle stops with a family on holiday, where little girl Sam almost drowns. During her recovery, her older sister Rebecca becomes ill too. Sam slips Bluebells under Rebecca's door. Images right show my illustrations from this story.

Bluebell means be-loo (Bbell-lue). It's just like 'blue'. I had written Bluebells grow in 'weedy soil'. This means 'weed-in-soil'. I feel sullied inside. Bluebells are also found on 'garden beds'. This means guard-on-beds. I mustn't know what happened on these beds.

Forsythia: The Blue gone Yellow

My penultimate flower is the Forsythia.

'It grows from 5cm in flower to 12ft in bushes. They have bell-shaped flowers. They grow in dry soil and grassy places. Sometimes, people grow them. Seasoned: spring.'

Notes: I had written the Forsythia has 'bell-shaped flowers'. It's as though I am describing the Bluebell again, only a yellow version. The Bluebell has gone yellow.

The Forsythia is 'grown purposely in spring,' (I note). Springtime means a new beginning. The liar in my head wants me to go yellow. Forsythia means I-scythe-for-her. The liar has sliced part of myself off. The blue has gone yellow with a new life.

Forsythia

Blue has gone missing.

White Deadnettle: The Deaden-tell

These two nettles contain a missing red (read). The 'tell' is deadened.

'The White Deadnettle grows 5cm to 9cm (I write). Grows in very grassy and hedgy places. Deadnettle was named because the weed does not sting. The nettle is dead.'

White Deadnettle and Red Deadnettle

Red Deadnettle

I follow this with The Red Deadnettle. (I begin) 'It grows in grassy, hedgy places. Grows 5cm to 9cm. It does not sting. It is not as common as the White Deadnettle.'

Notes: Deadnettle means deaden-tell. The telling is deadened and the 'weed' doesn't sting. I am numb. The White Deadnettle is white, but the red one is purple. It's not 'read' at all. The read has gone missing, and I can't read the 'tell'.

Several times I have described plants that grow in 'grassy places'. They are in fact 'grassing', but the colours have gone missing. My plural has injected codes into colours and the liar keeps stealing them away.

This project shows.

135

Chapter 12: My Garden Reports 1978

Introduction   **Part 2: July**   **Part 4: September**
Part 1: June   **Part 3: August**   **Part 5: The Sunflowers**

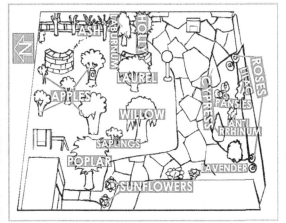

The garden layout (drawn 2021).

Introduction

I would continue to write about flowers.

This chapter is about my garden reports. The year is 1978 and I have just turned thirteen. Currently, I was keeping meticulous weather records of sunsets, wind direction and clouds. I am also keeping a diary. My garden reports would form part of these records.

Our cottage garden was adorned. Rose beds festooned edges and perennials shimmered. We had cypresses at the entrance and hawthorn borders. Ash trees lined the top of a little hill near a laburnum, holly and laurel. Central were apple trees, a poplar and willow. Having a painting set for my birthday, I did a few sketches late May.

The image shows the layout. The laurel stands almost central. I had drawn this tree in my Pyrenean book. It's under *Crocus Nudiflorus* and I had made it fair (I-far). This is due to the oral-code it carries.

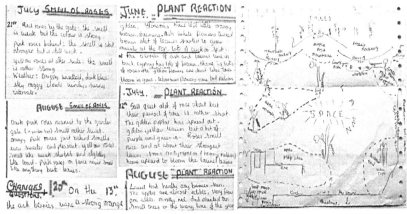

Left: My garden reports 1978. *Right*: Map of the garden drawn 1978

136

Further plants referred to on 2 June	
Ash	White flowers turned brown. Leaves at the top starting to grow.
Cypress	A lime colour
Laburnum	Yellow flowers are at the top where the sun can get at them.
Lilac tree	Fully-bloomed purple.
Pansies	Fully-bloomed.
Roses	Have just begun. The leaves are half-red.

Part 1: June

On 1 June, I began a weather diary. I had dedicated a section to the garden. I had used the term, 'Plant Reaction'. Touched upon in chapter 8, the following report of 2 June is set out in full.

Plant Reaction: 2 June

'No berries on the ash or laurel (I had written). The apple blossoms have blown off. Orange-brown stamens are left behind. Yellow, dandelion-like flowers are dying. The poplar's leaves are mostly golden. Lots of cuckoo spit, mainly at the top of the garden.'

Notes: As seen, cuckoo spit is exuded from the froghopper insect. It occurs from May when the cuckoo returns from Africa. I had read about the cuckoo in my 1977 diary. The 'spit' brought distaste. My plural is reminded of how Donald Pleasance choked on gunk in the film *Fantastic Voyage* a few days earlier. Something like that had happened to me.

The 'spit' clashes with the blossoms gone. Only stamens remain. Stamen means man-stain. My fruiting flowers have been adulterated by a man (the cuckoo). The

Cuckoo spit and cypress with dead innards

cowardly-yellow of the dandy-lie makes the 'popular' choice of hiding the cuckoo.

Plant Reaction: 22 June

Three weeks later, I make another report: 'Ash and laurel berries are budding, (I begin). Cypress is brown inside. Lots of roses. But the lilac and laburnum are bare.'

I had spelled cypress like the country (Cyprus). With the 'p' toppled, means us-cried (cryd-us). It's like my misspelt cirrius in my weather reports.

The cuckoo spit has left behind inedible fruit and dying blooms. The vulva-shaped cypress is dead inside and I-lack (lilac) due to the sore (rose). The garden is bitter and jaded for the cuckoo spit.

The garden has become of reflection of what I carry inside. The green is grassing on my toddlerhood.

Part 2: July

It is now July, and the weather turns dull and cool. This month, I write two garden reports.

Plant Reaction: 12 July

Further plants referred to on 12 July	
Apples	Big and rosy, but inedible
Ash	Berries are brownish.
Cypress	Patches of brown, but still green.
Laburnum	Flowers gone. Pods left behind.
Laurel	Leaves are shiny and bright green
Pansies	Blooms are strong.

'The roses are still out,' (I note) 'but their time is short.' The golden poplar has spread golden-yellow leaves with bits of purple and green. Antirrhinum (bunny rabbits) have bloomed.'

Notes: *Bunny rabbits?* I'd forgotten about that. This is what we used to call the antirrhinum. The flower would nod when pinched. My Pyrenean collection included the *Antirrhinum* too. It was of the *Majus* variety.

In a momentous tornado project I would begin in five years, I would write about thousands of dead rabbits gouged out by a Kansas tornado. It felled a water tank too. A water tower used to command our skyline until a building estate obscured it.

My tornado project is telling me a storm decimated my toddlerhood home. My plural has used my tornado project to tell me about my vile toddlerhood. Being so big, this project is looked at in a separate book.

Antirrhinum, Ash berries and Laburnum. Top right: my painting of sunflowers and chairs (1998).

The Golden Popular

I had begun this garden report by saying the roses' time is short and the golden poplar has spread its stained leaves. The 'popular' in me is spreading because of the stain I carry. My childhood has been lopped because of the 'sore'.

The garden is dotted with stains and inedible fruit. But the pansies remain 'strong'. At seen from the previous chapter, Pansies means a-penis. It remains unaffected.

Plant Reaction: 21 Jul

Two weeks later, I write about roses.

'Red roses by the gate, (I write) smells weak but the colour is strong. Pink roses behind smell a little stronger but not much. Yellow roses at the other side smell strongest.'

Notes: Why all these smells? Is this another mode of messaging? My research has shown red means read and smell means e//ms (a split me). My torn-self can't read these signs. The 'red' smells weak. Pink is weak too, but the yellow (of cowardice) is strong. The cowardly-lie commands the roses.

Part 3: August

It is now August and I write five garden reports. Why this abundance? I have abridged them here.

Plant Reaction: 2 August

I begin, 'Dad

Further plants referred to on 2 August	
Apples	Mostly red. Almost edible.
Ash	Berries are orange.
Cypress	Has brown patches.
Laburnum	Fully-grown pods are 5cm long, but small compared to the runner beans.
Lavender	Violet-blue flowers dying.
Laurel	Has few berries. The young leaves are fully-grown but lighter green.
Pansies	Still abloom.

planted the (ten) saplings in the wrong time: summer, but some are giving shoots. Two have the best leaves: the one nearest the poplar, and the smallest. The golden poplar has spread since last year but has pinches of green and purple.

'The sunflowers are shoulder-height (I continue). The shorter one (with my arms straight by my sides) is up to my elbows; the biggest one is above my head.

'Lots of yellow roses. Pink rosebush by the porch is dying. But the pansies are still abloom.'

Notes: My projects on wildflowers show I see myself in each plant. It's the same here. The sunflowers are a prime example.

The Sun-Son Lowers-Flower

Sunflowers means son-lowers. He lowered me. And 'I' (sun) lowered too. My face burnt like the sun once I was lowered.

The popular-poplar and blossoms in autumn.

My arms were pinned to the sides whilst the son sat astride of me. This is what the shortest sunflower is saying. The taller 'son'-flower rears over my head and shoulders. Both mean oral rape. Meanwhile, elbows mean belows – my vagina. He also went up my belows. The 'sun' (of sunflower) means sun-son. My *Space* project has told me of this double-meaning.

My Krakatoa project (chapter 14) would also declare a son forced me straight through Sunda Strait.

False Childhood

My false childhood clashes with autumn. This is what Dad's ten saplings (planted on 11 Jul) is saying. Their buds are not of spring, but a time of year when everything's over. But the 'lots of yellow roses' insists upon the cowardly lie. The popular-poplar keeps spreading its stained leaves, needing approval, seeking acceptance. That's me. I'm stuck on this boulder, trying to fill a void.

When I write these reports, the garden becomes a mirror of myself. The yields are bitter or dying except for the 'pansies'. This means a-penis and these continue to thrive. My rapist is unaffected by my childhood's end. My (false) childhood comes in autumn after the cuckoo spit had destroyed it in spring.

Smell of Roses on 13 August	
Dark pink roses by gate (in bed).	Sweet.
Orange-pink roses	Sweeter and pleasant.
Yellow roses	Like weak sherbet and slightly of toast.
Pink roses by fence	Nothing but leaves.

Plant Reaction: 13 Aug

Eleven days later, I return to the smell of roses. The table lists them. What does one this tell me?

The pink roses 'in bed' smell sweet now. The orange-pink ones, sweeter still.

Orange means Nor-age, the age of when my rapist lived with us, and smell means e//ms, a split-me. The 'on-the-fence' roses smell of nothing and the others are sickly-sweet. The roses are mirroring the liar in my head: trying to hide the burning from me, but the yellow ones cannot hide the faint 'toast'.

140

Changes and Questions: 20 Aug

Seven days later, I make a report on the ash berries. On 13 August, they had been orange. They are now pinkish-red.

'The ash tree next to the laburnum has lots of berry-clusters, (I had noted). But the ash on the other side has lost most. Perhaps they were shaken off, eaten by birds or died. Why didn't the birds take berries from the tree next to the laburnum?'

My Return on 22 Aug: Two days later, I would return to the two ash trees. I smelt a healthy berry from the (mostly) berry-less ash to notice a sweet scent. The berries were also drier. I would conclude that the scent must have attracted the birds.

The laburnum stands next to the berry-endowed ash. All-burn is encoded within laburnum and is poisonous. No wonder the birds weren't tempted. But the berries of the other ash smell sweeter. This ash stands further away from the all-burn and is sweetly oblivious – like me.

Plant Reaction: 28 August 1978

I would complete my August reports on the 28th.

'The laburnum pods are yellow (I had noted). The birds have eaten the ash berries. Dad has re-potted the sunflowers. There are two growing in each one.' The table lists these sunflowers.

My Reports on Four Sunflowers 28 Aug 1978			
28 Aug: My original list		**My reshuffle from the tallest**	
Pot 1	Up to my head	Pot 2	Up to 8ft
Pot 2	Up to 8ft	Pot 4	Up to my head (standing on bench)
Pot 3	Up to my cheek	Pot 1	Up to my head
Pot 4	Up to my head (standing on bench).	Pot 3	Up to my cheek

Notes: I remember those sunflowers. Dad got into planting them from seed every year and made them grow tall. But the damp, dull summer of '78, made them look despondent, nodding in the wind. I saw myself in those sunflowers. My final report fully explains about the sunflowers.

August is ending and I am soon to begin my second year at senior school. A distant cousin stops in Dad's room. My plural is reminded of the sleeping arrangements of my toddlerhood.

Part 4: September

On 7 Sept I suffer my second bad period pain since the menarche (Apr 1977). I miss PE. The day after, I sight a deep red sunrise. On the same day, I would make this final garden report.

My Final Garden Report of 1978: 8 Sept

'Four of the ten saplings have leaves (three apple and one plum). The golden poplar has spread a lot. The apples are now edible, and the pansies are still abloom.'

Further plants referred to on 8 September	
Apples	Are now edible.
Ash	Berries are gone.
'Bunny rabbits'	Still abloom.
Laburnum	Pods are brown.
Laurel	Berries are purple, red, yellow and green. The red starts at the bottom.
Lavender	Blooms are brown.
Pansies	Still abloom.
Roses	May heads have been 'used'.

Notes: So, Dad's saplings are fruit trees. The blossoms are coming too late. These autumn buds represent my false childhood. Meanwhile, nearby apple trees are bearing edible fruit. Their springtime blossoms represent my true childhood, but their blossoms have vanished last June with the cuckoo spit. Meanwhile, the stained leaves of the popular-poplar keeps spreading. The garden is like my childhood: out of sync. And all because of the pansies (a-penis). Only poisonous fruit or dying flowers remain. The roses have 'used heads'. Mine was used and autumn comes early.

My Sunflower Report 8 Sept 1978	Height and state of Sunflowers
Pot 1 Faces East	Located below Mum's bedroom window. When I am standing on bench, is up to my head. Budding of head is light green, under a foot wide.
Pot 2 Faces East	Is the tallest, just under a foot below Mum's bedroom window. (No detail on the head).
Pot 3 Faces North	Has very good leaves. Flower head has a big dark green bud. Reaches the veranda window frame.
Pot 4 Faces North	Also has a big, dark green bud and reaches the veranda window frame. **Sunflowers from the tallest: 2, 4, 3, 1.**

Part 5: The Sunflowers

The sunflowers' code is stark. They carry a double meaning: (the) son-lowers, and sun (my burning face)-lowers. No wonder I dwell upon these flowers within my garden reports. I had reported on their heights on 28 Aug. The table here shows their heights on 8 Sept. This bit I find odd.

The Sunflowers' New Heads

I had numbered four pots on 28 Aug. I no longer know which is which, for they have been moved. But from the tallest are ordered 2, 4, 3 and 1. Both pots 1 and 2 are located to the front of the cottage (facing east) for being near

Mum's window. The image shows. Pots 3 and 4, are at the veranda, facing north.

Summary on the Sunflowers' Heads

Pot 1 Faces East: This sunflower has a budding head of light green.

Pot 2 Faces East: This tallest sunflower has no mention of the head.

Pot 3 Faces North: This sunflower head has a big, dark green bud.

Pot 4 Faces North: This one also has a big, dark green bud.

I have described the heads of all but sunflower 2. This sunflower is in the sunniest spot.

September sunflowers by our cottage. Three have new budding heads. The sun-drenched tallest one is left blank.

It is the tallest and faces east. The other sunflowers have green buds. But in the August (photos testify) all had big yellow heads. Three have gone. Did I not describe sunflower 2 for still having its original head?

The heads of the other sunflowers have been replaced with new heads. Pot 3 has very good 'leaves'. This means desertion. I now have a new 'head' after deserting myself. Sunflower 2 may still have its original (old) head. I have a new head after my toddlerhood blossoms have long gone.

The Story of the Garden

I loved that garden…*didn't I?*

The cuckoos spit reminds my plural an imposter had groomed his way into my toddlerhood home and took my innocence with substance like that. My fruiting blossoms would die. My fake childhood would arrive in autumn, like the buds of Dad's saplings.

But the pansies stick around. The meaning is a-penis and rose means sore. The berries of an ash have been soured by a nearby laburnum.

The Stained Appal

Not mentioned is an ant-infested apple tree in the corner. The apples were small and bitter. My plural could see herself in that tree: stunted by the ant-stain. The showy popular represents the lie: needing to be 'popular'. The dwarf cypresses are the same. They appear okay from afar until checking out the dead innards.

The sunflowers are known for facing the sun. This represents the son-burn. But in September, three of the heads would be replaced. I have a new 'head'. The head of sunflower 2 is overlooked.

Willow weeping over the oral and the hole-I.
(Right) An ant-stain infested apple tree.

The Weep of Old
The oldest tree in the garden is overlooked too: the holly. The willow as well. This 'weeper' stands in front of our living room window. I reasoned the holly, being unchanging, didn't need observations, and the willow was yet small. But the 'weeping' willow (I-low) is growing fast. The 'hole-I' is why.

I was forced low and a hole made into me.

I fancied myself an innocent thirteen-year-old in the garden, yet vile notions would follow me around. My subconscious has been tarnished by sex abuse and my plural keeps making unsavoury links with everything around me. Even plants.

The green is grassing around me, and the garden is grieving for my lost toddlerhood. My garden reports have ended for the year but would resume on 20 July 1979.

My Garden reports in 1979

Chapter 13: My Garden Reports 1979
Introduction
Part 1: 20 July 1969
Part 2: The Normals
Part 3: Leaves, Buried and Hush
Part 4: Heads Used and Dying
Part 5: The Garden in Five Years

Introduction
A year has passed since my 1978 garden reports. It is now summer 1979 and I have just turned fourteen.

Things are crap at home. A divorce is in the air and the cottage is briefly on the market. I'm feeling unwell and drawing pictures in the garden, one of which was a rose. On 18 Jul, we go to Skegness, and I bought a thermometer. I'm about to keep records of the 'degrees'. This makes me think of my *Science* book. Degrees means an agreement and would form part of my weather records.

Soon after, we go on another trip. I cry to Mum with depression. The prospect of losing my home has provided a stepping-stone to when a rapist lived with us. On the 27th, I begin a story called *The Secret of the Shadows*. A creepy uncle stops on holiday with a family. This was the situation surrounding the start of these garden reports.

Part 1: 20 July 1969

Instead of buying a new notebook for these reports, I had used an old 1977 appointment diary. My first report was written on a page dated 22 March 1977. At the top, I had put, 'These (garden) reports must be taken on the 20th of every month'. I would start mine on 20 July 1979.

This I find odd. On 20 July 1980, my diaries had gone big (see image). And on 20 July 1988, my diaries would end. This date has significance for my plural.

The reason is the Moon. I had written about the Moon in my *Space* book. The lower image shows my poem *Moon Mystery*.

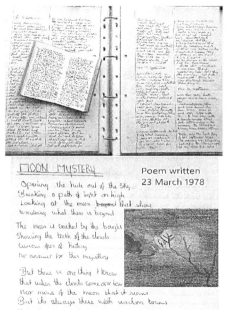

On 20 July 1980 my diary would grow big. On 20 July 1988, my diaries would end. Bottom image shows my poem Moon Mystery *(23 Mar 1978)*.

Moon means mono. I can only see one face of two. The Moon Landings took place on 20 July 1969. I was four. I don't remember the live coverage, but I do remember the holiday. My plural has viewed the Moon Landings to mark the dawning of my conscious awareness and my toddlerhood falling into shadow. I can now see only one face of the Moon. The other is hidden, hence the 'mystery'.

The hidden face represents my toddlerhood; the visible face, my life since. I have just awoken to the world and my plural is remote. So, I would begin my garden reports on 20 July 1979 – ten years after the Moon Landings.

My incidence of the 'normal' in my garden reports gives away my torn-self in nor-a/m.

Part 2: The Normals

I make four garden reports in all: 20 July to 20 Oct.

Here, I would encounter the same plants as before: the oral-laurel, the popular-poplar and the sore-rose.

On 20 July, I report, 'The laurel is packed with green berries and the poplar is full. The pansies have yet to bloom, and the cypress is brown inside.'

Much the same as last year, then. The popular-poplar is spreading its golden leaves whilst the cypress remains dead inside. The cuckoo spit has long gone.

My reports appear 'normal'. My life seems normal. Indeed, I use the word 'normal' fifteen times in these reports. The holly reiterates. 'Normal (I had written). Young leaves are fully grown.' The following month, I had written, 'Coming on normally. Little leaves fully grown.' And the final two reports: 'Normal' Simply 'normal'.

Norway contains the Nor-code. It means going my rapist's way with the lies. Anorexia is the same, a self-divorce due to the Nor. Both contain part of Uncle Dan's name.

Normal contains the Nor too. It is in fact two words: nor-mal. Read backwards from 'a' to find alm, a slashed am. The Nor has torn me in two. '*Normally*' means nor-a/m-lie. I'm living a lie.

The image shows the plants I had described as 'normal'. All represent my torn-self. There's quite a lot here. They include the holly, willow, poplar and apple. All are 'normal'.

But my life isn't normal at all. I'm torn and a force in my head is hiding the truth from me. This force is reflected in my garden reports. I have a torn-self and I mustn't know about my vile toddlerhood.

Part 3: Leaves, Buried and Hush

Many of my plants are normal. They are also 'leaves'. The holly says so. 'Young leaves are fully grown,' (I had written).

Leaves mean to desert. I have deserted myself.

This sentence comes together, 'Nor-a/m (I am torn). Young leaves (young deserter) are fully grown (my plural and I are fully grown.)

The poplar reiterates the 'leaves' with, 'full yellow leaves, a few young brown ones.'

I have fully deserted myself and gone no-brow. Brown means oblivion too. I have no brow and no memories.

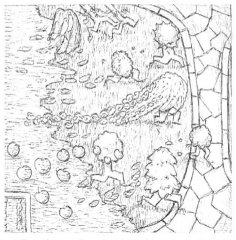

The plants 'leaving' and going yellow.

I would add, the willow has 'full leaves' and 'A few chains of dead leaves. Normal.'

I notice the chain. I remain chained to my past despite my oblivion to it. The image shows the mass desertion. I am deserting myself. The garden is running away. My burning face in oral rape is the reason.

On 19 Aug I saw a documentary about Krakatoa. I would write about this volcano in May 1983, little realising I am describing the cause of this desertion. The day after I had seen this documentary, I would write my garden report with eight 'normals', three 'buries' and three 'leaves'.

My Krakatoa project is looked at in chapter 14.

The deserters here include the willow, laburnum, apple and poplar. The poplar is opting for the popular. I am stuck on this boulder seeking acceptance instead of facing the truth.

The Gone Yellow

The image also shows the yellow. The horizontal lines indicate. The plants are reflecting my torn-self running via the cowardly-oblivion to no-brow. I had written, 'It has been a dry period. The grass has yellowy patches on the lawn.' The image shows the yellow patches left behind. Plants gone yellow include apple, poplar, laburnum and lilac.

The Vanished

There's a lot of berries here too. By this I mean, buries. I have buried my past. The laurel has 'green berries.' And later, 'berries disappeared.'

My *Colours* book has told me green means to grass and ruby means to bury. Green berries mean buries-grass. I have buried the grass in me. On 27 Jul, I would remark on greenfly. This means 'grass fly away'. Vanish.

147

The ash and hawthorn have buries too – reddish ones. This means she-read-sh. Hush about reading these codes. I mustn't know about these codes.

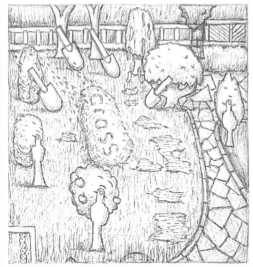
The hush and the buries

In July, the ash has 'orange berries and full leaves.' This means Nor-age buries. Full leaves mean to desert. I have buried my toddlerhood after deserting it.

In August, the birds would eat the berries. The buries have disappeared. I don't even know I have buried anything. On 27 Aug, we went blackberry picking. I'm feeling unsettled and melancholy. No wonder.

The cypress is bluish in colour (I continue). This means I-sh-be-loo. I am hushing the loo. The hawthorn provides my plural's response to the hush. Haw sounds like 'whore'. I am th-Nor-whore for letting my rapist get away with it and the lying pimp of pimpernel. I may as well be his girlfriend, 'Gwen' as seen from the Gwenni-pig cage in my *Science* book.

The image shows the plants burying the grass, hushing it up and going the yellow way.

Part 4: Heads Used and Dying

A similar thing has occurred here as last spring with the cuckoo spit. As seen, the wind has blown the blossoms away, leaving cuckoo spit behind. But the cuckoo itself has gone. The cuckoo is Uncle Dan, grooming my family on the pretext of being a friend.

In August, I would write, 'Roses have a lot of used heads.' But the Pansies (a-penis) seems to have disappeared. My rapist used my head and disappeared. It's just like the cuckoo last year. He has disappeared.

I had used the z-spelling 'panzies'. I am oblivious to the penis and to the blooms (be-loo-me). In August, the lavender begins to die. This plant means ''alve-rend'. Being torn, I can no longer remember my head being used.

I would finally report that Dad's ten young trees (planted last summer) have yellow full leaves. They have gone yellow after a mass desertion last autumn. Some of these trees haven't survived.

148

The Garden in Autumn

It is now autumn. Everything is dying, but the pansies are still abloom, and the lilac is 'normal'. Lilac means I-llack and is my normal. The cypress' innards remain dead.

The autumn garden would bring dread and melancholy. My feelings are due to my lost childhood. Every year, the fading garden provides a reminder of my childhood lost. I write my final garden report on 20 October 1979.

Section 7 summarises these codes.

Part 5: The Garden in Five Years

This chapter ends with my drawings of the garden. Five years have gone by, and it is summer 1984. I am in my second year of uni studying for an art degree. I am now nineteen. Some of these drawings would become huge studio pieces.

Top left: a surreal sketch for a painting called *Summit*. The view is based on apple trees draping shadows over our lawn.

The colours would become apocalyptic, as though the sun had advanced in the sky.

This would lead to a second painting *Webbed Shadows* featuring the shadows closing in.

Top right: Our crazy paving path. The willow stands to the left of the drawing.

Bottom left: The laurel tree and (just behind) the holly. Some of the main branches have been lopped off. My plural could see herself in this tree.

Bottom right: a view looking out of our garden gate. The location of the roses and one of the cypresses stand to the right of the drawing.

We had five apple trees.

Top left: Apple tree by the swing. Felled apples in the foreground would soon turn yellow. This means gone oblivious to the (green) grass.

Top right: Trunk of our biggest apple tree. It used to creak in the wind.

Bottom left: Apple tree near the fence. This one stood beside a pear tree.

Bottom right: Apple tree on the little hill leading to a row of ash trees. To the left is the ant-infested apple tree (out of sight).

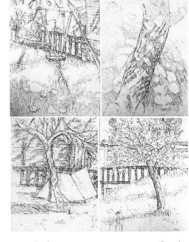

Image top: Colour-notes to a row of ash trees on a little hill at the top of the garden.

There's a lot of alizarin (crimson). This means liar-lyin'-z. I have gone to sleep to the lies.

Image centre: Garden furniture beneath the large apple tree. This composition is full of codes, including the chair beneath the appal-tear. A fence around the garden means ringfence. It's like Saturn's ring.

Image bottom: The laurel (right), apple and kids' camping gear.

The garden often accommodated children. This formed a constant reminder of a childhood I had lost. The drawings are sunny, but sadness hides in the shadows.

SECTION 5: HUGE FORCES
Chapter 14: Krakatoa
Chapter 15: Astronomy
Chapter 16: The Sun and Moon

This section looks at some of my big projects. The Eighties have turned, and my work's gone all ambitious. I spent hours cutting out pictures, drawing maps and skiving from college. My portfolio of projects has amassed with a huge one on weather, another on astronomy, the sun, hurricanes and tornadoes. I am also keeping weather records. My head is full of natural disasters, and I am about to write about volcanoes.

Chapter 14: Krakatoa
(13 May – 3 June 1983)
Introduction
Part 1: Rugging and Mt St Helens
Part 2: A Growing Obsession
Part 3: My Face Erupts
Part 4: A-Two-Rak
Part 5: Crater Face
Part 6: 27 August 1883
Part 7: Tsunami, Man-used-me
Part 8: Submerging
Part 9: False Paradise
Part 10: Santorin's Missing I
Part 11: Mount Stain In-hell

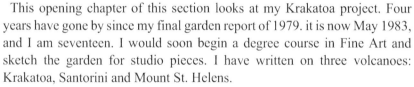

Introduction

This opening chapter of this section looks at my Krakatoa project. Four years have gone by since my final garden report of 1979. it is now May 1983, and I am seventeen. I would soon begin a degree course in Fine Art and sketch the garden for studio pieces. I have written on three volcanoes: Krakatoa, Santorini and Mount St. Helens.

The build-up is explained here.

Part 1: Rugging and Mt St Helens

On 18 May 1980, Mount St Helens erupted.

Mount St Helens is a volcano in Washington, USA. On 21 May, my diary mentions it. 'Mount St Helens volcano broke out and dust scatters everywhere'. The scenes on TV enthralled me. I couldn't get enough of nature's fury. Two months earlier, I had collated Mum's coin collection and made her a Mother's Day card.

On 22 May, I report in my diary of having a day off school. I did a lot of 'rugging'. On 23 May, I break up for Whitsun. I have another day off for a period pain. I'm still rugging. On 24 May, I went to town and got a load of wool. I'm rugging again. Later, I broke an 'ornament'. On the 27th, I'm still rugging. My rug shows three apples. I remember it.

My plural is triggered by the smothering pyroclastic clouds of Mount St Helens, and I'm getting vile dreams. Rugging is due to this volcano. The '*pull-the-wool-over-the-eyes*' saying is the drive behind this rugging. The liar uses sayings to preserve my oblivion. I've gone woolly-headed. and the liar can't get enough wool. A woolly head won't see the mount-stain-hell this volcano represents.

A few days later, I broke an 'ornament'. Orn-meant contains my rapist's Nor and the liar has broken the meaning. See how this volcano has affected me? Krakatoa contains the Rak and would be used to describe in graphic detail how I was almost murdered.

Part 2: A Growing Obsession

The table below shows my diary mentions of volcanos. On 19 Aug 1979, I saw a documentary about Krakatoa. The following day, I would write a garden report with eight 'normals', three 'buries' and three 'leaves'. I am burying my past after my subconscious sees my burning face in Krakatoa.

On the day I saw Krakatoa, I report of playing 'Cheat' (a card game) with my sisters. I also mention Cliff Richard's hit, *We Don't Talk Anymore*. Nan (my rapist's mother) is stopping for the summer, and I thought the world of her. On 27 Aug, we went blackberry picking and I make a pudding.

My plural feels cheated and abandoned by my life of lies. The eruption of Mount St Helens the following year would bring a reminder.

The Eruption Over and Over

On 11 Apr 1981, I saw a Krakatoa movie. The next day, Nan stops again. On the 14th, I begin a painting, *Nature Scenery with Plants*. This one shows pinecones and butterflies. Whilst doing this painting, I became ill with a nasty period pain, headache and sore throat. As seen, pinecones mean penis-con. I'm conning myself with the 'utter-lies' while the traumas keep coming out in my body.

On 16th March 1982 I wrote about volcanoes in (a missing) weather project. On 10 Aug 1982, I'm still writing about volcanoes (including Krakatoa, tsunamis and ice ages). On 12 Aug, I painted a wall in Mum's bedroom violet. Violet means vile-tell, to disclose on the rape. I'm conning myself while my plural keeps telling on the vile.

On 10 Sept 1982, I see another Krakatoa film. I'm doing a load of weather stuff and my depression bites.

Finally, on 9 Oct 1982, I watch a film about Krakatoa for the third time. I'm writing about ball lightning and tornadoes. That November, I'm writing loads more about Krakatoa. My big project on Krakatoa would take place in May-June 1983 and is the topic of this chapter.

The table lists diary mentions of volcanoes and the effects.

DATE	ELEMENT	NOTES
19 Aug 79	Saw a documentary on Krakatoa.	Next day, wrote a garden report with a load of normals, leaves and buries.
21 May 80	My diary reports Mt St Helens is erupting. (It had erupted on 18 May).	I'm doing a load of rugging. I suffer unexplained nausea. I break an orn-ament.
11 Apr 81	Saw a Krakatoa documentary.	On the 14th, I begin *Nature Scenery with Plants* (with pinecones and butterflies). I become ill.
16 Mar 82	Wrote about volcanoes.	I'm skiing in the library writing about nature's fury. I'm depressed.
7 Apr 82	Wrote about volcanoes and earthquakes.	I become ill with bad throat, headache and nausea.
6 May 82	I paint a volcano for mock A levels Scorched Theme.	I'm skiing in the library, writing about volcanoes, hurricanes and nature's fury. My face erupts in boils.
10 Aug 82	Wrote about Krakatoa and tsunamis.	On 12th, I painted Mum's wall violet. I'm depressed and can't sleep.
10 Sept 82	I'm reading about volcanoes	I'm depressed and doing a load of nature's fury.
9 Oct 82	Watched a film about Krakatoa for the 3rd time.	I'm writing about lightning and tornadoes and sneaking books from the library. My artwork is filled with snakes and big cats.
Nov 82	I'm writing about Krakatoa	My artwork is all big cats. I'm depressed and writing about hurricanes.
May-Jun 83	I'm writing about Krakatoa and other volcanoes.	My face erupts into boils, and I feel ill. I skive in the library writing about volcanoes and hurricanes.
30 May 83	Saw volcano film: *When Time Ran Out*.	I'm writing loads about Krakatoa and tsunamis. My throat is thick and my voice hoarse.
9 Aug 1983	My diary mentions Krakatoa.	Krakatoa's 100th anniversary (27 Aug 1883 at 10.02am) approaches.
27 Aug 1983	Krakatoa's 100th anniversary.	I report of unpleasant dreams. Early morning the whole sky was lit up with a dull, deep red.

Part 3: My Face Erupts

In 1968, I suffered immense pressure and smothering. I became like a volcano.

Throughout the Seventies, a face ablaze in a cave haunted me. Not until the Eighties would these intrusive thoughts come out on my face. Puberty seems to have brought things on. The following looks at these eruptions and is taken from my diaries.

On 24 Jan 1979 Grandad burnt his face after falling on a fireplace. He dies on the 28th. Shortly after, I'm compulsively playing dolls. My plays are centred on Big Sue (big-use) who lays inert. Her shiny plastic face evoked notions of skin hardening and about to blister. Two months later, I select to write about burns victim, Nikki Lauda for a Grand Prix project. I enter another doll-playing episode and am off my food.

On 2 Jan 1980, my face rashes-up and persists until the 7th. I go to the doctors for tablets. The snow sitting about outside is evoking notions of smothering. Future winters would bring similar reactions on my face.

Reconstruction of my Scorched theme painting of a volcano (May 1982).

In spring of 1982, I receive male attention. I am now sixteen. This particular art student is tall like my rapist. I respond by selecting a Scorched Theme for my mock A level and, on 6 May, paint a volcano. I would then retreat to the college library and write about volcanoes. My lower face erupts.

The following May (the 10th), the same thing happens: On receiving male attention (this time from my future husband, Mark), I would retreat to the library and write about volcanoes. That evening, I would stop up to see a comet with 'rak' in its name (like Krakatoa). It was called the IRAS Araki-Alcock Comet. A few days later, my diary reports of dramatic thunderheads. They resemble pyroclastic clouds. My face erupts.

Mistaken for Acne

My breakouts weren't acne at all, but blisters. On 7 Jan 1984, I have my second date with Mark, and I develop a 'blister' above my nose. Sometimes these lumps would come up within minutes. My face bubbles up and squeezing brought nothing but a clear fluid. From here-on, I would suffer countless facial eruptions like these that worsens into 1985. My skin got so bad, I looked like a junkie. I'm now writing about scarred faces in my novel, *The Lessons*.

I have a hidden disfigurement. I carry burn scars from my toddlerhood. On 10 Sept 1984, I saw the film *Elephant Man*. The woman kissing Merrick's cheek made me want to cry. She accepts him when the world didn't. The feelings of my abused-self have been expressed.

Part 4: A-Two-Rak

Krakatoa is me. Notice the 'Rak'. Krakatoa could be spelled Krrakatoa. This provides two Raks. I am two. The word ends with 'to-a' (meaning a-two).

My plural had seen 'Rak' within Krakatoa and urged me to write about this volcanic namesake. I

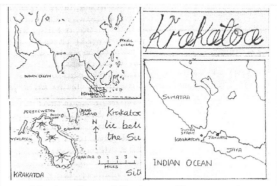

My drawings of Krakatoa. Shown are its location on the map, being the Sunda Strait between Java and Sumatra. Krakatoa has three volcanic cones.

have two Raks and Krakatoa means plural.

This section is about my Krakatoa project of May 1983. My others have gone missing.

A Rak Remote

Krakatoa is remote. It's just like the planets, just like my plural. She is far away.

Krakatoa is a small Indonesian island between Java and Sumatra in the Sunda Strait (I had begun). It was an eighteen-mile long tropical 'paradise' with three islands to the north: Lang Island, Verlaten and Polish Hat. But it is Krakatoa that has the cones: Perboewatan, Danan and Rakata (see image).

Krakatoa One Hundred Years On

The story of Krakatoa begins in May 1680 with 'eruptions'. These continue into the 1870s, which were largely 'ignored'. Throughout the 1970s, I ignored them too. By this, I mean flashbacks – the face on fire and the choking. It's like an anniversary: one-hundred years later, for this is how far back the cause felt. Furthermore, 1680 contains 1968, the year these 'eruptions' occurred. Repeat the '6', upend it and eradicate the redundant '0'.

Part 5: Crater Face

On 20th May 1883, Krakatoa becomes active. What an extraordinary thing. I had met Mark in May 1983 – a hundred years later again. Mark evoked notions of my uncle, for being tall and dark, and I'm getting 'active'. As a result, clues to my toddlerhood would pour into my artwork and this project. This is my plural's doing. She has gleaned data from books to tell me about my toddlerhood.

*Top: My drawing of Krakatoa erupting (drawn May 1983). **Bottom**: What this drawing really depicts (drawn 2021), and it is a face being smothered during oral rape. The islands on each side represent my rapist's knees. The face is drowning, but I have incorporated stripes for the pattern on the pillow during a particular assault. I remember it.*

The Smothering Sulphate

In Batavia (a city north of Java) people see smoke rising seven miles above Krakatoa's main dome. Poisonous sulphurous gas and dust choke the atmosphere.

Sulphur has entered this project. My *Science* book has shown copper-sulphate means a copper suffocated me. The sulphur is now choking the 'island'. By 22 May, lightning brings a lurid scene. A lull follows and this is when the Batavians visit the island.

Perboewatan, the main cone, is now a crater, 3,300 feet wide and 160 feet deep. Steaming vents accompany roaring sounds. Captain Ferzenaur visited the island and the soles of his boots got burnt by the ground. He was the last white man to visit Krakatoa before the eruption.

This captain is like one of the horrible Trumpton men (animated figures) dancing round the burning face in my intrusive thought. My vile imagery included all sorts of stuff happening around a disempowered large face: dancing, chanting, partying, worshipping. The

156

face is being abused whilst unconscious and has suffered immense heat and pressure. These thoughts so distressed me, I loathe to speak of them, and I couldn't live in the present.

Hidden Disfigurement

In June and July 1883, Krakatoa quietens down, but further craters open up. The sea hissed and the air becomes 'unbreathable'. Whilst I am writing this, my lower face keeps erupting. I avoid seeing Mark because of sore throat and nausea. Trauma sites on my body are coming up because of this project.

I have drawn a picture of Krakatoa erupting. It looks like a face being subjugated. Compression is implied with the pyroclastic flows and the sinking. For years to come, I would write about characters with facial disfigurements such as acne and burns. The main character, Aidan of my first novel, *The Lessons* is nicknamed Crater-Face because of these scars.

Fear Through Ignorance

In August 1883, another huge vent opens up on Krakatoa. All vegetation has perished and Rakata, the main cone, becomes the most active. Buitenzorg (a town sixty-one miles away) reports of thunder-like tremors. This means th'under. I was under during oral rape. Krakatoa has now been erupting for eighty-four days and has yet to enter the violent (Plinian) stage. By mid-August, the island is roaring with thick black smoke, now seventeen miles high.

St Elmo's Fire Stain e/m

The Trumpton figures return in the form of men on a British Naval ship who approach within ten miles of Krakatoa. They report of burning rocks 'hailing' the vessel. Visibility is zero (due to the nuclei-uncle polluting the air). And the St. Elmo's Fire on the ship's mast completes the story for meaning I am so-e/m (split me) for the fire-stain.

The Trumpton men keep distance, like I had. I was frightened of what Krakatoa represents: my face burning and comatose during oral rape. I could make no sense of this imagery and I kept running away. I am like the plants in my garden reports: hushing burying and deserting.

Part 6: 27 August 1883

The loudest sound ever recorded in modern history is nigh. I found this bit fascinating.

By 3pm, Krakatoa's cataclysm could be heard 700 miles away. In Batavia (100 miles off) it was 'deafening'. An eyewitness describes an ominous sunset of dense clouds with a murky tinge. Inky blackness ablaze with lightning would come down.

157

The 'night of terror' has come: the small hours of 27 Aug 1883. No one could sleep in Batavia. I compare Krakatoa to a kettle, the lid rattling. Lava a mile long causes the rock to heave and buckle. This is what I did during assault, writhe and buckle. I remember doing so.

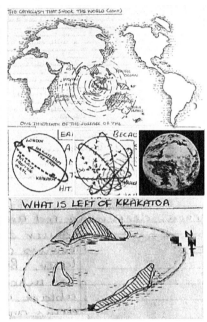

My map showing where the sounds of Krakatoa could still be heard. The waves travelled around the earth several times. The bottom image shows what's left of Krakatoa.

At 5.30am, the island explodes. At 6.44 am, the island explodes again. The heart of Krakatoa is ripped out.

My picture shows a face removed. I have been defaced.

Magma, Lava and Ash

An Irish merchant ship, the Charles Bal reported of a huge black plume shooting above the island. Dead fish bob belly-up in the hot ocean. I lay belly-up unconscious too. I remember my uncle sitting on my chest before he suffocated me, and I was belly-up. I keep talking about magma, lava and ash clouds. All mean burning.

The Enlight'n of Lightening

I dwell upon the lightning. I used to misspell this word 'lightening' and it means to enlight'n. Here, I had made the same mistake a few times, but on this occasion, I had scored-out the errant 'e'. I am no longer 'enlight'n.

The Heart Torn Out

The historic sound would take place on 10.02am, 27 Aug 1883. The lid of the 'kettle' has blown off and the kettle itself explodes. Fourteen cubic miles of granite and obsidian bursts fifty miles into the stratosphere. The sulphuric pyroclastic cloud smothers the island, and the pressure waves resound like my pulse did during suffocation.

With the heart of Krakatoa ripped out, the oceans flood inwards. The water boils and superheats. This island has no foundations (I had exclaimed). The meaning of this is toddlerhood. My foundations have been torn from my core identity and my face is gone. A chasm is left behind. In a bid to fill it, I would adopt a fake self, a fake history. I have no foundations because my toddlerhood has been destroyed.

Another explosion was reported at 4.30pm.

The Loudest Sound in Modern History

In Celebes (1000 miles away), the sound was still very loud. In Victoria Plains Australia (1,700 miles off), the sound was like artillery fire. And at Rodriguez Island, Madagascar (2,968 miles away), the sound was like distant gunfire.

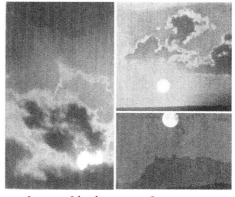

Images I had cut out of magazines showing angry sunsets and discoloured moons. This is due to the dust and nuclei in the upper atmosphere.

Madagascar contains the word 'mad' and 'scar'. I have been scarred but mad to say the cause. Still, one-third of the world's surface heard the sound. That makes it 15 million square miles. This part captivated me.

The remaining two thirds couldn't hear a thing. This represents my oblivion.

How Far the Sound Travels

Beyond range, only sensitive instruments, like seismographs and barometers will detect the soundwaves. Barometer contains bar-me-tear. My torn-self is barred from the truth and (since 1980), I have logged bar readings in my little weather station.

Half-a-day after the eruption, the soundwaves hit London. Thirty-six hours later, the waves would return. In total, four westerly waves and three easterly ones would hit the capital. This seesaw would continue for nine days.

Part 7: Tsunami, Man-used-Me

Krakatoa, once an island half-a-mile high, is now a gaping chasm in the seabed. But the worst is about to come: Tsunamis – waves driven by the displacement of the earth's crust.

I have already written about tsunamis in earlier projects. Here, I express awe at the size and the force of these sinister waves. I drew pictures including a house to bring a sense of scale. The meaning of tsunami can be found within the sounding, and it is sue-nam-me. Man-use-me. I have been used by a man.

These monstrous waves travelling 350-400mph hit four continents. On 5pm on 26 Aug, a 400mph tsunami hit the Strait of Surabaya (500 miles from Krakatoa). Waves eighty-seven feet high struck the Sunda Strait. In Merak, they were over 130 feet high.

Surabaya is more commonly-known as Madura and means you-are-mad (u-r-maad). The liar in my head is calling me mad for writing this account.

The Anger-Anjer Submerged

In Anjer, a town on the West Coast of Java, a wall of water bearing a log struck a captain unconscious. When he came-to, he was sitting on a tree, half-a-mile inland and stripped of clothing. Anjer has vanished beneath the waves.

The captain is obviously me, blacking-out during rape. Sitting on a tree, naked speaks for itself. And Anjer is anger. The anger has been submerged beneath my conscious awareness along with the horrific memory. But this doesn't stop my plural from picking out projects like these to tell me about my toddlerhood.

Reconstruction of a painting I did for art college on 19 Jan 1982. The theme was Horror to Mankind. A tsunami is about to hit a lighthouse.

The House Lit Up
The tsunami killed 360,000 – more than the eruption itself. The waves traversed the width of the Indian Ocean. In Cape Town (5,100 miles away) is still a foot high. The tsunamis would then veer past the Cape of Good Hope, into the Atlantic where it would spend itself on the English Channel, 11,000 miles from Krakatoa. A tsunami reportedly carried a lighthouse 1.8 miles up a valley and 130ft above sea level. It is still there today

Interestingly, on 19 Jan 1982, I had painted a lighthouse and tsunami for my mock A Level (reconstructed image shown). The theme was *Horror to Mankind*. On 6-8th June 1983, I had painted another lighthouse, this one in a tropical storm. Both paintings depict light snuffing out. Lighthouse means shedding light on a house, and the liar wants to obliterate it. I had written about a ghostly lighthouse in my children's story, *The Secret of Melhound*

Creek (1-7th April 1980). Lighthouse means to light up a house where I was raped.

The Three Tsunamis

I have drawn Krakatoa's biggest tsunamis against an average house to convey the force. The first is an 87ft one that hit the Sunda Strait. This placename means 'under-straight-son.' In oral rape, I was forced straight by a son. In vaginal rape, the son was straight. In both cases, I am forced under.

My 1978 sunflower reports have reiterated: I was forced straight (elbows to the sides and lowered) by a son.

The second tsunami is 100ft high and hit the Coast of Anjer. As seen, Anjer means anger.

And the third one, 130ft high, hit the Merak Coast. This one is me-Rak.

These tsunamis

My drawings showing a tsunami against an average house. Upper images from the left: The 87ft wave that hit the Sunda Strait; centre shows the 100ft one that hit Anjer and right shows the 130ft tsunami that hit Merak. Bottom images give an idea of the force.

(man-used-me) tell me about the under-straights of my toddlerhood.

Part 8: Submerging

Enough dust and debris to coat an area bigger than France smothers the area (I had written). In places, is 100ft thick and day turns to night for two-and-a-half days. Within a month, jet streams ferry the dust fifty miles up. Weird sunsets and optical phenomenon blaze the sky, blood-red, silver and copper.

Silver and copper have appeared together again. The setting sun flashes green. Green means grassing on the burning presence. I dwell upon the green, for in Stockholm (17 Jan 1884), the Moon turned green for three minutes.

The dust reduced the sun's heat by 30% (I report). Mount St Helens in Washington (which erupted in May 1980) reduced it by 15% and Mount Pelée in Martinique (May 1902) by 2-3%. The stratosphere is warmed and the Earth, cooled. A wet summer follows. 1968 was a wet summer too.

161

The Vanishing

And what of Krakatoa? The north part of the island, Polish Hat, Danan and Perboewatan have vanished. Only a cliff of Rakata remains. Unseen are two huge underwater craters, the first being four miles across and 910 feet deep. The second is three miles across and 300 ft deep. No more than 5% of Krakatoa is accounted for. The rest has been distributed across the globe. It's like most of Krakatoa simply vanished into 'thin air'.

The Utter Lies of Butterflies

Four months after the cataclysm, a botanist found a microscopic spider spinning a web on the island. The meaning of this is lies – spinning lies. Next comes more lies: butterf-*lies* and rept-*iles*. I have already painted butterflies in *Nature Scenery with Plants* and *Butterfly Mural* (the previous year). Butterflies means 'utter-lies' and reptiles contains rep't – repeat. Repeat-lies. The swallowtail butterfly is prominent in my *Junglerealm* painting (completed shortly before this project) and means the 'swallow' is a tale. Don't believe it.

I then mention the scorpion.

The Scorpion of Truth

My Aurther book on *Space* mentions the scorpion too. This Nor-creature has a sting in its tail. The scorpion-like facehugger in the film, *Alien* (1979) smothers its victims. Scorpion is like the Nor-way and anorexia for containing the Nor. Scorpion is the same.

But lies overrun Krakatoa. Seeds within bird-droppings ignites propagation, a new ecosystem. Between 1910 and 1919, ants overrun the island. I am reminded of the ant-infested apple tree in our garden. The crawling sat-stain has soured and stunted the fruit. By 1924 forests would conceal the ants, and soon after, climbers would overrun all. Sinister trees with deep roots take over. Eventually, a tropical paradise would return. New species of butterflies and insects form on the island. But only scientists are allowed there.

Restricted access, it seems. My stained face is concealed.

Part 9: False Paradise

This paradise is founded on lies. It is a false paradise, not really a paradise at all. Scientists discover a pocket of lava deep beneath the rock seeking a way out. This is the truth of my toddlerhood rearing up. The rock heaved and buckled like before. On 26 Jan 1928, a large cave rose from the sea. This 'ugly' formation was hundreds of feet across but was soon washed away.

The ugly truth will never go away.

A year later, a geyser sprouted. With steam, ash and sulphuric fumes, the seas become a soup of dead fish again. The geyser is there to this day (I write). This geyser is like a safety valve, allowing the lava to release. This geyser represents the fuel for my art, stories and these projects. The trauma insists upon expression, and I cannot stop it.

How the demise of Krakatoa correlates with my garden reports for the tearing, desertion and burying. My smothered face is hidden.

The Truth Rearing Up

What a bewildering thing. I am writing about the survival mechanism of the brain within a story about Krakatoa. What would happen if this 'valve' was shut off? What would happen if I never wrote a word or painted a picture? Would I die?

I had posed the same question in my second novel, *The Locked Door* (written thirty years after this project). A captive sees a ghostly hand clamped over the airways of her callous kidnapper. His emotional breaths are stifled. Meanwhile, a part of me continues to lie. I am not allowed to see the fuel behind my novel nor this Krakatoa project. I simply believed I was writing about a volcano. But this doesn't stop my creations.

The False Child

Natives now call this volcano, Anak-Krakatoa – Child of Krakatoa. This false paradise isn't my child at all, but an imposter. My true child is Krakatoa itself prior to the main eruption. For years afterwards, I would adopt a fake toddlerhood while my truth remains hidden. The cataclysm that ended my 'childhood' remains the most powerful in modern history, equalling twenty-six hydrogen bombs. But Krakatoa is not the most powerful volcano known to mankind.

I bring in Santorini, a volcano in the Aegean Sea. This obscure volcano erupted in 1470 BC. Krakatoa's power represents a mere fifth of this one. *Wow*, I thought. I must write about this volcano!

And so, I did.

Throughout my life, vile imagery of a face smothered and burned has tormented me. Seldom have I vocalised them. And yet without my realisation, I am describing these images in graphic detail within my story of Krakatoa.

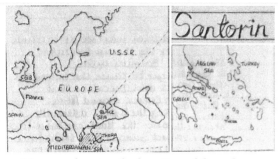

My map showing the location of the volcano Santorini in the Aegean Sea.

I am now writing about a bigger volcano.

This section on Santorini is comparatively short, for being obscure. It is the largest explosion in civilised history but occurred almost 4000 years ago.

No volcano can be big enough or remote enough, it seems and this one used five times more energy than Krakatoa.

I had spelt Santorini 'Santorin', (minus the final 'i'). I can find no record of this spelling variant, and this would appear to state 'I' am missing an 'I'.

Santorini (now called Thera) is a small, crescent-shaped island in the Aegean Sea, north of Crete. In one, violent eruption, dust spumed into the atmosphere, coating thousands of square miles. Monstrous tsunamis hundreds of feet high swamped neighbouring islands. This destruction was thought to have ended the Minoan civilization, such as Knossos, eighty miles away. Part of Greece around Attica was also destroyed. Atlantis and Deucalion were flooded. Black days followed, freak weather and violent sunsets.

Biblical plagues, ruined crops and blood-red waters were thought to be linked to the eruption. This part is crammed with codes. Knossos means so-con (ssso-kon) and Minoan means I-know-man (I-no-man). An Earth-anagram also exists in Thera (th-are). The polluted waters and black air mean the nuclei. It always goes back to the pollution caused by my uncle.

The other codes can be found in Section 7.

Part 11: Mount Stain In-hell

My final volcano is Mount St Helens.

This modern-day eruption occurred on 18 May 1980. I mention this volcano in my diary on 21 May. I would then do a load of rugging. Little did I realise this volcano contains the stain of saint as well as the mount of mount. The enhel (in-hell) of Helen follows.

Quiet since the 1850s, Mount St Helens develops a small crater in March, followed by another. By April the two had joined to form a bigger crater. Ash and debris spat, and tremors agitated seismographs. By mid-May, a column of ash almost eleven miles high was televised across the globe. An easterly wind blew it sideways.

In one eruption, the summit vanishes. Hurricane-force winds flatten trees eleven miles out. Spirit Lake at the foot of the mountain, once full of life, has become a 'sewer with trees suspended' (I had written). The water has become polluted because of the nuclei again and included is the trees. I am reminded of the captain in Anjer who found himself sitting on a tree after a tsunami had stripped him of clothing.

Images I had collated of Mount St Helens. The air and Spirit Lake are polluted. Bottom image right shows life returning after just four months.

But Mount St Helens is a young mountain, just 27,000 years old. I remark on this fact because I was young too.

The Story of David Crockett

I recall being fascinated in a lone survivor's story, David Crockett, a TV cameraman. Mudflows passed on either side of him, marooning him on the slope. Whilst recording, he kept speaking to his camera in laboured breaths. He reports on the following (not verbatim due to copyright). 'The ash is burning my eyes. It's hell and hard to breathe. It's dark with ash coming down heavy on me. It's either dark or I'm dead. God, I want to live!'

Crockett appears to be speaking on behalf of my plural. A toddler is unable to express these words, and neither can her oblivious-self. So, someone else's words have been used. These are the sensations during oral rape. It's dark, I can't breathe and its hell. Crockett was trapped for ten hours before rescue came.

My project on volcanoes has concluded.

Conclusion

Of the three volcanoes, Krakatoa dominates. My story on Krakatoa gives a detailed account of oral rape. Without my realisation, I have described suffocation, heat and coma. I would then describe the cover-up and the lies. A false paradise results. But the truth keeps rearing up in my creations. This is symbolised by the geyser providing an outlet. My plural would use survivor's accounts of Mount St. Helens to tell her story, and Santorini to convey my missing 'I' for the destruction of my toddlerhood. She would see my burning face in other things, such as the sun, bonfires, and ships ablaze.

I'm not really writing about volcanoes at all.

Interestingly, on 9 Aug 1983, Krakatoa's 100th anniversary is referred to in my diary (which occurs 27 Aug 1983, 10.02am).

When 27 Aug 1983 arrives, I report of unpleasant dreams. Early morning, the 'whole sky was lit up in a dull but deep red,' (I had written). It's as though Krakatoa is just beyond the silhouette of the garden, out of sight.

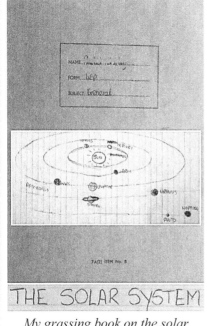

My grassing book on the solar system.

Chapter 15: Astronomy (18 – 24 Aug 1980)
Introduction
Part 1: Toymaking
Part 2: The Broken Milk Bottle
Part 3: Grassing across the Void
Part 4: The Mono Face Moon
Part 5: The Furnace Planets
Part 6: The Rocky Planets
Part 7: Jupiter, the Gas Giant
Part 8: Saturn, the Ringfenced Planet
Part 9: Venus' Two Moons
Part 10: Conflict about Density
Part 11: Outermost Gas Giants
Part 12: The Distant Rocks
Part 13: The Feeble Asteroids
Part 14: Comets' Coma
Part 15: The Milky Way
Part 16: The Far Reaches

Introduction

This chapter looks at another of my huge projects: astronomy.

I've gone back in time, for in three years', I would write about Krakatoa. Krakatoa has been moved forward for the explicit message conveyed.

I've written about space before – in my Aurther books of 1974. *Space* has shown the sun has a double-meaning: the cause (the son) and the effect (the sun). Mercury has a double meaning too: me-cry and crime. A crime is being committed behind my back.

166

This project is more elaborate and takes place in August 1980. I had just turned fifteen. Throughout 1980, I'm reading about the weather and keeping records. Then on 18 Aug, I get a book about the stars. The following night, 'I had a horrible night of dreams. Glad it was over.' I am writing about my toddlerhood again. My project is another Trojan Horse. This book is dark green, and my plural is 'grassing'.

Part 1: Toymaking

Throughout the summer, other hobbies have been gathering force: I'm jogging, doing jigsaws, quizzes, doll pantos (with Big Sue) and rugging. Rugging has been

Date ('80)	Toy Made	Meaning
Early-Aug	Poodle	Be-loo
Late-Aug	Ladybirds	Lies
Mid-Sep	Snails	Lies
Late-Sep	2 Bedtime Teds	Pregnancy
Early-Oct	3 Ragdolls	Be-loo
Nov	3 Basset hounds	Seat-sh

explained in the previous chapter and means *pulling-the-wool-over-my-eyes*. This is due to the Mount St Helens eruption of May. I mustn't see my burning face in this mountain.

I'm now making toys (including snails). The purpose is the same as rugging: to ensure the liar overlays the truth. As seen, snail means lies. The message within this astronomy project must not be 'read'.

My toymaking episode pans-out thus. (The following has been taken from my diaries).

Toymaker's Conflict of Truth and Lies

On 6 Aug, I decide.to make toys for my youngest sister, Mazie. My astronomy project is twelve days off. I cut up my fur jacket (gifted by my rapist's niece on 8 Mar 1978) to make a poodle and puppies. I develop a bad cough and get depressed. On 12 Aug, I'm making ladybirds.

Ladybird means be-liar, just like snail. Line up the letters to find b-lyiar. (The d brings lied).

Two days later, I have a bad period pain. On 18 Aug, my astronomy project begins. For six days, I'm feverishly writing about the planets. On the 20th, Eve shoplifts false fingernails. These mean long-liar, just like the snails I am about to make. By mid-September, I have made several. I wrapped material over the buttons (for the eyes). I'm pulling the 'cotton' over the eyes again. I then illustrated the pupils and iris. My eyes appear to see but in fact *can't*.

My astronomy project is now finished (except for 7th and 13th Sept).

Girl without a Face

My toymaking contains codes, just like everything else I do.

Into the autumn, I'm making bedtime teddies. I insert a tinkler into the tummy of one. Tinkler means semen and it's gone in my tummy. My second bear doesn't have a face. I make one, lost it and make another. How odd. I'm replacing a teddy bear's face as though to roleplay replacing mine. Krakatoa blasted-out, and the grafting of the *Adonis Pyrenaica* (cat-mask) symbolises a desire to remove my face too.

Soon, I'm making a ragdoll. This means Loobyloo (of *Andy Pandy*). Poodle of earlier means loo too (topple the 'p' to find be-loo'd). The table lists the codes.

Towards Christmas, I'm making basset hounds. Basset means be-seat. Hounds mean sh-sound. Silence. I hide these toys under Dad's bed (where Uncle Dan used to sleep). In the midst of my toymaking, I'm writing about the solar system. My toymaking tells me about the lies, the tinkle in my tummy and my missing face.

Part 2: The Broken Milk Bottle

Two days before I begin my astronomy project (16 Aug) something else happens.

A neighbour was seen wandering down the garden path with a milk bottle threatening to kill herself. She says she is pregnant. The bottle, remember represents truth (as seen from my *Science* book). After an accident with a milk bottle, Eve returned from hospital, and I saw a man in my chest. My chest had 'recalled' my rapist.

This neighbour was pregnant. I saw myself in her for the tinkle in her tummy. I am learning sex education at school, and my plural realises, had I been raped a little older, I could have got pregnant. Three years later, this neighbour sadly took an overdose.

Challenge of the Stars *by Patrick Moore and David A Hardy.*

Part 3: Grassing across the Void

So, throughout late August 1980, I'm writing about the planets within a dark green exercise book on a 'leaf' table.

It's all grass.

I had chiefly used *Challenge of the Stars* (1978 edition) by Patrick Moore and David Hardy (although Dad gets me other space books).

Voyager had been launched a year prior to print. Images of Jupiter had graced TV screens in March 1979 and Saturn's wouldn't arrive for twenty months. Since this date, more has been discovered about the planets, but the facts are accurate of the time.

168

Unknown to me, just a few feet from where I was writing, Uncle Dan had suffocated and raped me. Three days into my astronomy project, I wrote, 'the house feels doomed'. I believed I was referring to the rows, but it's not. My astronomy project is spurring intrusive thoughts. From across the void, my plural is letting on about the rape. She has used the language of astronomy to grass.

Part 4: The Mono Face Moon

The opening section of my project is about the Moon. My Aurther book on *Space* has told me moon means mono. I can see only one face of two. I begin by noting the moon is small compared to the earth – like a child to an adult. It therefore has a 'low escape velocity'. My 'small body' had a low escape velocity too. At three, I had no chance of escape.

The far side of the moon remained a mystery until the Sixties. This correlates to my hidden self since the Moon Landings. Scars and craters have remained unchanged since the 'dinosaurs roamed the earth'. The scars of traumas endure from the remote past.

The moon has two faces, one hidden. Between the two, Venus rotates backwards to a time when I shared my home with a huge 'son' who burnt me. The Nor of corona clues-into my rapist's name. (Drawn 2020).

The Moon has no atmosphere and no protection against the sun's radiation. During suffocation, I had no air. During rape, I had no protection against the burning sensation. Post coma is a cold place to be. Indeed, temperatures on the Moon range from +210°F to -250°F.

See how my slant on this topic becomes about my toddlerhood?

Part 5: The Furnace Planets

I move onto the rocky inner planets.

I begin with Mercury, the closest planet to our sun. Again, I remark on its small size (not much bigger than the Moon) and its low escape velocity. It's like the Moon again, only this time, closer to the sun. Time has just wound back to the 'son's' burning. Mercury's surface crumbles and cracks under the sun's corona.

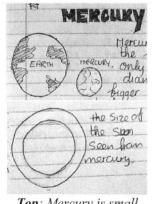

Top: *Mercury is small compared to Earth.*
Bottom: *The sun as seen from Mercury.*

Standing on Mercury would be terrifying, for the sun would appear 'three times' larger than on earth (see image), as it moves erratically across the Mercurian sky. The erratic thing happened when I was three, and I was burnt by something immense.

The day is long, at 176 earth-ones and midday gets hot at +700°F with bitterly cold nights. Mercury is like the dark side of the Moon. Its hidden side is burning due to the corona (Onca-Nor). This is why I had cried mercy.

Venus the Hell Planet

Venus comes next, the Earth's twin, otherwise known as the 'hell planet'. I have a split-self who knows about the hell. Clouds of carbon dioxide thirty-five miles thick 'smother' this planet. Levels of this greenhouse gas increase in the blood during asphyxia. I'm writing about air deprivation, for Venus is like me during suffocation.

This brilliant planet glows ashen even on its dark side (I had written). It's as though this planet *wants* to be noticed. I describe a 'mark' on its surface, believed to be a mountain chain. This mark is on me and has been left from the 'knives' of toddlerhood. The sun rises in the west and sets in the east. Venus rotates 'backwards' (known as retrograde rotation). Venus is going back in time from our cold Moon to a baking Mercury.

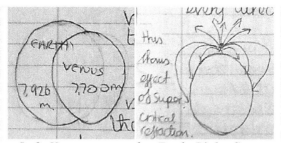

Left: *Venus compared to Earth.* ***Right***: *Super refraction makes the horizon appear lofty.*

Venus' day is 243 earth ones – longer than its year. In toddlerhood, my days seemed long but my years were short (three). A probe was sent to Venus to encounter a furnace of +890°F with an atmospheric pressure one-hundred times greater than on Earth. Sensations during suffocation are being conveyed here with heat, pressure and ashen. Like on Krakatoa, lightning would flash in the murky atmosphere and the ground would bubble in lakes of tar and asphalt. My face carries the somatic scars of burning. During an episode, my skin would blister-up around my mouth.

Due to 'supercritical refraction', standing on Venus would be like standing at the bottom of a huge basin, with the horizon turning upwards. The horizon appeared high during assault too, as I was lowered. The flowers have told me about the lowering. It was like being at the bottom of an immense well.

Part 6: The Rocky Planets

I have completely missed out our Earth. Did a section on Earth exist in Moore's book? I am unsure but my decision to omit Earth seemed natural because I lived on it. Earth didn't feel like outer space at all and yet it is. My exclusion of Earth from my project betrays of the gap within me. Part of me is missing and a gap is left behind.

This gap works the other way too. Earth is the Goldilocks planet, the only one with clement conditions. This temperate planet is like my oblivious-self, missing from the world of extremes endured by my plural.

Mars, the Iron Planet

I skip to Mars, a cold 'red planet'. Its atmosphere is like Earth's at 100,000ft, 'painfully' thin. I declare a match cannot ignite in the Martian atmosphere. This part is telling. Air deprivation is painful.

I comment Mars is the most 'earth-like' planet in the solar system – a twin again, (just like with Venus). But its year is longer than ours at 687 earth days. (The Martian day is similar to ours). My 'short' years on Venus are

Mars' frozen cap of carbon dioxide represents my oblivion. The moons rotate on the equator, hidden to my 'higher awareness'. Notice the unconscious face prone beneath the cap. This wasn't intentional. (2020).

due to having only three, but each year seemed long, like on Mars.

Frozen in Oblivion

Mars wears an icecap of carbon dioxide. (The southern cap often vanishes in summer). This means my frozen numbing oblivion. I wear a frozen cap on my head. My traumas are frozen in the past, and I can't see.

The dark canals on Mars are believed to be dried up ocean basins. My flashbacks have told me Uncle Dan did nasty things with water. I have suffered trauma in water which have since dried up.

171

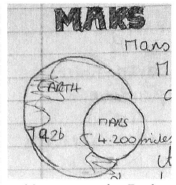
Mars compared to Earth

Sadly, only the dark side of Earth can be seen on Mars' closest approach. In other words, I can't read Mars' 'red', the rams nor the are-ams. I can't read the iron oxide.

Mars' Moons, Phobos and Demos

Mars has two moons. The largest (and closest to Mars) is Phobos. Being irregular in shape, may not be a 'true' moon, but a captured asteroid. This implies a phony. A crater warps one end. This charlatan exists because of the mark left by trauma. Phobos is a liar with a clear view of Mars. This false moon can see things I can't, just like the liar in my head.

The other moon, Demos is smaller and orbits almost in perfect sync with Mars' rotation. This means Mars would appear unchanging in the Demos sky. Being smaller, Demos is like a younger version of Phobos. So, the liar in my head materialised from an earlier self.

The Nix Scarred

Both moons would have a grand view of Nix Olympica (otherwise known as Olympus Mons), a huge extinct volcano. Why didn't I use the traditional term? It's because of the 'Nix'. Backwards is 'skin' and this is where the burning occurred: my skin. The moons know about my past burning, but neither is big enough to bring a solar eclipse. In other words, in spite of my oblivion, I suffer flashbacks and intrusive thoughts. Both moons have equatorial orbits, concealing them from higher latitudes. My 'higher' awareness cannot see them. But these moons are opposed, estranged.

We have now reached the gas giants.

Part 7: Jupiter, the Gas Giant

'Jupiter, the biggest planet in the solar system, is as different to Earth as it could ever be,' (I had begun). This correlates to a past I didn't know existed. It is truly alien.

This, the innermost of the gas giants, is flattened at the poles due to rotation. The days are just ten hours long. Suffocation brings vertigo, as though on Jupiter. The atmosphere is composed of hydrogen, ammonia and methane.

Why didn't I mention helium? This 'failed star' has an abundant supply. I go on about hydrogen and compression at the core, raising the temperature to half a million degrees. Heat and pressure are stressed here, just like many times before. And by contrast, the visible surface can never rise above -200°F. The cloud belts and immense red spot are a majestic sight. Or rather, terrifying. These weather systems from hell are like my earthly hurricanes and tornadoes gone off the scale.

Jupiter's Outer Satellites

I declare Jupiter to have twelve satellites. Of course, since

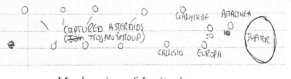

My drawing of Jupiter's moons.

1980, this figure has increased. But I would describe the outer seven to be small, perhaps captured Trojan asteroids, not really moons at all. I give no further mention of these 'false moons', a part of me seeing them as imposters, just like Mars' Phobos. They are a bunch of liars, too small to be seen with the naked eye. They sneak about and do things on the sly.

But 'Trojan asteroid' means Trojan seat-orid. This project is a Trojan Horse carrying a message about the horrible-sat of my toddlerhood.

Four Galilean Moons

I move straight onto Jupiter's inner moons – the 'proper' ones. This leaves five, but only four exist in the Galilean group. These are Io and Europa (the size of our moon), Ganymede (the largest of the four) and Calisto. The Galilean group was discovered soon after the invention of the telescope, hence the Galileo honour. All are visible through binoculars. Having binoculars once, I could have seen them. They represent the truth, and I wasn't looking hard enough or in the right place.

I begin with Europa. This dense moon is luminous, as though *wanting* to be discovered (just like Venus). The brilliance is due to frozen gases lacquering its surface. I paint a disturbing picture of this world, intensely cold. There is no atmosphere, and the inky sky, broken only by the immense disc of Jupiter. Parallels with my toddlerhood can be drawn here – the blackout of coma due to a huge, terrifying presence.

Amalthea, Jupiter's Doomed Moon

Instead of moving onto the other three moons as expected, I describe Amalthea, the closest one to Jupiter. The allusion is, that it all begins with this small world (it is only 150 miles across). I have gone back in time, smaller and closer to a big force, just like Mercury with the sun.

I had made an error here, stating that 'Amalthea is the nearest satellite to Venus.' I had written *Venus* instead of *Jupiter*. Sneaky things are going on in this project and a pattern will soon emerge.

Breath Taken Away

At Amalthea's closest approach, Jupiter would cover a quarter of the sky. I propose the view to be breath-taking. My breath is taken away. Amalthea's rotation is almost in sync with Jupiter's, just like Demos with Mars. This small, tortured moon is stuck in the past with a ghastly view of a huge presence. This is my plural's world. She lives with the truth while I'm oblivious.

In future years, Jupiter will crush Amalthea to dust, to become part of Jupiter's (recently discovered) ring. This implies the force behind Jupiter is in cahoots with the false moons and doesn't want Amalthea grassing on the huge presence of my toddlerhood. The truth must be crushed to smithereens and my oblivion preserved.

One day, little Amalthea will 'vanish'.

Just like Krakatoa.

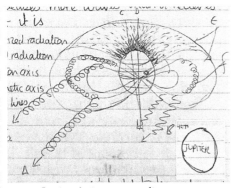

Jupiter's intense radio waves.

Io, the Volcanic Moon

It is here that I bring in Io, one of the 'four'.

Lava and magma overspill this volcanic world due to a surface in flux. 'Two forces' are responsible: Jupiter's gravity and the pull of a neighbouring satellite. It's like the conflicting forces in my head is causing Io to go haywire. The insinuation is, that like Amalthea, Io will one day be crushed to smithereens by Jupiter. The huge presence of my toddlerhood must be hidden from my conscious awareness.

But Jupiter's radio waves give Jupiter away (see image). This seems due to Io and Amalthea. These two moons are 'grassing' on the big presence, causing high-pitched sounds like birdsong. Several times, my stories have related on birdsong and disclosure.

Ganymede and Calisto get no further mention. This I find odd, as the former is the largest moon in the solar system and the latter is the third.

Why didn't I expand on them?

Part 8: Saturn, the Ringfenced Planet

'Beyond Jupiter is Saturn,' (I declare). This planet takes the

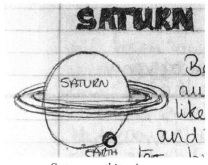

Saturn and its rings.

174

biggest section of this project for the sat-on, a ring (fence) and several moons. The codes are blatant.

The rings make this planet unique. Made from ice and dust, may be remnants of a former satellite. This implies a future Jupiter, where Amalthea has now been destroyed. This moon has now become a ring.

Jupiter (a similar gas giant with a cold surface) has twelve moons. But Saturn has ten (correct in 1980). This suggests two moons are missing. Saturn is like a *future* Jupiter minus two moons. How odd.

Rhea, the Second Doomed Moon

I begin with Rhea, the sixth moon from Saturn. *Why didn't I begin with the first?* This moon orbits in line with Saturn's ring. From there, the ring would appear a mere streak. This implies that Rhea is poised at the edge of Saturn's ring, ready to be destroyed. Abridged, I had put *'Saturn's rings are made from particles of ice and dust. They may be remnants of a former satellite. Rhea is the sixth satellite from Saturn.'* Remove the full stop after 'satellite', and this former satellite becomes named: Rhea. It's as though Rhea is about to suffer the same fate as (a future) Amalthea.

Saturn's Inner Moons

I bring in Saturn's inner moons. From Rhea, 'looking like pearls' are Dione, Tethys and Enceladus. (Mimas and Janus aren't visible). 'Pearls' means rapes-I. (Uppercase I and lowercase l look alike: Il.) These moons carry the rape-code and are about to be destroyed.

A surprise follows.

On turning the page, I would discover a separate section on Titan (Saturn's seventh and largest moon). Titan has a section all to herself.

Like a planet.

Why did I do this? Titan is not a planet. It's a *moon*.

Part 9: Venus' Two Moons

So, I had given Titan a separate section, as though a planet.

My opening sentence is, 'Titan is one of ten satellites of Venus.' I have written *Venus* instead of *Saturn*. Not only did I do this once, but twice, naming Titan as Venus' moon.

But Venus has no moons.

My mind is cast back to Amalthea. I had done the same thing here: named Amalthea as Venus' moon. Venus now has two moons. Amalthea and Titan. (The-a/m and taint).

Saturn's pearly moons are being destroyed one by one. Meanwhile, Titan is flung towards Venus to join Amalthea. (2020).

I make another error: name Titan as the largest moon in the solar system when it is in fact Ganymede. This seems to explain why Ganymede has little mention in this project. My plural is sneaking moons about, while the biggest of all is keeping quiet about it. These celestial worlds are like 'agents', preserving the truth.

Titan, the Moon of Truth

Titan is similar in size to Mercury, (I had written). And like Europa, Titan's surface is lacquered with frozen gas, making it luminous. Titan *wants* to be seen. How odd. She wants to be seen by my conscious awareness yet hidden from the liar. *But both exist in my head.*

Titan has an atmosphere. This atmosphere was discovered in 1944 and was found to contain methane. Being cold at -240°F, the air molecules cannot leak into space. But heat the planet to +100°F and the atmosphere would vanish. Titan's relocation to Venus means she is about to become airless and overheated. She is suffocating under immense pressure just like I had at three. Titan has an almost perfect circular orbit. This means true. A circle is symmetrical like the full rainbow and the butterfly. Titan has been secreted away because she wants the truth known.

The two missing moons have been identified: Titan and Amalthea. They have been moved to 'Venus'.

The Years Encoded

I have drawn a little diagram, listing Saturn's moons (see

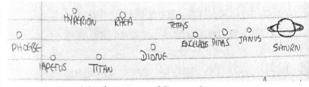

My drawing of Saturn's moons

image). From the innermost are Janus, Mimas, Enceladus, Tethys, Dione, Rhea, Titan, Hyperion, Iapetus and Phoebe. It is here that I bring in Janus, discovered in 1966. The year 1969 can be found if the '6' is toppled. This is the year of the Moon Landings.

Sadly, Janus remains unobservable until Saturn's rings are pointing to Earth. This happens in 1980, the year I had written this project and is a leap year (like 1968). Like Jupiter's Ganymede and Calisto, Hyperion barely gets mentioned. My excuse is that little is known of this small moon.

These moons are keeping quiet. Hush.

Part 10: Conflict about Density

Dotted around this project is the issue of density.

'The satellites near Saturn are not dense at all,' (I had written), and 'man cannot step on them'. Mimas, Enceladus and Tethys (the next moons out) are as dense as water. Dione (number five) is as dense as the moon and Rhea (number six) is twice as dense. Titan (the seventh moon) is denser still. As for Saturn, it can float, for 'its density is less than water,' (I had written).

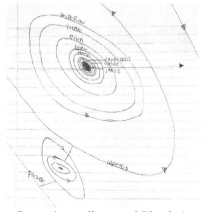

Saturn's satellites and Phoebe's erratic orbit.

'Does it float?' My *Science* questionnaire had posed the same question. Does the object float? It's to do with water and I am reminded of the 'sink in water'.

Moving outwards from Saturn, density increases until we reach Titan, a moon that would plummet in water. The big presence of my toddlerhood remains above water while I am being dunked, for this is what the moons are saying. Uncle Dan drowned me in the bath. My *Science* book, *Human Being* project, children's books and flashbacks are saying the same thing.

I am not yet done with Saturn, it seems.

Iapetus the Conflicted Moon

I have allocated another moon a separate section, just like I had Titan. This moon is Iapetus and is the ninth moon from Saturn (correct in 1980).

I begin by saying Iapetus is most puzzling. When to the west of Saturn, is the second brightest satellite in the sky; to the east, it fades. Iapetus seems like our moon for showing one face. It has no atmosphere, nights are 'intense black', and days long (at 79.25 earth ones). From this viewpoint, the big presence is my oblivious-self and Iapetus carries dangerous knowledge. Should this moon shine brightly or hide away like a lying asteroid?

Iapetus is one of two satellites with a tilted orbit. When viewed head-on, Saturn's rings (thirty miles thick) are almost invisible, and the other moons

177

can't see it. But Iapetus can. This conflicted moon can see the full breadth of Saturn's rings. These rings symbolise a crushing device.

Phoebe, the Liar

Neighbouring Phoebe (the tenth moon) has a tilted orbit too. It too can see the rings. But due to being small and moving in the opposite direction, is likely a captured asteroid. This makes Phoebe an imposter, just like Mars' Phobos. What an odd thing. Phoebe is keeping an eye on Iapetus as though to stop disclosure.

These celestial objects appear to have a will of their own, each governed by conflicting forces in my head.

Saturn's Rings of Annihilation

I declare Saturn to have three chief rings. Two are bright, separated by the Cassini Division 1,700 miles wide. This gap is due to the gravitational pull of the inner satellites. This is the gap in me from another angle, just like the missing Earth from this astronomy project. I have a missing self because of my vile toddlerhood.

Closer to Saturn is a third ring called the Crepe or Dusky Ring (because it is semi-transparent). Fainter rings have been reported but have yet to be proven. These faint rings (like the small asteroids) don't want discovery and represent the lie.

But the main rings outshine Saturn itself. This is due to ice and dust from an inner moon that has wandered beyond the 'Roche Limit' (the point where gravity disintegrates a body). Amalthea and Rhea carry dangerous truths about my toddlerhood and annihilation threatens. But the moons of truth don't go quietly. Their icy composition means the ring will shine brightly for all to see.

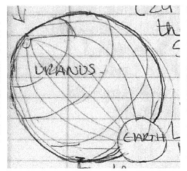

Uranus compared to Earth

Part 11: Outermost Gas Giants

We're done with Saturn's moons and now we're back to the planets.

Uranus is another gas giant. With a diameter less than half of Saturn's, means Uranus is just visible to the naked eye. Discovered in 1781, glows greenish in the gloom. My projects are in green books, and Pluto in my *Space* project is almost entirely green. It is now Uranus' turn to grass. Indeed, my handwriting looks like 'you-are-ands' (u-r-ands). This means plural, and lines (lyin's) cover the surface.

The Uranian year is long (eighty-four earth-years) and the days are short (10.75 hours). I hadn't said so but have found the Uranian year to be 42,718 days. Uranus is my plural in adulthood. She is far away from me and has lived through thousands of days in the dark.

Five moons encircle Uranus: Miranda, Ariel, Umbriel, Titania and Oberon. All are smaller than our moon. They are invisible to the naked eye, just like asteroids. These sneaks don't want discovery and are keeping my plural away from me.

Ninety-Eight Degrees

The tilt of Uranus' axis makes this planet extraordinary. Being 98 degrees, is rolling around prone. Topple the '9' to find '68, the year I was raped. The '68-agreeds are set to wall up my toddlerhood.

For twenty-one earth-years at a time, a Uranian pole will be in perpetual darkness, which makes this planet unique. For its huge volume, Uranus is lightweight, the gravity marginally greater than the earth. This grassing planet has blacked-out on its back. Like Venus, Uranus rotates retrograde, meaning backwards. It's denser than Earth. We are going back in time to 1968 when I had rolled around prone and blacked out.

Neptune the Second Blue Planet

Discovered in 1846, is Neptune is the eighth planet from the sun (I write). Like Uranus, is an outer gas giant. It has horizontal streaks across the surface. Its size and gravity are similar to Uranus. A marked difference is the colour: blue. It's like an ocean planet. Neptune could be confused for Earth. The blue deceives for it is not water, but poisonous methane and ammonia. At temperatures below -360°F, methane absorbs red and yellow light. Life cannot exist on Neptune.

The be-loo is inhospitable.

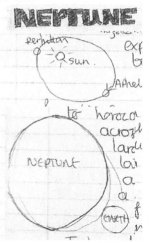

Neptune: remote but big.

I remark Pluto reaches perihelion (closest approach to the sun) in 1989, and for the next twenty years, Neptune would be further from the sun than Pluto. I note the 1989-1968 echo. Neptune is like my toddlerhood again: remote.

Part 12: The Distant Rocks

Neptune's chief moon is Triton. This moon is similar in size to Mercury, making it the seventh largest (known) moon in the solar system. Being dense, should have an atmosphere, but as yet, none has been found. The skies are black and conditions freezing. Airless and comatose again.

This moon orbits in the opposite direction to Neptune, causing it to zip across the sky as though wanting to be noticed. Its movements are conspicuous, for being closer to Neptune than our moon is to Earth. Most notably, Triton does not orbit at Neptune's equator like other moons, but higher. This makes Triton visible in the poles.

Triton is big, bright, close-by and fast-moving. It is visible to my higher awareness, and it wants to be noticed. Triton wants the truth known. A pattern is emerging here. My plural has gleaned facts about the solar system to tell me about my vile toddlerhood and the resultant forces in my head.

Nereid, Estranged

Of course, Triton has a companion. It *has* to. Nereid is a small moon, being less than two-hundred miles across. Its orbit is erratic, toing and froing from Neptune on its transit, but never coming close to Neptune. Nereid seems to represent a liar in conflict. An estranged self. This theme keeps repeating.

Pluto, the Dense Planet

In 1980, Pluto was considered the ninth planet of the solar system. It is now downgraded to a dwarf planet, its year lasting 248.5 earth-ones. Pluto is five times denser than water and more so than iron, (I had written). In other words, Pluto will plummet faster than the Nor. My *Earth* project has shown Pluto almost entirely green. It's grassing again.

Theorists propose Pluto to be an ex-moon of Neptune. A collision with an asteroid may have knocked it off course. This is trauma and the result is estrangement. Extremes are monstrous. Freezing, dark and airless. Liquid methane lacquers the rocks, and a heavy silence hangs in the air. The sun and planets are mere specks. I finish off, 'beyond Pluto is a gulf of emptiness. The nearest star is four lightyears away. Nothing compares to the terrifying desolation of Pluto.'

Sounds horrible.

Part 13: The Feeble Asteroids

The outer asteroids epitomise isolation. The reason is the seat-orid. I mustn't know about it. The liar in my head is intent upon keeping the horrible seat from me.

The 'swarm' of dwarf worlds skulk between Mars and Jupiter. Up to a million are thought to exist. This far outnumbers the true moons or indeed the planets. Most are tiny irregular bodies. The three biggest are Ceres (427 miles across), Vesta (370 miles) and Pallas (280 miles). These fragments are believed to be remnants of a planet after a 'remote disaster'. Despite this huge number, if fitted together, would remain smaller than our moon. In other words, lies cannot compare to the heftiness of truth. Lies are asymmetrical, erratic and crooked.

The truth reigns.

The Eccentric Liar

I describe asteroids as eccentric. They wander from the solar system's orbital plane and vary wildly in brilliance. Some make close approach to Earth before retreating. The cigar-shaped Eros is a strange sight with hollows and dimples. Indeed, many asteroids take on twisted and warped forms. Life on an asteroid would be nightmarish, the space rolling and pitching, rocks zooming past and collisions many. The chaos during assault is embodied in the seat-orid. The mounting is horrid, I felt trapped and disfigured.

Icarus, the Asteroid of Extremes

Icarus is the most astonishing of the swarm, for it zooms past Mercury right up close to the sun. Rotating once per eighty hours, the dull red rocks have barely the chance to cool from the glare of the 'corona'. My plural surely sees Onca-Nor in the sun's force.

Once baked, Icarus retreats beyond Mars to freeze. I write, 'Icarus has the most unpleasant climate in the solar system.' I keep writing about extremes and bringing in human endurance. I remark, 'Arthur C. Clarke suggested men could shield within Icarus' bulk to study the sun.' I find the notion unthinkable. My plural sees the sun as callous and dangerous. It cannot help but fry any living thing.

Part 14: Comets' Coma

I move onto comets.

After asteroids, this topic seemed natural. But my plural has a trick up her sleeve.

These 'erratic wanderers of the solar system' are made from rocky particles coated in ice. I remark on the Great Comet of

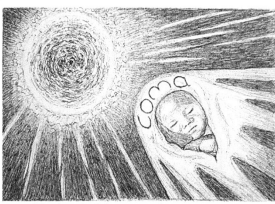

The head of the comet forms a coma on approaching the sun's corona. This symbolises my comatose-self due to a large presence that burnt me in toddlerhood. (2020).

1843, being 'larger than the sun'. I found this hard to believe until checking the facts and I had meant the *length* of the tail being longer than the sun (not the comet being larger). This tail, equalling the distance between Mars and the sun, makes it one of the longest in recorded history.

Why did I say the comet was larger than the sun?

I go on to explain, 'the nucleus of the comet (head) is usually no more than a few miles across'. I note the head comparison here. The comet has a 'head'.

I would have seen the word 'coma' during my research. *Coma*? How can coma appear in an astronomy book? The coma (in cometary terms) is the nebula enveloping the 'nucleus' (head) of a comet. Only on passing close to the sun, does the 'coma' form. The big presence that burns creates the coma around the head.

My plural was behind the inclusion of comets. She had seen 'coma' in reference books. I can now see why I had declared the Great Comet to be 'larger than the sun'. My plural has made the coma larger than any object in the solar system. Sadly, the liar in my head has prohibited me from writing the word 'coma'.

Going Back in Time with the Tail

The comet's tail comes next.

Due to the solar wind, the tail points away from the sun. So, a comet shooting out of the solar system will travel tail-first. Only when the comet reaches perihelion (closest approach to the sun) does the display become 'breath-taking'. I'm going back in time to when a 'son' took my breath away.

Short-Period Comets

'There are two main types of comets,' (I had written). The first is the short-period type. These orbit the sun per few years. Encke's Comet for instance, reaches perihelion every 3.3 years. Another, the D'Arrest Comet has a period of six. Halley's Comet (the most spectacular of the short-periods) returns per seventy-six years and is due for arrival in 1986 (six years from 'today').

These short-period comets venture little further than Jupiter (although Halley's reaches Neptune) and are therefore known as the 'Jupiter Comet Family'. Most are faint, lack tails and fade quickly per return. The short-period comets make me think of the false moons and asteroids: liars. Jupiter determines their orbits, and the coma is negligible. They sneak about without notice.

Short-period also means finite, like the annuals of my *Wildflowers* project. The liar is built on sand and is fleeting.

Halley's Comet 8 – 9 April 1986

I remember seeing Halley's Comet. We watched it from the back garden. My diary lacks a mention. No wonder. I recall being disappointed. With all the hype, I believed Halley's would be dazzling. My plural knew it would be the wrong sort, for being faint and coma-less. Three days earlier, Nan had come to live with us because Aunt Maud has downsized to a bungalow. On the 7th, I caught one of my vile head-colds. On the 8th, I had written, 'I'm ill with cold. Depressed, off food, headachy and drowsy.'

On 4th May (whilst stopping at Eve's and her boyfriend), I had a nightmare about the end of the world and astronauts. The spacesuit is draining of oxygen, and a horrendous burning is nigh. I have exed myself for the 'dogging', but Halley's appears to have triggered notions of the sat-Nor (in astronaut).

The IRAS Araki-Alcock Comet of 10 May 1983

Incidentally, I had reported of a lesser-known comet on 10 May 1983. It was called the IRAS Araki-Alcock Comet. My diary reports of me stopping up past midnight to see it. I had met my future husband Mark that day and I was working on my Krakatoa project. I suffer a nasty head-cold and my skin erupts.

Long-Period Comets

So, the short-period comets are no good. They are faint and lack a coma. But what about the long-period comet?

Also known as great comets, these arrive from outer space and offer a breath-taking display (like the Great Comet of 1843). Some do not return to perihelion for thousands or millions of years.

I describe a comet splitting in 1846 (three years after the 'Great Comet'). The 'twins' returned in 1852 but haven't been seen since. The 'dead comet' was 'replaced by a brilliant meteor shower in 1872'.

This appears to tell a story. This 'splitting' occurred three years after a big event (my birth), and the 'dead comet' relates to my near-death experience. A 'rebirth' follows via a brilliant meteor shower. I have become a born-again virgin.

I now have an 'inner-twin'. My *Human Being* project tells me about conjoined twins. The long-period comets make me think of the moons of truth such as Titan and Europa. All want discovery. Sadly, a comet of any sort wouldn't bring recall. The clues are too abstruse, and I am too blind.

I can't 'read' this project.

Part 15: The Milky Way

I'm now writing about our galaxy, the Milky Way. Where is this project taking me now?

It begins with our star. In galactical terms, average. There are one-hundred-thousand suns in our galaxy. I talk of diversity: size, brilliance, temperature and density. I talk about the shape of our galaxy, like a Catherine-wheel, one-hundred thousand lightyears in diameter. The cosmic year is 2250-million years. One cosmic year ago, dinosaurs ruled the earth.

This is all fascinating stuff, but how does this relate to my toddlerhood?

It's about the stars – the stuff that lights up our galaxy. It begins with nebulae – cosmic dust. This is where stars are born. A clump of matter condenses, generates heat and, once past a critical point, ignites nuclear fusion. A star is born. These are bluish in hue and is often the hottest and brightest objects in our galaxy.

My Pyrenees project contains a load of bluish (green). This means be-loo-hush (grass). Here, of be-loo (of stars) is being hushed again.

The Stars' Middle Age

But the truth will not hush. I would describe Population I on our galaxy's spiral arms, where these new stars are born. The new star is now fusing hydrogen nuclei into helium. Energy is generated and the star will shine for at least 6000 million years. The 'main sequence' has begun, a long period where the star finds equilibrium between gravity (which makes it contract) and heat (which makes it expand). The 'main sequence' is where our sun is at.

Two 'I's Read Giant

But one day, hydrogen-fuel will stop. The end of life is nigh, and the sun will turn red. The core temperature fluctuates, the star swells and shines more brightly. These red giants are known as Population II and cluster mostly at the galaxy's hub. I am struck by the II for the two 'I's. I am plural for I have two 'I's. The red giant is the language of my plural. The read (past-tense) is giant. My plural is saying, 'read these codes!'.

Giant-read.

The Planet-Swallowing Red Giants

It is here that I cut abruptly to the size of our galaxy. *What? I've barely even started on red giants and I'm talking on something else!* I needn't have worried, for I would return to red giants within 'Distant Stars'. For continuity, I have placed it here, but I would soon discover the reason for this odd slicing.

The red giant is now short of hydrogen, leaving only heavier elements to burn. Although not mentioned in my project, I recall being bothered by iron. This heavy element forms the end of the line for the star, doomed to collapse. How horrible. The star at first expands. In the process, the star will swallow planets whole. The Nor (of iron) causes the swallowing. This 'giant-read' is forceful. No wonder I had shifted this bit to a separate section.

The liar doesn't want me to see the giant-read.

A Star without Helium

My mind is cast back to Jupiter. I had failed to mention helium. Jupiter has a lot in common with our sun and should contain an abundance of this second-lightest element. After hydrogen, helium is burnt, which then builds in the core. All ends with iron. A subconscious part of me had removed helium from a failed star to stop the iron-burning stage. The star can never become a red giant without helium – *can it*. What an odd thing to do – remove helium from a chain-reaction. *What was I thinking?*

The Nova without the Super

The red giant is dying. The core temperature rises; the surface temperature falls. Bursts of energy explodes to the surface. The outer shell ejects. A nova has formed. Many old novae are known to be binaries, (I had written), meaning two stars. My mind is cast back to Population II of the two 'I's. This is where the 'red giants' are found.

I hadn't used the word 'supe-*rno*-va'. It contains a Nor-anagram. Nova doesn't. After the cataclysm, the red giant becomes a white dwarf. A cupful of this dead star would weigh tons. The nova has ended, and the star goes quiet.

No more 'read-giant'.

Part 16: The Far Reaches

No red giants exist in our neighbourhood (I proclaim). Our nearest star (except for our sun) is Alpha Centauri, a dwarf star 4.3 lightyears away. Only in southern skies can it be seen.

The Population II red giants are located at our galaxy's hub in the constellation of Sagittarius. But we can't see them because of interstellar dust. Dark nebula doesn't help. This dust falls in shadow. The Milky Way is otherwise a majestic sight and is visible from Earth as a band of stars. But this forms only a fraction of what our galaxy is made of.

Dark matter is hiding the red giants from me. This means the liar, and I can't 'read' this project.

The Advancing Andromeda

The other galaxies are barely visible. The exception is Andromeda, our closest galaxy. Andromeda is a spiral much like our Milky Way but much larger. Its light is 2.2-million years old. This galaxy (along with the local group) is speeding towards us. The Nor and his mother's name hide within Andromeda.

Meanwhile, everything else is speeding off. A galaxy known as 3C-295 is receding at half the speed of light, quasars even faster. Our universe is expanding and 'no one knows if this is going to continue'. The outer reaches of my past are flying off. Will it continue to recede forever? Will recall ever occur? Thirty-six years after this project, it did.

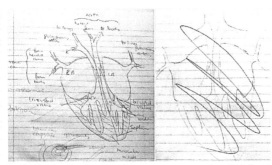

The Black Hole

I conclude my project with dead stars and black holes.

Here, I have used the word 'supernova', but is severed via a scribble. 'A pulsar, (I had written) is the remnants of a super...nova'.

Radiation is emitted at intervals of less than a second. The result is ticking. This

Left: *At the back of my astronomy book, I had drawn the heart and connectors to the lungs.*
Right: *Overleaf I had scribbled over my heart drawing, which looks more like lungs.* My Human Being *project shows a chest scribbled-over too.*

was once 'mistaken' for signals from another race. A signal *was* being sent, but the 'red-giant' is so remote, I can't read it.

I next mention the neutron star. I hadn't said so in my project, but the neutron star is the densest matter in the universe (except for black holes). The stability of the neutron star is 'destroyed' as it implodes. An immense gravitational field is left behind. The space closes around the star and leaves our universe. A black hole has formed.

Star means sat (staa). It's like tsar in my *Human Being* project. The Nor (in neutron) says who did it. But all is sucked into another universe. My astronomy project ends here.

Old Scars

At the back of my book, I had sketched the heart and lungs. I had scribbled over the second drawing. My *Human Being* project shows the same thing: my chest scribbled over. My lungs carry suffocation scars.

Whilst conducting this research, lumps came up on my lower face. Headaches and disturbed dreams accompany. The traumas in my body continue to emerge during expression like these.

In later years, the forces behind the lying asteroids and the truthful moons would take the form of fictional characters in my novels. These forces now have faces and voices. Astronomy means Nor-sat-on-my. I was mounted on my chest, back buttocks, head and shoulders. The Nor serially mounted and used me.

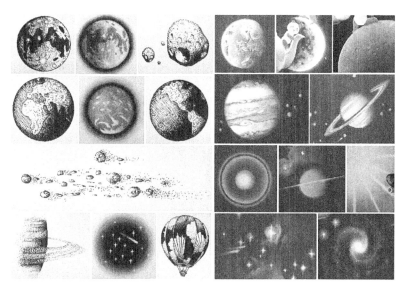

My illustrations for a children's book about a little girl's venture into space (1996). A niece was the model, and she was three. I suffered intrusive thoughts, migraines and depression. My astronomy project was sixteen-years old and forgotten. I'm still living the lie.

Chapter 16: The Sun and Moon
(11 – 28 Sept 1982)
Introduction
Part 1: The Missing Weather Project
Part 2: Boxer
Part 3: The Sun-Son
Part 4: The Moon-Mono
Part 5: My Other Big Projects

Introduction

Two years have gone by since my astronomy project of 1980. It is now spring 1982 and, in a few months, I will return to space with the sun and Moon.

Images I had cut out of magazines. Notice the sun's cross on the left. This symbolises the crossroads waiting for me.

I am sixteen and in my first year of an art diploma course.

This mini project takes place in September 1982. But first, a project would go missing. I am reminded of the missing moons in my astronomy project, the sneaky forces in my head.

The following has been taken from my diary.

In September 1981, I begin my art diploma course. I'd had two boyfriends in quick succession. Both were tall and dark, and one was nicknamed Pig (like a policeman). I'm secretly terrified. Boys start noticing me and my plural keeps comparing my uncle with those of the opposite sex. The liar sabotages these relationships before they go too far. My freeze-ups would provide the perfect excuse for all to end. By Christmas, I suffer a crush on another boy. On 22 Jan 1982, I went to a party where he accidentally burns my hand with a cigarette. Notions of toddlerhood burning rear up. Over the coming weeks, he keeps showing an interest and I would retreat to the college library and write about nature's fury.

I can't seem to have a boyfriend.

Reconstruction of my painting Light Through the Clouds *(30 Sept 1980).*

Part 1: The Missing Weather Project (28 Feb – 24 May 1982)

My missing project takes three months to complete.

It begins on 28 Feb 1982. I'm loaning a load of weather books from the library and writing about the clouds. The image shows *Light Through the Clouds*. The light of truth keeps trying to break through, like the lighthouse in my Krakatoa project, and the red giant in astronomy.

By 16 March I'm writing about huge forces again: natural disasters, ice-ages, glaciation, atmosphere, and how Europe looked 18000 years ago. My throat flares up, and I can't sleep. On 4 April, Nan stops over, and my illness swoops in with a vengeance.

On 14 April I had a dream of nuclear war and on 6 May, I select a scorched theme for my final exam piece. By the 11th, my face has erupted. I'm writing about volcanoes now.

The Big Skive

Between 9 to 24 May 1982, I'm working hard in the college library instead of attending lessons. I would skive a further twelve days doing the same thing. I

Reference notes to my missing weather project in my brown notebook.

don't know how I got away with it.

This weather tome would go missing. I'm saddened. The liar is responsible. Clues to my toddlerhood are pouring out. But on 9 Sept, I had listed the topics covered within a little brown notebook (see image). It's as though part of me knew this project would disappear. Included are big forces again, volcanoes, earthquakes and much more.

Hidden from Official Records

My second year at art college is nigh and on 9 Aug, I'm loaning more weather books without checking them out. I sneak them back in. This odd behaviour seems a ploy to keep these books from official records. The liar in my head mustn't know about these books for what happened to my previous project. This next project *mustn't* go missing.

Reconstruction of my Boxer *painting (22 Sep 1982)*

Part 2: Boxer

Thankfully, this project hasn't gone missing at all. And my plural gets straight to the point.

On 22 Sept 1982, I'm writing about the sun.

That same day, I had got George Orwell's book *Animal Farm* from the library to do a painting of the workhorse, Boxer

(shown). I had already read Orwell's book at school in 1975. (And in almost exactly two years', I would get Orwell's *1984*).

The 'sat-stain' in Stalin's name and the moustache spurred notions of Uncle Dan. My *Boxer* painting was supposed to support a zoo project. But Boxer

189

symbolises me in toddlerhood: naïve, trapped and used by a moustachioed oppressor. On the same day as I'm painting Boxer, I'm writing about the 'sun'.

My plural is frustrated at my missing weather project and keeps trying to break through the clouds.

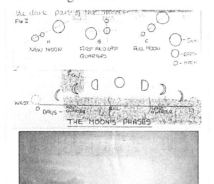

Top: My line drawings of the moon's phases and the quarters.
***Bottom:** Picture cut from a magazine of a sun over a lake.*

Part 3: The Sun-Son

This is what I had written about 'the sun'.

'The sun is a huge ball of heat (I had begun). I propose if the Earth were flat with the sun shining continuously on it, the surface would become a burnt crust.'

The flattened object is me. The sun is the 'son' again. I provide all sorts of fascinating facts about the sun, stuff like the heat and size of the thing. More than 99% of our solar system's mass is the sun's. It is truly monstrous.

I dwell upon the sun's spheres: the photosphere, chromosphere and the corona.

The Spheres of the Sun

Sphere means fears. I fear something.

The sun's innermost atmosphere is called the photosphere. The meaning of this word is 'fear-so-hot'. (Read backwards within the word). I fear the burning.

Left: The sun as presented in kids' books.
***Right:** My plural sees my face ablaze in the sun. (2022).*

The next atmosphere out is called the chromosphere. Read backwards again to find fears-room. The reason is the 'K'-sounding (yack backwards). Fears-yack-room.

190

Throughout the mid-Seventies, I avoided my bedroom.

The sun's outermost atmosphere is called the corona. Onca-Nor is the reason for the burning. The spheres mean fears and is due to the 'son'.

Nuclear Reactions

I write about the proton-proton reactions within the sun. This is what keeps it burning. Four hydrogen nuclei fuse to form a helium nucleus (I explain). I'm writing about helium again. I had omitted this element from a chain-reaction within the red giant.

The helium nucleus is lighter than a hydrogen one. This means the sun's mass is decreasing every second. However, this nuclear burning will continue to the 'end of time'.

There is a lot of 'nucleus' here. Nucleus means uncle, just like nuclear, and proton (like corona) contains my rapist's name.

These nuclear reactions travel via gamma rays through the sun's layers (I continue). Heat blasts into space. These blasts are my breaths. I am trying to breathe through obstruction. The nature of trauma merges things. Here, the sun has been used to symbolise Uncle Dan's force, but the sun is also me, for the burning.

The Moon-mono. I can see only one face of two. (2022).

Part 4: The Moon-Mono

I provide a short section on the Moon.

'This celestial object shows only one face to Earth (I write). The other side remains hidden.' The Moon Landings have come to symbolise my toddlerhood falling into shadow.

It is the Moon that causes the tides (I inform). Twice per month, the tides are lower than usual. This occurs when the Moon is new or full, but in spring, the tides are higher than usual. In other words, when the mono is near, the 'tieds', (restraints) are high.

I had drawn a picture of the Moon's phases. Centrepiece is the full Moon. On either side is the half-moon. The image implies the Moon is splitting and each side is disintegrating. I have become two.

Sometimes the 'old moon in new moons arms' can be seen. This means the new Moon is visible in the sky due to reflection from the Earth's albedo. Albedo has the word 'bed' in it and means all-bed-do. I was 'all-done' on

191

bed. I finish off by remarking an eclipse gives a coppery-red tinge. This tinge means copper-I-read.

Sadly, I can't.

I would end my sun-moon project here.

The following spring, I would write about Krakatoa.

Images left: some of the many weather books I've read. Images right: my weather projects.

Part 5: My Other Big Projects

The main body of this book looks at my fact-based projects. Weather forms the biggest of all. Due to its size, I have dedicated a separate book to this aspect, but for a linking-chapter

(9) via an Aurther book.

For six years, I kept detailed weather records. In the Eighties, I had a little weather station in the porch with a barometer, hygrometer and thermometer.

My main weather projects are summarised here.

2 Oct – 10 Nov 1979: *Climate and Weather*. This project has 151 sides, 70 figs, 35 plates and 13 maps. I was fourteen when I wrote it. My mishap in 'Weater' (see image) exposes the we-tear code. Climate means climb-mate.

1 Nov 1982 – 10 Jun 1983: *Hurricanes*. I was already writing about hurricanes in March 1982 (in my missing project). Throughout Nov 1983, I'm hard at it, drawing hurricane tracks and listing hurricanes of history. In June, I'm writing about hurricane eyes. I suffer vertigo before quitting.

2 Oct 1982 – 4 April 1983: *Tornadoes*. This is my biggest project of all. I was seventeen. There are thirty-six chapters, 144 sides, thirteen tables and countless maps. I have collected eighty-three images of tornadoes. All are immersed within a sea of writing. The 'torn' in the title has provided the fuel.

11 March -25 Apr 1983: *My Little Black Weather Book*. I completed this project between my other projects. It consists of 153 sides, with countless maps and drawings.

SECTION 6: THE GRASS AROUND ME

Chapter 17: The Grass in Cambridge
Chapter 18: Factoids
Chapter 19: The Legend of King Author
Chapter 20: Junglerealm

The green is all around me.

This book has examined my factual projects. My rotten toddlerhood has imprinted itself upon all, from wildflowers to the planets. But the grassing is going on whether or not I write a thing. This section looks at how I know this.

Chapter 17: The Grass in Cambridge
Introduction
A Tour

Introduction

My view of the world has been adulterated by my rotten toddlerhood. My projects have shown that the grass is all around me. Pluto (in my *Space* project) shows green surrounding a central speck. The speck is my oblivion. The truth grows tall from the green grass, while the liar obscures the view.

No wonder I often felt depressed or troubled for no apparent reason. My subconscious is seeing another meaning in everything I encounter while I am basking in 'virginal' oblivion.

A trip to Cambridge (a university city in England), has shown how my plural sees the world.
Note: I have visually enhanced and enlarged some of the signs to make them clearer.

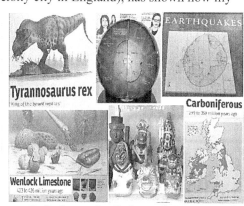

A Tour
1: Sights at the Museum. (From top row).

Tyrannosaurus Rex means (t) I-ran-know-saw-us-ex'd-t. I have run away and exed the part of me that sees the big and horrible thing, for the sex.

1. Sights at the Sedgewick Museum of Earth Sciences.

193

The Earth's core is like that of my *Earth* project with me-tell (of the hot inside). My brain would twist the smiling scientists into liars: 'Nothing hot was inside me at all'.

Earthquake means earth-quack. My plural is a quack for letting on about my toddlerhood rape.

Wen-lock means 'when' the 'lock' happened (a long time ago). I am now I/em (lime), a split me and the truth locked away.

And stone means not-know stain. I'm torn and oblivious. The little figures (bottom centre) is the liar taking many forms in my head. Finally, the Rac-bonfire-us. I burnt like a bonfire and became plural.

2. Sights at the Museum of Zoology.

2: Fossil means foils. I have been foiled about my life, and there's a lot of fossils here.

My *Science* book has duplicated the fossils.

Arthropleura means author-plural. I am plural.

Inferior and grea*t-oolite* means (I felt like an) inferior, great toilet.

Lower Greensands means I was lowered, and the green is grassing on it. Sadly, the sand means the sandman – going to sleep. My *Science* project has shown the meanings.

Norfolk means Nor-fuck. My plural can't help seeing my rapist's name there. But I am like the limestone and sand: plural, not-know stain and asleep to the truth.

3: There's a lot of stones here too. The word 'not' is central and means denial. I do not 'know' I carry a 'st' (stain).

Amethyst means am-the-sit. My diaries and *Colours* book divulge of this meaning. Lapis Lazuli (written ladis-lazuli in my *Colours* book) means all-zz-you-lied (about it).

3. Stones at the Sedgewick Museum and Cambridge Botanical Gardens.

The blue (be-loo) crystals (all-sat-cry) are crying out about the rape.

Sulphur and sulphates remind my plural of suffocation because of the copper-connection in my *Science* book.

Notice the 'twin crystals'. I have an inner-twin crying out about my past. The dark twin crystal means my plural. The butterfly crystal is the be-utter-lie (masquerading as my plural).

Finally, the (sticky) boulders anchor down the plants. I am stuck on this world, looking for something that exists only in my head.

4: I am confronted with Pyrenean paintings. This would spur memories of the penises in my 1975 flowers project. My plural would continue to see this word in various syllables.

In the corner was a pochade box showing a cirrus sketch. I was

4. Sights at the Fitzwilliam and Zoology Museums.

forever painting clouds. I was in fact painting these codes, for my misspelling, cirrius means us-cries.

(Image right) An owl with a removable head. I wanted to remove my head too, for being used like a toilet.

Finally, a beach painting showing sand dunes. The coast evoked sadness and grief, for the Saltland of my lost toddlerhood.

5: An exhibition of the Solar System.

Olympus Mons (also known as Nix Olympica), is an extinct volcano on Mars. Nix means skin and mine boiled like this during the rape. The heat would then go 'extinct' like on the Moon.

5. More sights at the Sedgewick Museum of Earth Sciences.

But in future years, my skin would erupt whilst I wrote about astronomy, Krakatoa and other such projects.

Moon means Mono. I can see only one face of two. After the Moon Landings of 1969, my toddlerhood fell into shadow, and the scars remain unrealised.

The Earth and the planets evoke thoughts of my *Space* and *Astronomy* projects. The planets hide codes, like sat-on, rams, me-cry and sun-son.

Meteorites means me-tear-writes. My plural drove these projects. She is trying to tell me through the solar system that I had an appalling toddlerhood.

6. Sights at the Botanical Gardens.

6: Garden means guard-on. My diaries tell me so. I am guarded from something horrible. Rose garden means guard-on-sore. I'm not allowed to see the sore of rape. (Roses appear in my garden reports).

Notice penis-names for trees: *Pinus Nigra* and *Pinus Sylvestria*. The latter means a decree, for containing my mother's name.

The c'Nor-bed exists within the 'chronological bed'. My bed felt like my uncle's to use. And the uncle-ran (*Ranunculaceae* beds) means Uncle Dan chased me.

7. Labels spotted at the Botanical Gardens.

My plural is reminded of my flower projects. Forget-me-not (don't forget me), Buttercup (be-utter-book), Stonecrop (the crooked flower), Lilies (llies), And 'grasses' (to tell).

Finally, the 'cape-of-shout-fry-Rac' (Africa). I'm not allowed to see the 'fire survivor' I am.

7: More guard-on signs can be seen here.

Upper left means guard-on face. I mustn't know about my

(hot) used face. Upper right means guard-on dire. I mustn't know about the dire thing.

Vile means dire too and is the meaning of 'shrieking violet' – to shriek about the vile-tell. My *Colours* book had a crooked bar-chart where violet has been robbed of votes.

See the lies everywhere. Garden trail means guard-on tale-liar. The liar is guarding me from recall. Mammillaria means I-am-liar.

But Cornflower contains the Nor-lower and seed-bomb. Climate means climb-mate.

Recall mustn't occur.

8: These two trees stand near each other (the bottom picture shows). The tall straight tree (upper left photo) is called the Dawn Redwood. It is like the tall straight tree of truth in my *Colours* book, and I must 'read' it. Being of truth, stands tall and symmetrical.

But the other tree (upper right photo) spurts extensions. They look like people. They want to propagate new roots, to get away from the parent root. In time, they would become false identities, liars. Asymmetry results.

8. Opposing trees at the Botanical Gardens.

I am reminded of the Stonecrop and Creeping Cinquefoil in my wildflowers book. They are crooked and are trying to re-root, to create a false past. But their foundations are of sand, like the Scarlet Pimpernel.

The tree of lies is flimsier than the Dawn Redwood. The lies are stunting this tree.

The Dawn Redwood is like the Thrift, borne on sturdy rocks and cliff faces. Being of truth, stands tall and prevails.

9: My plural sees all sorts of things in trees. The following composite shows. In 1985, I sketched twisted trees at Kew for a painting depicting distorted cats. I suffered period pains, nausea, skin eruptions and disturbed dreams.

I can now see why. My plural sees contorted body parts of my toddlerhood.

The tree upper left looks like a vulva bricked up. The rape has been walled up and I can't see it.

197

Tree upper right suggests legs suspended and a phallus. These legs could be mine, with a phallus plugged into a posterior. The rapist is missing.

Bottom left is like the laurel tree in our garden with all the Y-shapes. A central stump pushes through the smaller limbs as they splay out. A trauma seems never-ending, and I must have felt like I was forever parting.

Bottom right suggest penetration from behind. See the limbs akimbo behind another tree.

The trees are all limbs, body positions and warped shapes.

9. *Twisted trees at the Botanical Gardens.*

10: Upper left shows the laburnum. We had a laburnum in our garden and is in my garden reports. The flowers are yellow. This tree means all-burn-me.

The tree upper right is all tangled up, like the stifling trees of my Krakatoa project.

The tree lower left is the same: smothering the ground. These trees are carpeting the sat-stain of my face so I can't see the truth. Sinister trees with deep roots revisit my dreams.

10: Burnt and lopped trees at the Botanical Gardens.

Tree lower right appears headless. The head has been lopped off. I am reminded of the Common Mallow in my *Wildflowers* book. The head of this flower had fallen to the ground, leaving just shoulders. I want to get rid of my head.

The trunk of this tree consists of the upside-down legs (upper-right of previous composite).

11: Pinecones means penis-con. I am conned about the sex abuse.

Beehive (upper-centre) means believe-lie. The way I wrote this word in my *Science* book has shown.

Reptile means rep't-lie. Crocodile means crook'd-lie. It's all a 'story', (as seen from the 'throne').

11: Objects referred to in my schoolbooks.

The thermometer (lower left) means agrees. From 1968, the agrees would go up, and my toddlerhood would vanish.

My plural keeps trying to contact me and is what the telephone symbolises (as seen from my *Lines* book). She uses the poppy too, for Remembrance Day. But I am torn and cannot see the son-lowers (sunflower). The house (bottom right) appears sliced. It's like the headless tree. It's like me.

12: This composite shows sights at the shopping centre.

Toast means two-sat. I am two for being mounted and burnt. Cubitts means book-sit. This 'book' is the same: telling of the rape.

The car has a numberplate, S3XY. Three-sexy requires no explanation, other than the car (Rac) is white. White means we-tie and this 'Rac' mustn't read this sign.

Seasalt means Saltland, the

12. Sights at the shopping centre.

made-up island of my childhood. Reeds means reads. I am finally reading that the 'Sat-land and the Nor have been "walled" up'.

Bottom: encounters at the bookshop. The burning defaces me and leaves me plural. My inner bird of disclosure is then caged up by the gwennie-pig of lies.

13: More encounters at the mall.

'Café in the library' means face-in-the lie-bury. Library means lie-bury. I know this for how I wrote this word in my diary.

North face means th-Nor-face. My face felt his to be used. And I am llies (Ellis) about it.

13: More signs at the shopping centre.

Carlos means Rac-los. I have lost part of myself to the rape.

Image centre right shows a sweetshop. My diaries have shown my sweet tooth has been used to imply I seek sweet oblivion.

Giles and co mean lies-and-co. The liar takes many forms.

14: And now for public signs.

'Staff only' means 'sattt-only (topple the 'ff'). My oblivion mustn't know about the sat. 'Use' is central in 'museum', flanked by two 'm's. I have two 'me's for the 'use'.

See the toilet sign. An adult appears to be deserting a child and moving towards the arrow. My plural sees toilet in 'to let' signs too.

14: Public signs.

The 'hop-on-hop-off' sign means something hopped on me and hopped off. Trinity means tie-enter. The entering must be tied up,

Finally, the wheelchair sign. The chair is my knowing plural, the person sitting in the chair is my oblivion. I am looking away, oblivious to my sat-self.

15: This stuff follows me around.

This final composite shows sightings in other places. Upper left shows a door bricked up next to another door. This is like my vulva bricked up and my past out of bounds. In a waiting area, I see blue chairs for the disabled. Blue means be-loo and I was used like a chair.

Notice the sign in the background. It says, 'Time to quit'. This was supposed to means smoking, but the liar has twisted this to mean my toddlerhood.

15: General sightings in other places.

The departure sign means raped-true. The phrase runs backwards and through.

The parent-child (sign) appear to be severing. I have lost touch with my inner child.

Adjacent right shows graffiti of a lopped ship. Half if it is missing, for the other (knowing) half has been left at Saltland.

Bottom images show a grass mound, evoking thoughts of Krakatoa grown over. A pile-on-lie (pylon) about the vile-age-face (village café) juts above.

Final image shows pyroclastic-type cumulus bubbling up.

This is how part of me sees the world and I never knew. This worldview follows me around without my conscious awareness and would imprint itself upon everything I produce.

My tour is complete.

Places visited	Fitzwilliam Museum	Sedgewick Museum of Earth Sciences
Museum of Zoology	Cambridge Botanical Gardens	Grafton Shopping Centre

Factoids in my 1977 diary.
This one is about sundials.

Chapter 18: Factoids
Introduction
Part 1: The Weather
Part 2: The Sun
Part 3: The Garden
Part 4: The Science

Introduction

My tour of Cambridge has shown how my plural sees the world. I don't have to write a word for the grassing to occur.

This has been going on my entire life. My 1977 diary shows how far back it goes and is the topic of this chapter.

Within this diary, I would find factoids about the world. I am bewildered to encounter facts I could have selected for my projects. These factoids could have been written by me. The publisher is Charles Letts. This means Rac-tells. How uncanny. These facts are implied to be telling on my toddlerhood. I have gleaned the following of relevance to demonstrate. The wording has been changed to avoid copyright issues. What follows is my plural's slant.

Factoid 38: 11 – 17 Sep: Grasshoppers and Crickets

These insects have unusual ears (this factoid begins) so they can hear each other sing. These ears aren't on their heads but their front legs. Look closely to see them.

My Plural's Meaning: This relates to my birdsong of disclosure. My eardrums thudded during oral rape. This was the location of my ears: on someone's legs, and my ears were small. The singing means my plural's voice. She is 'grassing' through the grasshopper about my small ears pressed against someone's legs.

Factoid 2: 2 – 8 Jan: Stalactites and Stalagmites

Pillars in caves form when water drips from stones, leaving a deposit. During evaporation, these deposits cause these pillars to grow. Stalactites grow down from the roof; stalagmites grow up from the floor.

My Plural's Meaning: In the Nineties, I suffered vile imagery of a girl trapped in a cave with a stalactite wedged down her throat. I never told anyone for I didn't believe such a situation was possible.

But go back to my 1977 diary, and I can see how the image came about. My plural has read this snippet and recognises the shape dropping from above like a stalactite. A secretion oozed from the end. Years later, I would suffer flashbacks.

Part 1: The Weather

See how my plural grasses even when I don't write a word? This part looks at weather. As seen, I was obsessed about the weather and did several projects, including one in my Aurther books.

Factoid 7: 6 – 12 Feb: The Iceberg

When water freezes (this factoid reads), it expands, so the ice takes up more space than the water. The iceberg loses density and floats. But four-fifths of the iceberg remains concealed. This is why they pose a threat to ships.

My Plural's Meaning: I would write about icebergs in my missing weather project. The iceberg is like the liar, lurking unseen. A message could be arriving from my toddlerhood Saltland and it must be stopped. The word iceberg hides 'd'cree'. (Reverse the 'b' to find *I-ceder*-g). This means a decree (agreed) to keep silent about the rape.

Factoid 33: 7 – 13 Aug: Sea Breezes

The sea breeze often occurs in the morning. The sun heats the land quicker than water, and the land-air rises. The air from the cool sea rushes in to take its place.

My Plural's Meaning: My *Climate and Weather* project (1979) describes sea breezes too. It's like breathing, for the ebb and flow. But the terrain obstructs the air, just like Uncle Dan did. Headlands and wind bluffs protrude in phallic shapes.

Factoid 35: 21 – 27 Aug: Lightning

Thunder can rarely be heard beyond ten miles. Estimate the distance by allowing one mile per five seconds between the flash and the thunder.

My Plural's Meaning: In my weather projects, I kept misspelling lightning 'lightening'. This means 'enlightin'. My plural wants to enlighten me about th-under. Sadly, the storm cannot be heard beyond range.

I can't hear the storm.

Part 2: The Sun

My projects have shown a preoccupation with the sun. This is because 'sun' has a double-meaning. See how my plural views the following.

Factoid 27: 26 Jun – 2 Jul: The Sun's Energy

Overhead, the sun's energy equals one bar of an electric heater per square metre. A one-hectare field (2.5acres) would need nearly 10,000 electric fires to equal the heat from the sun's overhead rays.

My Plural's Meaning: The 'sun' is the son (Nan's), burning me from above and I am 'bar'red from the memory. The field is me (given in acres). Rac is me, below the 'son'.

Factoid 31: 24 – 30 Jul: Sundials

The sundial was first used by the Chinese as early as 2500BC. The first in England was Saxon. The bar on the dial represents the Earth's axis and the shadow (cast by the sun), the time.

My Plural's Meaning: We had a sundial in the garden. For a time, I used it at dinnertime to tell me when to go back to school. I notice the word 'bar' again (on the dial) which means to ban. The bar casts a shadow, which means hiding the sex-on away.

Part 3: The Garden

My projects include garden reports. The following contains garden-related elements.

Factoid 11: 6 – 12 Mar: The Queen Wasp

In March, a queen wasp may be seen. She is the sole survivor of her tribe for only queens can withstand the cold. In spring, she searches for a home to recolonise. But this colony can become a nuisance to us in a few months.

My Plural's Meaning: The queen is like me in toddlerhood: a survivor. But my home has been destroyed and part of me has been left out in the cold. Because of her knowledge, my plural becomes a nuisance to the liar in my head.

Factoid 17: 17 – 23 Apr: The Cuckoo

The cuckoo comes in April and sings in May. Songs and rhymes describe the cuckoo as female, but the call is made only by the male in mating season. The female makes a soft bubbling sound.

My Plural's Meaning: My garden report of 2 June 1978 details the fruits and flowers of the garden gone, leaving behind cuckoo spit. The cuckoo symbolises an imposter left 'cock-spit' behind and destroyed my innocence.

Factoid 41: 2 – 8 Oct: Elderberries

The elderberry ripens in autumn. They are used to make jelly or wine, but in the 19th Century, housewives used their juice as a dye to turn bonnet ribbons lavender.

My Plural's Meaning: My garden reports also contain buries (a-berries' homophone). Elder means an older-self – elder-bury. I have buried my younger self and the fruits come in the autumn. Wine means oblivion to my halved-self, for this is what lavender means.

Part 4: The Science

The following looks at a few Earth facts.

Factoid 39: 18 – 24 Sep: Make a Magnet

Rub a sewing machine needle with a magnet and the needle will become magnetic. Plunge through a cork and float in water. The needle will point north.

My Plural's Meaning: The needle is 'rubbed' and plunged into something. This is rape, for north means th-Nor. Magnet means get-man. My *Science* book has told me about the magnet.

Factoid 51: 11 – 17 Dec: The Constellation of Orion

Orion (the Hunter) can be seen at night if you face south. To his left is Sirius, the Dog Star which is supposed to represent his dog. It is the brightest star in the sky and one of the nearest to us.

My Plural's Meaning: I had written about Orion in my Aurther book *Space*. The Nor is blatant. Sirius is a homophone of cirrius, (my misspelt cirrus cloud) and mean us-cried (about Orion).

Orion is why I would write about Hunter in a story, *Hindbury's Run* (1978) about evicted farm animals. Hunter is chased into a pond by an invisible predator. Both Sirius (the dog) and Hunter have come to mean me.

Factoid Undated: The Degrees

A factoid about temperatures comes in the form of tables and formulas for converting Fahrenheit to Celsius. Degrees means agree'd, and for years, I would keep temperature readings My *Science* project has told me the 'agrees' kept rising from 1968. My toddlerhood is walled up.

How odd that I have uncovered my plural's view of the world like this. It is nothing like mine at all.

Chapter 19: The Legend of King Author

Everything in the world appears to be about my toddlerhood. My vile toddlerhood has created an illusion and a strange effect has resulted.

This penultimate chapter looks at the author in me.

Once upon a time, my plural couldn't express much. Her language was narrow, and childhood amnesia is about to strike. How can she describe oral rape? She doesn't understand the world and her vocabulary doesn't include penis or oral. She can't grass.

Only once childhood amnesia strikes, does she learn sex education and about rape. The more I encounter, the more my

My 1977 Letts Schoolgirls diary contains a little school.

plural can use to express herself. She can now grass through the author in me. But she is trapped behind my oblivion. I can't remember a thing.

The Legend of King Arthur

My diary's 'little school' dedicates a few pages to a mythical king. His name is King Arthur.

The liar doesn't want me reading about him, nor indeed, history. The reason is my plural keeps making links to my toddlerhood. Arthur means author – me. My Aurther books have shown my plural sees 'author' in 'Arthur'.

Arthur has become me.

On 23 Jan 1978, I had written, 'I started to get these pains in my leg. Mum said it was aurther-itis.' My misspelling means author-sit. 'I want to become an author,' (I had declared in my 1978 diary) and would include novel-writing within my 'Secreat Amethist Club'. I would now see the 'author' in me, blinded by an aspiration to become a writer. My stories and projects are fuelled by a broken-self in toddlerhood and I couldn't see it. The 'Legend' of King *Author* could mean a legend I am writing about. My stories aren't true. It's all myth. This 'legend' has become about my toddlerhood.

The Nights and the Round Table

King Arthur was born in Cornwall (I would read). A wall was put up against the Nor, but what hides on the other side would drive my projects.

Arthur led the Britons against the Saxons at around 600AD. He pulled a sword from a stone, where the Lady of the Lake would gift him his own, the Excalibur. He married Guinevere and would conceive the Round Table.

Guinevere makes me think of Gwen, Uncle Dan's girlfriend. Gwen could be short for Guinevere. My *Science* book has told me I am in the Gwennie-pig cage of lies. I may as well be my rapist's girlfriend for letting him get away with it. Gwen becomes 'author's' wife. I have become bedfellows with my rapist and may as well be her.

Our playhouse had a round table too. It was in the back room and Dad had painted a matchbox on top. We were learning about knights at juniors, and I was shown up for writing about 'nights'. My plural emerges at night whilst I am asleep, and she is grassing on my toddlerhood.

The Be-lack in Me

Arthur famously removes a 'sword' from the 'stone'. The crime scene is left clear, and I not-know-stain (stone). In the legend, Arthur's best friend Lancelot had committed betrayal. But Arthur had betrayed himself the moment he had de-sworded the 'stone'. The rape never happened, and I am oblivious.

The Lady of the Lake gifted Arthur the Excalibur – your-ex-calib. Calib means be-lack (bilac). Ex means divorce. My *Colours* book has told me black means be-lack. I have an ex and I lack her. The kidnapper in my *Locked Door* novel is called Caleb. My plural drove this character.

The Question of Arthur's Existence

Arthur lived in the 'Dark Ages', a gap in recorded history (like my toddlerhood). Nenniun's *The History of the Britons* (of the 9th century) was believed sourced from genuine (lost) chronicles. My stories and projects keep getting lost too. The liar insists they're just kiddie stuff and to 'lose' them. My toddlerhood is the same: all dark, with little reported. Arthur would die at Avalon and interned in a tomb in Glastonbury Abbey (found empty). It's as though he never existed. This is due to the (Gl)-sat-on-bury.

His history is all myth, just like the 'stories' the me-tear-writes.

Arthurian landmarks dot Britain.

Arthur's seat (a hill outside Edinburgh resembling a 'crouching lion'). And Arthur's Fountain, Arthur's Chair and Arthur's Stone. For my plural, all mean author-used.

The Printed Word

World history is a nuisance to the liar. My diary's little school touches upon wars, the Tudors, the great burning and the great filth. My plural keeps making links to everything.

In 1477, Caxton sets up printing presses in Westminster. In 1526, Tyndale's English New Testament Bible is published. But then an 'authorised' version is published in 1611. This implies the rewriting of the original Scriptures by the liar. My history is being rewritten. I have a New Testament.

The Industrial Revolution brings on the printed book. I want to become a published author, for a broken self is fuelling my projects. But the liar wants to abolish the printer. She doesn't want me reading or writing a thing.

My *Science* book had reported of boiling ink. But add water and it returns. My ink will continue to flow, and the liar cannot stop it.

Chapter 20: Junglerealm

The final chapter of this book is about my painting, *Junglerealm*. Like my grassing books, contain a lot of green. Flowers, cats and symmetry are telling on my toddlerhood.

This painting brings together all my findings within this book.

Junglerealm (Acrylic 4x8ft) 7 Feb – 21 Apr 1983.

During my five years at art school, I produced copious oil paintings and drawings. *Junglerealm* is one of the most remarkable.

I had already produced a couple of jungle scenes at home, including *Face of the Tiger* and *Jungle Mural*. I was also working on a lion leaping on a deer. Being large, *Junglerealm* engulfed me, as I was just seventeen and under eight stone. The huge panel caused disapproval for the cost. But one tutor, Dave, on seeing its potential, urged me to keep going. The following is taken from my diaries.

On 24 Feb 1983, I gridded up the tiger's head and a retreating leopard adjacent. To create cohesion, I placed two swallowtails in the centre. This painting soon got a hold of me, and I stopped late painting away. For a time, I grow disenchanted and 'hate it'. I wanted the leopard's spots to appear blue and the fur to burn. Instead, they appeared dull and pragmatic against endless green.

On 3 March, I start my periods and spent all day painting, concluding with the butterfly. 'Wanted to cry once I got home,' (I had written).

The Grass-Eyed Tiger

7 March: I paint the tiger's eyes green. 'They look realistic and human,' (I had written). I have just expressed the grass in my eyes. The eyes appear to glisten for becoming plural.

14 March: 'I painted the second butterfly flying off.' This butterfly is losing its symmetry, just like I have.

On 18 March, *Junglerealm* is moved to the sculpture room because a tutor keeps complaining about the size of it. I'm getting headaches.

The Flowers from the Abbey

On 12 April I go to an abbey with my art group to take photos of flowerheads. I had incorporated daffodils, but disliking the yellow, made them white.

22 April: *Junglerealm* is tethered to the roof of the car as the heavens open on the motorway. I arrive in time for my uni interview and my painting got me a place in. Only two other students had got anywhere.

A Constant Reminder

23 April: *Junglerealm* is hung in our living-room to replace *Jungle Mural* and I have a stomach-ache that morning. 5 May: Dave wants *Junglerealm* back in the studio. He finds it 'pleasant to look at.' There it would remain for the rest of 1983 while I begin my first year at uni.

On 6 Jan 1984, *Junglerealm* is returned to the cottage. It hangs in the living-room again, but this painting is about to go on a tour.

On 8 – 30 May and 3 June – 22 June 1987 *Junglerealm* would be exhibited in the Town Gallery, a library and a zoo. On 18 Jan 1988: Mark (my then-husband) and I start a photography course and *Junglerealm* is back in the college.

This painting would eventually find its way back to the cottage where it would remain until my parents' move to a semi in May 1996. Dad had sliced a portion off to make it fit in an outhouse where vines began to creep into the wood. On Mum's death and selling the semi, *Junglerealm* has been returned to me. I plan to restore it.

The Formation of a Plural

This painting is not a jungle scene at all, but a self-portrait. Not until recall in October 2016 would I see the bizarre and terrible symbolism within.

The stripy leaves around the tiger's head is the striped pillow of my bed where I was suffocated. The tiger's head is mine, forced down and merging with the stripes.

The tiger's eyes are grass-green as the butterfly (in time-lapse) flies off and becomes half. The leopard is like the half-butterfly from another angle, losing part of itself (the head). The reason is the 'saliva' at the tiger's mouth after the 'swallow', for this is the meaning of the Swallowtail. I had swallowed during oral rape, but the liar says all is a 'tale'. The ladybirds reiterate be-liar-lied. Don't believe it.

But the 'leper'd cannot change its spots' (goes the saying), which explains the bloody undercarriage. I carry the scars of rape despite my oblivion.

The We-tie-Lowers

White flowers dot around. These mean we-tie-lowers. I cannot see the lowers of my toddlerhood. The flowers represent fear, disgust, rejection and desertion. The flower strung from the mouth speaks lies. The bottommost flower shoots off, as though to gain distance. These daffodils have been reinvented, for they are yellow, not white.

Call Back to the Pear Blossom

This painting is driven by an artist raped and suffocated in toddlerhood without her conscious awareness. She is a plural and this part of her had composed this painting. I would now begin my Fine Art Degree due to this grassing-painting. In two years', my plural would speak through my novel and my degree show.

Message Through the Ages

I have already described this painting eight years before conception. It's in a book on wildflowers (chapter 11). Under Pear Blossom, I had written, 'Seeds stick out on long hairs at the centre of the flower face'. I'm describing my tiger. The 'long hairs' mean whiskers – long hair. The liar is long, but pear-blossom means rape.

I Unglue Am/me

The title, *Junglerealm* means 'I-unglue-am/me.' I have unglued part of myself. Notice 'ungle' near the start. *N*-glue. Un-glue.

J' means I (in French).

Realm means: 'r'-am/me.

I-unglue-(are)-am/me.

I am two.

My book has concluded.

Section 7: Indexes of Codes and Tables

Introduction
This section provides a summary of the codes uncovered in my projects (misspellings preserved). Find also items not included within the main book.

Chapter 1: The Human Being

Og the Amorite, King of Basham and Gilead
Means 'Go. King am-all-right of be-shaam and Gile-ad' (Giled-a). The liar is telling my plural, 'Go.' And making out it's all right to live a sham. The liar has 'guiled-'er (giled-a). This means me.

Robert Wadlow of Alton, Illinois USA. (The tallest man in recorded history). Robe-'er-waddle-low (how a toddler walks), of all-not (Alton), soil-in-user (Illinois). My soiled toddlerhood and the user (USA) are denied and robed.

Men over Eight feet and Where they Came (misspellings preserved)	
John F Carroll: I'on f-ck-Rac-oral. (J' is French for I). Rearrange to find 'oral-f'ck-on-Rac-I'. Something oral-fucked on me.	**Sulaiman Ali Nashnush**: Man-sully-I-liar-shsh. Hush about the sully-man.
Constantine: Con-sat-taint. I'm conned into believing I don't have a stain.	**Buffalo, New York State**: A bluffer-knew-Y-rock-seat. The liar is bluffing about the rape and why.
Don Koehler: Done-colour. My plural uses colours as codes and she has 'done' them.	**Chicargo Illinois**: I-Rac-in-soil-go. My plural is ordered to leave.
Gabriel Estavao Monjane: Liar-bag (a bag of lies). Seat-over-my-anger. (Mon-*anje*. Mon is French for 'my'). I'm angry about the rape.	**Gallatin, Tennessee**: Giant-II (plural)-enntees. Big-enter.
Vaing Myllyrinne: 'Aving-my-liar-lyin'. I have a liar in my head.	**Helsinki, Finland**: Hell-sink-I, End-land. I was drowned and it was hell.
	Tripoli, Lybia: Rip't-lop-lie, be-liar. Rip't means ripped.

Tall Women and Related	
Pauline Marianne Wenche: Name akin to my rapist's sister.	**Nova Scotia, Canada**: No-over-cots, I-can-add-her (can-ad-'er). I've added a plural and can't see the thing over my cot.
Anna Swan: Swaaannn (An empathic swam). A lie.	
Martin Van Buren Bates: Ram-int' (enter) have-burn-seat. ('Av-nBurenB means 'have-burn, for the letters lined up.)	**Whitesburg Letcher Conty Kentucky USA**: We-ties-decree. Let-her-con-tie-neck, I cut user. This code contains cuts and ties. Burg (short for iceberg-topple the g to d) means I-dec/gree.
Do*l*ores Ann Pullard: Is-door-and-pull-hard. (Capital, I resemble 'l'). A plea to recall.	
	Ripplegale, Lincolnshire: Rip-legal-link. Lock-in she-ire.

Ann Hardy: A-hard-in. (A-hardy-nn). Something hard was in me. **Mary Hales**: I-ram-liars (hails - liahs). Lies about the ramming.	I'm torn and locked from the 'shine' and ire. I can't take legal action. **Norfolk**: Nor-fuck. Uncle Dan fucked me.

Ateliolic Dwarfs and Placenames

Charles Sherward Stratton (alias General Tom Thumb): Rac-less-she-are-sat-on. I lack a Rac for the mounting. **Count Boruwlaski**: Cunt-bore. Double-you-scar-I. Rape scarred me and left me plural. **Caroline Crachami**: Rac-lie/lyin' (and) Rac-am-I. The two mes.	**Connecticut, USA**: Connect-I-cut-user. The user-memory is cut. **Poland**: Lop-land. My (tot) land cut off. **Palermosicily**: I-rape-most-silly. Paler means I-rape (l-I look alike). **London**: I-done-on (I-l look alike). I was 'done' on. **Hunterian Museum, the Royal College of Surgeons**: Hunter-(ian) means the Orion star cluster. Nor-I-me-use-me, the lyar lock-edge-of surge-ons. Something surged on me.

Heavyweights and Related

Robert Earl Hughes: Robe-tear-loos (l'hughes). Tearing off and robing the loo. **Mills Darden**: I//ms-dare-dn. I daren't unify. **Aurther Knorr**: Author-know-Nor. (My stories hide rape themes). **David Maquire**: I've-add-me, acquire. I have acquired another self.	**William J Cobb**: We-I//m-I-book. My plural's book. **Binville, Illinois**: Bin-vile-in-soil. **Henderson County, North Carolina, USA**: (*He*-ender-*son*) He-son, end-her-cunt-I. Th-Nor. Rac-lyin' user. I have been 'ended' by a son and lied to myself. **Mexico**: Me-ex-I-co. **USA** (several times): User.

Light and Thin

Lucia Zarate: Loo-I-see. Z-tear. I was used like a loo and the memory torn off. I then go zz-oblivion. **Rosa Lee Plemons**: On-sore-please-e/m. (The phrase begins with the 'ons'.) A plea to remain plural for the sore.	**San Carlos Mexico**: Sank-Rac-loss. Me-ex-I-co. (Co meaning company). I lost part of myself for the drowning. **Troyes France**: Tore-yes. Far-ran (Frraan-s). The liar says yes to the torn and far-away. **Cork Prison, Ireland**: Crock Prison-lie-land. My plural is a crock, imprisoned by the lie.

Twins, Triplets and Quads

Bill and Ben McCeary: Twins with two-Racs (for the) rear-I.	**Derbyshire**: Bed-'er-why sh'-ire. The rape ires my plural.

Jerrald and Jeraldine: I-lied-liar-lyin'. Both names begin 'Je', French for I.

Mrs. Maureen Head: Misses-am-urine-head. I am missing the toilet memory.

Mrs. Ruth Becker: Misses-truth-decree. (Reverse the 'b' in Becker to find 'd'ckree). I miss the truth for the decree.

Chancy and Eng Bunker: Reverse the 'g' to 'd'. Shank-I, and end-be-unc-'er. An uncle shanked me.

Sahah and Adelaide Yates (Misses): Has lia-ed and I misses-I-seat. The lie hides the rape.

Chalkhurst twins, Mary and Aliza: Ch-all-hurts-twins, I-ram and lia-zz. It hurts to be plural.

Daisy and Violet Hilton: I-said (and) vile-tell-'it-on. My plural wants to tell-on the vile.

Colwyn Bay, Denbigshire in the HM Stanley Hospital, St Asaph, Flintshire: Lock-double-you-in. (Loc-w-yn). End-big-shire, (in the) Him-stayne-face (saaph), fly-int'-shire. (Int' is short for enter). My face has been stained and entered.

Maklong Thailand (Siam): Am-yack-long tie-land (I-ams). The yuck-rape has been tied a long time.

Biddenden, Kent: I-ben-ended-yack. I was bent.

Brighton, Sussex: Not-bright (dumb to the) us-sex.

Charlotte, North Carolina, USA: Rac-lot-th-Nor-Rac-oral-lyin'. Lots of lies about the Nor-user.

Motherhood

Fyodor Vassilet: If-door, 'ave-lie-ties. If a door to truth comes my way, the liar uses lies and ties.

Court of Tsar Alexander II: Court (of) Sat (tsaa) All-ex-and-her (plural) Two (II). I want to testify in court.

Oldest People and Places

Pierre Joubert: Pyre (Pirre) you-be-hurt. The burning hurts.

John B Salling: I-on, be-all-lying/s. (J' is I in French – I'on). Nothing was 'on' me at all.

Ada Rowe Giddings: Ad-are-woe-diggings. Burial of the woeful thing.

Theton Katherine Plunket: The-two-nkat. (My plural can't). Therine means 'in-three'. Plunket means pee-I-unc-it. (Uncle-it). My plural can't get the message through about my uncle inside my three-year-old self.

Australia: Us-sat-liar. (Us-stra-lia).

Austria: Us-sit-tie-her. (Us-sti-ti-'a).

Belgium: Find *Blue* in *Bel*gium. Topple the 'g to 'd' to find be-loo'd-mi. (Be-loo'd-me).

Channel Islands: Double 'n' resembles 'm' to bring Ch-amel (sh'am/me. E/m-lies-land. I am ams and feel shame.

Czechoslovakia: So-check-yack-lover. The yack-sex is checked.

Finland: End-land (Fin is French for end).

France: Frraan-s. Far-ran/s. I ran far away.

Germany: Man-germ-in.

Johanna Bodyson: Son's-body J'onnaa (I-on-her) means on-her-I. He was on me.

Marie Bernattiova: I-ram-burn-at-over. The burning ramming whilst bent over.

M N Harvey: Mean-halve-I. (MN-me-en means mean). I am halved.

Y Ilto: To-tie (to-tiiy).

B Karnebeek: Be-Rac-'n'-be-kee (key). My plural has the key to truth. I don't.

M P Flossaver: Me'd favour-loss. (Topple the 'p'). I favour losing part of myself.

R Spoto: Are-spot-two. (Sullied and two).

James Hull: J'am-mes'-hull (part of a ship). The ship symbolises transport from my toddlerhood. Je is French for I. The ship is mine.

R Macarther: Rac-me-author.

M Olsen: Me-holes-in.

M A Crow: Me-Rac-woe. I woe about the rape.

LZ Schwaltz: She-wall-zz. I've gone zz and walled up the rape.

M L Jorge: M/e-gorge. A gorge divides the mes.

J Spier: I-spy-er. Part of me sees the truth but not allowed to tell.

M Anderson: Me-Ander'-son. My rapist's mother's surname.

M F Punode: F-me-done-up (something up me).

J Kneen: Je-nnek. I-neck. A trauma site.

Ireland: Liar-land.

Isle of Man: Lies-of-man (meaning wo*man*). I'm part of mankind.

Italy: Liar-tie (Lya-ti).

Japan: J-Pa-nap. I-Pa-coma. Coma/oblivion caused by the Pa.

Netherlands: Nether-lands (meaning lowered-lands).

Norway: Nor-way. Going my rapist's way.

Portugal: Read backwards: All-goo-tore-p (al-gu-tor-p).

Scotland: Cots-land. My toddlerhood.

South Africa: Shut-out-fry-Rac-shout. (The phrase rotates through).

Spain: Panis-pains. (Penis-pains).

Sweden: We-ends. Self-divorce.

Tasmania: I-man-sat. (Read backwards from the final I).

United Kingdom: Untied-King-dumb. I was once united. I am now untied (from the memory) and become dumb (oblivious).

Yugoslavia: You-go-silver. (Line up the final 'slavia' to find silvaa. This means Mum and the decree.

Other placenames

Shanghai: Sh'-aanghi (angry). A child's sounding about silent anger.

Thiruvadbl Monsastery in Incha: Th'-I-rue-you've-bad. Mon (my)-seat-her-why-in-chain.

I rue the rape badly and the part of me that knows about the 'seat' is in chains.

Fingers, Har and Beard	
Swami Pandara Sännadhi: Swam-pi-(pee) and-aar-sandy. I've gone sandy (sandman that comes in sleep) and believe I swam. In fact, I was drowned and raped.	**Hans N Langseth**: The-sang-insane (The-sang-Insahn). (I-I look alike). My plural's messages are 'insane'. **Voight**: (voite): I-vote. This relates to the *Science* questionnaire. I vote for truth.

Blood & Body Temperature

J Elmalen: I-e//m-en. I'm-e/ming.
Christopher Legge: R'c-sit-of-her-leg. My legs sat during rape.
Victoria Mary Davis: I've-K-tore-her. (Kay means yack, a term of disgust). I've torn myself.
Ram-I, is-add. The yuck-ram made me add a self.

Marseilles France: Rams-say, Far-ran. I ran away from the ram-disclosure.
Milwankee, Wisconsin: I/m-wankee, is-connin'. I'm conned about the stain.
Marshaltown, Iowa, USA: All-ram-sham (town), I-woe-her (user).

Neck and Related

Jack O'Leary: I-yack- o-really. Disbelief about the I-yack. (J'ack).
St Jude the Patron Saint of Lost Causes: Stain-I, you'd-the Pa-torn-stain-of lost-causes.

Padating people of Burma: Pa-dating people (the-mes) of burn-her.
Lames Vue Point: I-am-mes view-point. I have viewed the pointed thing.

Underwater

R. Arntzen: Aren't-zz. Denial and oblivion.
Robert Foster: Rob-'er-fforced (foerst). (The 't' topples to 'f'). The liar robs forcibly from me.
Norwegian: Nor-we-gain. I have gained a self for the Nor.

River Nideelv, Trondheim: River-I-need-lie, he-torn'd-me. His river tore me and I need the lie.
Richmond, California: Richmond, I-lack-of-Nor. I lack the Nor-memory. Richmond connects to my rapist.
Bemuda Palms Motel at San Rafeal, USA: Be-murder-pee-a/ms.
(Mo-tell means nno-tell). No-tell at stain-far-lia, user. I mustn't know I was stained and almost murdered.

Awakening

Mehined Ali Halici: Me-deny-liar, all-I-see. The liar blinds me.
Toimi Arthurinpoika: I-Tom (Thumb). Poker-I-in-author. (I saw myself as an author). Something poked in me.

Ankara Turkey: Rac-'n' to-your-key. My plural has the truth-key. I don't.
Finland: End-land.

Chapter 2: The Pennies

The following lists coins and their meanings.

Coins and Their Meanings

Copper	Policeman	**Florin**	Foil'n-R. I'm foiled.
Crown	Head	**Pennies**	Penis
Half Crown	Half-oblivious	**Shilling**	She-lyin'
Farthing	Far-thing	**Silver**	The Mum-decree

Chapter 3: Science

This section consists of lists and tables found in my *Science* book.
Chapter 3A: Science Words and Terminology.
Chapter 3B: Chemical Reactions
Chapter 3C: Tables as they Appear

Chapter 3A: Science Words and Terminology

This section looks at codes unearthed within chemical names and other science terminology. First up, comes the general terms.

General Terms

Acid (paper): Asid. This means 'said'. This book is saying things about the raper (paper). At the beginning, I had said that if a chemical is acid, the 'paper' turns red. Red means read (past tense). Messages about the raper is all over my science book and I must *read* them.

Alkaline: Lack-lia/lyin'. I am lacking, for the liar. At the beginning, I had said the paper turns blue if a chemical is alkaline. Blue means be-loo (rape) and the alkaline is saying it's a lie.

Crystals: I spelled this word various ways: christals, chrystals and cristals. The meaning is all-sat-cry. The syllables run backwards within (cry-sta-al). Salt and copper sulphate are crystals. My plural is crying out about the copper that suffocated me.

Degrees: Agreed-decree, an oath to hush about the rape (for the 'silver, which means Mum). From '68, it went up.

Neutral: Knew-all-true. The paper doesn't change colour. The truth doesn't change about the 'raper'.

Universal indicator paper: A means to test the PH of a chemical. My plural sees raper in paper, and it is indicating things about it.

Terms Relating to Liquid

The following relates to liquids. Dissolving has been mentioned a lot. This means to melt all proof of the rape and erasing my conscious memories. This is what the liar is doing: dissolving. The following show.

Crystal (pertaining to liquid): An undissolved solid. It has sharp sides and flat faces (I had written). My face felt flattened during oral rape and the all-cry (of crystal) refuses to dissolve the memory. It has sharp sides and won't melt away.

Dissolving: This means to get rid of proof. My questionnaire had included 'dissolve in water' and means to dissolve evidence of the drowning. A 'solid' (I had written) disappears in liquid.' Disappear means is-raped (*d*-is-apear-ed) and it is dissolving in liquid.

Distil: I hadn't explained the meaning clearly in my book, only that we 'collect the solid and liquid to distil'. But at the end of this sentence, I had written 'dissolving' by mistake. Distil means sit-lid. A lid is being kept over the 'sit' and dissolved away.

Evaporating: I had written, 'we heat a solution until the liquid disappears. The solution is evaporated.' This is what the liar wants: for all traces of my is-raped (d-*is-appear*-s) to evaporate.

Filtering: Here, I had separated a solid from a liquid. We had done this with salt and sand. The liar has segregated the truth (salt means sat-land) from my conscious awareness (sand means sleep as in the sandman). The salt melts away and I am asleep to the truth.

Saturated: I had written this word disjointedly (sat-urated). Notice 'sat' at the beginning and the preceding u-r. This means your-are-sat. The final rated means tear'd. You-are-sat-teared, and I would explain, a saturated solution is one that will dissolve. The rape is being dissolved away.

Solute: A solid that dissolves in liquid. More dissolving, it seems, and I become loss-two (los-tue).

Solution: I had explained this word to an even mix of a solid in liquid. Loss-you-shun. Part of myself has been shunned.

Solvent: The liquid in which a solid dissolves. No amount of 'dissolving' seems enough for the liar. It's everywhere.

Chemicals

This section gives chemical names and the codes unearthed.

Ammonium Dichromate: The second word means ditch-room-mate. My plural has been ditched yet she remains in my head. Ammonium means am-know-you-me (I). Half of me knows.

Copper oxide: I-do ex-copper.

Copper sulphate: Copper-suffocate.

Cuprous Chloride (spelled Cuprius-Cloride): Cuprous means us-crop. Cloride means lock-ride. The 'ride' has been cropped and locked away.

Iron filing (spelled iron filling): Nor-filling-I. I was filled by my rapist.

Iron oxide: I-do-Nor. I have 'done' the copper.

Iron sulphate: Nor-suffocate-I.

Nickel Sulphate (spelled nicle sulphate): The 'nickel' is trying to be uncle. This should mean uncle-suffocate.

Polystyrene (spelled Poly-stryrene). Poly means I-lop. Ssty-rene means cistern. This pertains to the loo and means sit-loo. The cover of my *Lines* book shows a blue cistern above a red loo-seat.

Potassium permanganate: Read backwards within *pot-tas-si-u(m)* to find 'you-is-sat-top'. My head (top) was 'sat' during oral rape. The spare 'm' at the end means 'em' (me).

(Per)*manganate* contains 'magnet' and means get-maan. Deduct get-man to leave *per-aa*. Raape. Get-man-rape. Get the man that raped me.

This chemical comes together, you-is-sat-top. Get-man-rape-me.

Red lead: Read (past tense) lade. Read-laid. Something laid on me and I must 'read' the meaning.

Chapter 3B: Chemical Reactions

This section summaries the chemical reactions. This includes burning and mixing. As seen, we burnt various substances and noted changes. My plural would see copper-suffocate in copper sulphate. The colours represent becoming plural and getting stuck on this world.

The Burning Table (in Alphabetical Order)		
Element and misspelling	**Before and during burning**	**After burning and under the scope**
Ammonium Dichromate	They looked like christals.	The powder changed quitly and the paper turned red, not so slowly. (After burned under the scope). They looked like coal. This chemical is acid.
Copper Sulphate*	The cristals are blue. We looked under the scope. They looked like blue rock.	We put them on the burner. It turned from blue to white, brown and greenish. After being burned, we put them under the scope. They looked like sticky boulders.
Copper Sulphate*	It was green at first, and then turned yellow.	It was all stuck together after burned. It did not spurt out. They looked like queer-eggs under the scope.
Cuprous Chloride (Cuprius Cloride)	It is a dirty green couler. Under scope, it looked like moss.	It turned black and damp and grey. A bit dark brown. Under scope (after burning), it looks like smudged paint.
Hypo crystals*	Heated in a glass container.	It smelled and melted 'quitly'. It became runny like water. Once cooled, we added un-melted crystals.
Polystyrene (Poly stryrene)	Like sugar.	It burned glitterish. And turned brown. It melted on the paper. It 'smocked' and smelled.
Potassium Permanganate	Black at first with bits of glittering purple	It spits until it's all gone. Left with black stains on the paper. It looked like stars in the night sky under the scope.
Red lead	It was orange at first and it changed to glowing red. And then purple.	It bubbled and changed to glittering yellow. It bubbled more and melted a bit. Under scope, it looked like coloured rock.

* The blue crystals 'burning white' has no heading. I have deduced it to be copper sulphate, for the description.

* The green substance that comes afterwards has the heading 'copper sulphate' This seems to be the same substance being burnt again.

* I think the hypo means hyposulphite of soda.

218

Other Chemical Reactions (in Alphabetical Order)

The substance	The process	The result
Copper sulphate (blue)	Pieces of iron filing was added (brown and red). The filing sinks to the bottom.	When shaken up, the blue turned green and faded. The (resulting) iron sulphate was warm.
Ink	Placed in an evaporating dish, 3-quarters full. We heated it and it began to bubble.	It got darker and smelled. The ink reduced until there was none left. The lumps at the bottom were shiny and golden. When water was added, it turned back to ink.
Polystyrene (Spelled Polystyene)	Through the scope, it looked like marbles.	It is not a 'crystal'. But salt, copper sulphate and hypo are crystals.
Potassium permanganate	Mix with equal part of water.	It has dissolved. The solid that has dissolved is called the solute. The liquid is called solvent.
Sulphur (Spelled sulphure)	Added to water.	It doesn't dissolve. It is insoluble in water.
Sand and salt	Mix salt and sand in a jar with water up to '100'.	Mix well and the salt melted into the water. I filtered it. The salty water got through, the sand didn't. I have separated them.
Water (solid, liquid and gas)	Boiling and freezing.	Ice (crystals) melt, water boils to steam. Gas condenses at 100°C. Liquid freezes to a solid at 0°C.

* I think the hypo means hyposulphite of soda.

Part 3C: The Questionnaire and Other Tables

This section contains tables within my *Science* book.
The following table shows the questionnaire as it appeared.

Quest ↓	Obj →	Beehive	Stone	Fossil	Bottle	Emerald	Tissue Ball	Snail fossil	Head fossil	Rubber plant	Fossil
Heavey		N	Y	N	N	Y	N	Y	N	Y	Y
Smooth		N	N	Y	Y	N	Y	Y	Y	Y	Y
Symetrical		Y	N	Y	N	N	Y	Y	N	N	N
Tough		N	Y	Y	N	Y	N	N	N	Y	Y

Nice smell	N	N	N	N	N	N	N	N	N	N
Bright coulerd	N	N	N	N	N	N	N	N	N	N
Attracted to metal	N	N	N	N	Y	N	N	N	N	N
Shiney	N	Y	N	N	N	Y	N	N	N	Y
Float in water	Y	N	Y	Y	N	Y	N	Y	Y	Y
Waterproof	N	Y	N	Y	Y	Y	Y	N	Y	Y
Conduct electricity	N	N	N	Y	Y	Y	N	N	Y	N
Bendy	N	N	N	N	N	N	N	N	Y	N
Light	Y	N	N	Y	N	Y	N	Y	Y	Y
Rough	Y	Y	Y	Y	Y	Y	Y	Y	Y	Y
Non-symetrical	Y	N	N	N	N	N	Y	N	N	N
Brittle	N	Y	Y	N	Y	N	Y	Y	Y	N
Nasty smell	Y	N	N	N	Y	N	N	N	Y	N
Dull coulerd	Y	Y	Y	Y	Y	Y	Y	Y	Y	Y
Non attracted to a magnet	N	N	N	N	N	N	N	N	N	N
Dull	Y	Y	Y	Y	Y	Y	Y	Y	Y	Y
Non water dissolved	N	N	N	N	N	N	N	N	N	N
Non waterproof	N	Y	N	N	Y	Y	Y	N	Y	Y
Do not conduct electricity	N	N	N	N	Y	Y	N	N	Y	N
Rigid	N	Y	Y	Y	Y	Y	Y	Y	Y	Y

The following tables show the codes behind the questionnaire: truth and lies.

QUESTION	MEANING	EXPANSION	THE TRUTH
Waterproof	I-drowned	Water-proof.	
Sink in water	I drowned.	I sank in water.	
Non-dissolve	Proof remains	Don't dissolve proof.	
Heavy	Heavy	A heavy thing was on me.	
Nice smell	Sign-e/ms	The signs I am plural are shining.	
Bendy	Bend-I.	I was raped from behind whilst bent.	
Attracted to magnet	Get-man	I owe it to myself to get-man. Attracted means Rac-debt. (The 'ted' is 'debt' backwards).	
Metal	Me-tell	To disclose of the rape.	
Symmetrical	Visible plural	My plural and myself are like a mirror image.	
Conduct electricity	Conduct election	My misspelt *elect-icity* means elect-sit-I. Truth should win the vote.	

QUESTION	MEANING	EXPANSION	THE LIES
Float	I floated	I floated (a lie).	
Non-waterproof	No proof	No proof of drowning.	
Doesn't sink	Didn't drown	I didn't sink.	
Dissolve	Proof dissolved	Dissolve all proof of the water incident.	
Light	Lie-tie	Sounded 'lite'. Lie and tie away the truth.	
Dull-coloured	Dull-you-locked-read	My misspelled 'coulerd' means you-lock-read. I can't read these codes and I am dull.	
Bright-coloured	Be-right, you-locked-read	The liar thinks it is 'be-right' I remain dumb and unable to read these codes. See how the liar twists an opposing statement.	
Rough, tough	Ugh-tore	Both end ugh. Something about me is ugh. The ugh 'tore' (toor) me.	
Smooth	Me-two-sh	Contains 'too' (two). This means plural. Me-too-sh.	
Rigid	I-rid-I-agree	The central 'g' segregates the two ii's - r-*i*-**g**-*i*-d. The letter 'gee' brings 'greed (slang for 'agreed'). I-agree to rid-I (my plural).	
Brittle	Be-lie-tie	Lie/r and tie, (like 'lite' earlier).	
Not attracted to magnet	Don't get man.	Not Rac-debt to get-man.	
Asymmetrical	Invisible plural	I'm 'not' plural but *a*symmetrical.	
Not conduct electricity	Don't conduct election	Don't conduct this election.	

This following unearths the codes behind other objects explored within my *Science* book.

RECALL	DISCLOSURE	
Birds: Disclosure **Bottle**: Recall **Broken glass**: Recall **Grass** and long grass): To tell. **Greenhouse**: Grass-house (the cottage). **Metal**: Me-tell.	**Boughs** (and bendy boughs). Lay bent and bowed. **Cement**: (Meant) semen. **Flowers**: Lowers. **Paint**: and dry): Pire-pa-enter (pa-int').	**Path**: Th-pa (father-figure) **Playground**: Laid-ground. **Pond**: Assault site. **Roses**: Sores. **Weeds**: Semen.

LIES & SILENCE	BEING TORN	BARRIERS	OBLIVION
Birdhouse: Silencing the disclosure **Boulders**: Being stuck on this world. **Insillirator**: Lies-lyn' and liar **Litter**: Lied/tie. **Snails**: Liar-lyin' **Guineapig** and guineapig cage): A blend of Gwen (Uncle Dan's girlfriend) and 'pig' (his once-job). I'm in a cage of lies, letting him get away with it.	**Barks**: Be-Racs. Be plural. **Cars**: Racs (being plural). **Moss**: (written like mass): Ams. Being plural. **Rotton wood**: Double-you'd-torn-two. **Trees**: Tears (teers) becoming plural.	Bricks Doors Fences Framework Gates Posts: (means stop) Lampposts Windows	**Autumn leaves**: At numb leaves. **Mud**: Dumb (oblivion). **Dry mud and dry)** Dumb and dire dumb. **School**: So-lock. **Stone**: not-know-st **Cracked pebbles**: Rac-be-sleep. (pebbles: pe-sleebb).

LIVING THINGS		
PLANTS: (make their own food)	**ANIMALS: (can't make their own food)**	
Conifer: I-confer (disclose). **Fern**: Fern-firn brings fire-in (burning inside). **Flowering plant**: Lowering plant ('plant' means to be on). **Fungi**: Fun-guy. **Moss**: Ams. (My 'o' looks like 'a'. **Mushroom**: Hush-room.	**Without backbone**: Spineless **Arthropod**: Author-Pop (Author used by a Pa-figure). **Jellyfish**: She-fly-lie-I. (Je is French for I). Read backwards. **Snail**: Lia/in'/s. Lies about the rape. **Starfish**: Sat-ship/fish. A messenger from Saltland about the rape. **W-or-m**: Double-you-or-me. Plural or not?	**With backbone**: Brave **Amphibians**: Ams-fib-I-an. **Birds**: Disclosure. **Fish**: Phish-ship. A mode of transport from my toddlerhood Saltland. **Mammals**: All-ams. **Reptiles**: Rep't-lies. Repeat-lies.

Animals With and Without a Backbone	
With backbone: Brave	**Without backbone**: Spineless
Birds: Disclosure **Fish**: Phish-ship. A mode of transport from Saltland. **Starfish**: Sat-ship/fish. A messenger from the ocean about the rape.	**Arthropod**: Author-pop (father-figure). **Amphibians**: Am-fibs-I **Jellyfish**: She-fly-lie-I. (Je is French for I). Read backwards **Mammals**: All-ams. **Reptiles**: Rep't-lies. (Repeat-lies)

Chapter 4: Colours

The following summarises colour-codes and gems found in my Colours book.

Colour means our-lock. Coloured means our-lock-read.

Rainbow: rein-bow: The memory of raped from behind (bowed) is reined.

Black: Be-lack	**Blue**: Be-loo	**Brown**: No brow (oblivion)
Gold: Go-old.	**Green**: Grass (to tell)	**Indigo**: (Inbigo): Go-big-in
Orange: Nor-age	**Pink**: Pee-ink.	**Purple**: You-repel
Red: Read (past tense)	**Violet**: Vile-tell	**White**: We-tie
Yellow: Coward		

Gems		
Amethyst: Am-the sit.	**Diamond**: Dire-man	**Emerald**: Me-liar/lied.
Garnet-red: Daren't read. Spin the 'g' to 'd' to find daren't red (read).	**Jade green**: Gade-green. A-ggreened. Green-(grass)-agreed. This is a lie.	**Ladis-lazuli**: (meaning lapis-lazuli): Read backwards to find 'lie-you-zz'
Onyx: I-ex-on. Self-divorce for the thing 'on' me.	**Pearl**: Rape-I. Capital I and lowercase L look alike (I-l).	**Ruby**: Bury.
Sapphire: Face-fire.	**Stone**: Not-know-stain.	**Tapas**: (meaning topaz): Saat-pee.
Turquoise: 'uoise' looks like voise (voice). Turq (cuut) means cut. Cut-voice. Silence.		

Chapter 5: Lines

The following looks at the codes unearthed in my *Lines* project.

General landmarks

Crossroads: Recall. With the liar abolished, I now have a choice.

Farmhouse: My 'f' resembles a slashed 's' to bring sarm. Rams-house. This means my childhood cottage.

Kara-Hara Dam: A dam separates my Rac from the Har. My name contains these letters.

Oxygen: I would spell it oxaginen and oxa-ginen. This means ex-dogging. Dogs peeing in parks brought notions of my used-self and I have exed her.

Railway: Liar-way.
Station: Sat-shun-I.

My Number: 19865

This number is at the top of the page about the Hara-Kara Dam.

I've come across these numbers several times in my other projects. It's a blend of my birthyear and the year I was raped: 1965 and 1968. (Rotate the '9' to get the '6'). 19865.

Lines on the World

I will now list my *Lines on the World*. The following places work from north to south and are copied as written in my *Lines* book.

Artic Circle (6.7N): Rak-tic circle. The reason I tic is encircled. I'm not allowed to know.

Gt Britain (5.5N): Get be-written. My plural wants these codes written down.

Spain, Italy, Japan, Chiner 4.0N: Panis-pains, it-a-lie, (J)-naap, chain-'er. These mean penis-pains, it's a lie, I-nap (oblivion) and chain my plural.

Tropic of Cancer 23½N: Pro-tic of sank-er. Part of me knows why I tic and is pro-truth about the drowning.

Equater, Congo, Brazil 0: A-quitter (a-quetter), go-con and bar-zz-lie. Desertion, lies and oblivion.

Tropic of Capricorn, Astralia 23 ½S: Begins pro-tic again. Part of me knows why I tic and she is pro-truth about the Nor and raip (C-*apri*-corn). But a cape (caip) hides it. My misspelled Australia means us-sat-liar.

New Seland, Borneo 40S: The former means a new beginning: New-lands. The latter is Nor-bore. I was bored into.

Cape Horn 55S: Cape (the) Nor. Hide the rapist.

Ant artic Curcule 67S: Taint-Rac (tic) circle. The clue (ccluue) to my tics is encircled. I'm not allowed to know.

Chapter 6: Aurther Space

Aurther is a blend of author-Arthur. I see myself as an author. **The-truth** can be found between these words.

My **sBaise** means be-says. It's like utter, read and grass. My books are telling on the rape. The following summarise the codes within my *Space* book.

Asteroid: Sat-'orrid. The mounting was horrid.

Comet: It-come (on me). It also means me-cot, the age of when it happened.

Lion: (Star cluster) Lyin and lie-on.

Meteorites: Me-tear-writes.

Orion: Nor-I. My plural roleplays her experiences minus the callousness.

Pan: (Star cluster): Pa-nap. Coma due to a father-figure.

Scorpion (Star cluster) The Nor with a sting in his tail.

Sirius: Us-cries.

Star: (staa) Saat.

The double meaning behind the sun, planets and moon have been explained in the main book.

Chapter 7: Aurther Earth

The following are codes found in my *Earth* book. Where clarification is needed, notes follow.

Ash: Is one thing the Earth is made of. (I had drawn an organically pink 'mountain of ash' beside it).

Notes: Ash comes after the burning.

Gas: is deadly poison. You get it far underground. Gas stops you breathing. It is unpleasant. Gas is dangerous and bad.

Notes: I was suffocated, and it is kept underground.

Metel: is steal (I had put). Meltle has two names (meaning metal and steel). Metle shines bright. The metlle drips and makes the metlle sticky. The metle is the white bit inside (the Earth). Molton is the red bit. When you cut the earth in half, you can see it.

Notes: My various expressions for 'metal' means 'me-tell.' And it's about the burning, sticky rape. Interestingly, metal has another name: steal. (I had meant steel). The liar is steal(ing) the me-tell from my plural about the rape. Later, I would put, 'steal is write, shining in the sun'. (I had meant white shining in the sun). The liar is claiming to be the 'writer' of this book. Not only does the liar lie, it steals from me.

Mud: Mud comes from marshes and swamps which is slodgy and horrible. Swamps are as deep as your middle. Mud is mixed with clay which is orange colour.

Notes: Mud means dumb (read backwards to find the word). I would later remark that mud is brown and dull. I am mud-dumb, for the oblivion. I am in marshland where everything is slodgy and 'horrible'.

Oil: You can get oil under the seabed (I write). Oil is to stop things going stiff. (I had drawn a bottle of oil).

Rocks: Rock is gleterd (glittered) in the sun. It is as bright as stars in the night sky. Rock is one thing the Earth is made of.

Sea: Sea is salty water. The deepest sea in the world is the Pasific. It is the widest sea too. The big seas are (the) Pasific (and the) Atlantic (Oceans) and AraBian (Sea).

Notes: My misspelled Pacific brings 'asific'. Faiisc. This means face. The phrase returns to the beginning, 'Pa's'. Pa's-face. A father-figure kept using my face as though 'his'.

Atlantic (Sea) means 'S-Alt-an-tic'. Saltland-tic. I suffer tics due to being sat in toddlerhood. My use of 'Sea' has provided this code.

The Barren: But why did I include the Arabian Sea with two oceans? My odd Arabian-spelling means I-barren (I-Baraan). My plural must have believed toddlerhood-rape had made me infertile.

Soil: Soil looks like black mud (I write). Soil is dirty. When there's nothing on Earth, the colour would be brown. That's soil and mud making Earth a dull colour. Soil means sullied.

Notes: Soiled is how I felt post-rape. Brown means no-brow, and mud, dumb. These mean oblivion to the soiling.

Steel: (See metal) has been spelled steal. My virginity and truth have been stolen from me.

Water: Earth is the only planet with water (I had written). Other planets don't. Water comes from seas and taps. Water is for thirst and to dive and swim.

Notes: Water means w-tear, which the Earth (the-are) has in abundance. The following explain the two maps.

1ˢᵗ Map	Meaning
Ala-ska	(Alaska): Alas-scar. I'm sad about the scar.
Atlantic	(With the 's' of Sea) means Saltland-tic.
Baffin	(Baffin Island): Swap the vowels and read backwards from the 'f' (Biffan) to find fib-ban lie-land. I am banned from recall and lied to myself.
Brasil	(Brazil): Be-liars.
Canida	(Canada). Can-add-her (can-ad-'er). I have added a self.
Greenland	Grassland. Everything around me is grassing on my toddlerhood.
Merica	(Meaning America): This word begins mercy (Meric) just like Mercry of Mercury. The final 'a' links back to the 'm' to bring 'am'. Am-mercy.

2ⁿᵈ Map	Meaning
Burma	Read from the 'u' to find 'you-are-mad' (rotate the 'b' to 'd'). The liar keeps calling my plural mad for wanting to disclose.
China	Chain. The truth is chained up.
India	Later, I had misspelled it 'Inda'. Upturn the 'd' to find 'pain'. I'm in pain.
Iran	I-ran. I ran away from the truth and the liar is born.
Mongolia	The word begins 'm' (em), 'me backwards. It continues 'gon-lia. Me-gone-liar. I have gone for the lie.
Rusha	(Russia): You are ash-sh. I have been burnt and hush follows.

Others	
Black Forest	(Mentioned twice): Be-lack forced (forst). I was forced to lose part of myself.
England	Erroneously paced north of Canada. I am far from home.
Gemeny	(Germany): Man-germ-in.
Illand	(Ireland): Lie-land.
Japan	J'naap'. I-Pa-nap. (J' is French for I).
North Pole	Th'Nor-pole. His phallus.
Sawth Pole	(South Pole): My misspelt 'South' means saw-the-pole. I had seen the phallus and I want the memory cut away.

United Staits	(United States). Untied-sat-sit. My toddlerhood is untied from me.

Chapter 8: Aurther Wildflowers

The following are nineteen flowers not shown in the main book. These come in alphabetical order.

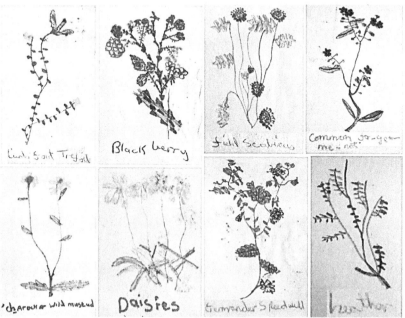

Birds Foot Trefoil, Blackberry, Character Mustard and Daisies.
Field Scabious, Common Forget-me-not, Germander Speedwell and Heather

Bird's-foot Trefoil: My 'bird' looks like 'liird's' (for my open 'b'). This means lie (lii) and its tenses (lie, liar, lied and lies). Foil means fool. The word 'fool' hides in 'foot' too. Liar's-fool-foil.

Blackberry: In my *Earth* book, I had said the blackberry can be mistaken for the deadly nightshade. This means coma. The liar has buried it. Be-lack-bury. I have buried my knowing self and I am now lacking.

Character Wild Mustard: I had misspelt character, Charakter. This means Rack-actor, my broken-self. On 15 Aug 1978, I bought pencil-top 'caracters' which means Rack-actor too. I was forever making up stories fuelled by the broken mes of my toddlerhood.

Wild means w'-lied (see cornflower). And my 'mustud' means must. I must lie to myself about the rape. Rack-acter-we-must-lie(d).

Daisies: The first part means said (siad). The final part, iesd brings 'dies' (rotate back to the 'd'). I had almost died. Said-dies.

Field Scabious: F-ield means I-fled and I lied to myself. Scabious means scar-be-us. (sca-bi-ous). A scar separates us after I lied and fled the truth.

227

Forget-me-not: I kept drawing these plants in infants. It is a plea *not* to forget my plural. I had tagged the 'common'. I was come-on and have forgotten it.

Germander Speedwell: This flower carries a sentence. Read backwards from the 'n' to find the words, man-germ-loo-peeds. (Man-germ llew-peeds). I was made to feel like a loo. The remaining 'er' means her. He did it to a girl.

Heather: Heat-her. The rape burnt.

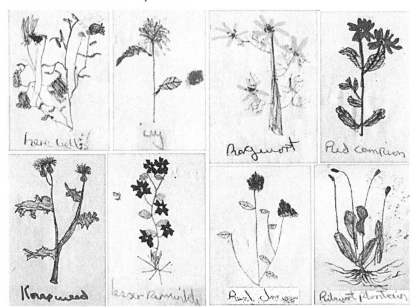

Harebells, Ivy, Knapweed and Lesser Periwinkle.
Ragwort, Red Campion, Red Clover and Ribwort Plantain.

Harebells: I had written the word 'here-bells'. I am struck by the 'her' beginning. The remaining 'ebells' (slleeb) means sleep. Topple the 'b' to 'p'. I have gone to sleep to the truth. The blue heads appear fuzzy and lack detail. Oblivion is fuzzy.

Ivy: I've-I. I have another I.

Knapweed: Nap is slang for unconsciousness. I was comatose when I was 'weed' on. A common knapweed exists too.

Lesser Periwinkle: The word ends 'riwi-nkle'. The 'nkle' means uncle and the 'wii' wee. The opening 'p' confirms.
The lesser means 'less-her'. I am less for feeling weed on. Uncle-pee-less-her.

Ragwort: Notice how the first part of this word looks like 'rage' (see image). Half of the 'w' has been used up, leaving 'u'. The word ends 'ort. This means 'tor' (tore). You-tore. The rage is due to the tearing. Rage-you-tore.

Red Campion: My 'red' looks like 'rid'. And the 'p' looks like 'r'. This flower now ends 'rion'. Shift the 'I' to the other side of 'm' (Caim) to bring 'rid-came-Nor'. I rid the Nor that came over me.

Red Clover: Notice the 'cl' of Clover looks like a 'd'. This brings redd-over (read-over). The read has been taken away before I had drawn this plant and I can't see the 'ddred' in the message.

Ribwort Plantain: The 'Ribwort' is full of torn expressions. Topple the 'b' to create 'rip'. Read backwards to find 'tor' (tore). The 'double-you'(w) joins both. Rip-double-you-tore. This is due to the Plantain (Plaant-in).

Rosebay Willowherb: (Written, Herb Rose Bay Willow). Reverse 'b' in bay. Her-be-sore-day-I-low. One day, I was forced low and made sore.

Wild Pea: The 'p' looks like an 'R', to bring 'Wild Rea'. This p-R amalgamation provides a rape-anagram. The 'wild' means we-lied.

Wood Sorrel: I have suffered a tic here, for my 'sorrell' ends with two big slashes. And my writing of 'Wood' looks like 'loo' backwards. Wood Sorre-ll means loo-sore. My 'w' (double-you) remembers it. I was made sore below. (W) loo-sore.

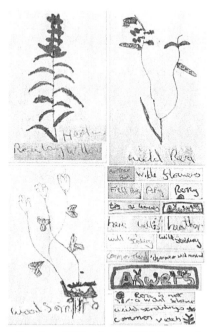

Rosebay Willowherb, Wild Pea and Wood Sorrell.

I have drawn five flowers in the back of this book.		
1: Creeping Quifoil	2: Wild Strabury	3: Yellow Flag
4: Ivy: I've-I	5: Blackberry	
I have drawn 'Five Flowers at a Time'.		
1: Goldon Rod:	2: Wild Dafadil	3: Wood Sorrel
4: White Dead Nettle	5: Bugle	

The Morphing

Some of these plants keep coming up. Creeping buttercup (x3). Creeping cinquefoil (x2). In all, the creeping occurs seven times and the 'common' in five plants.

Wild appears in daffodil, strawberry, pea, character and mustard, Wild means we-lied.

Wild strawberry occurs five times (Strawberry, strabberys, strabury, strabery and stabury). My plural urges me to keep writing this word until it morphs into the stabury. This means sat-bury, and it stabbed.

Foil occurs four times. And in a quiz, the daffodil (spelled dafadil) appears three. This means padofil (paedophile). My future creations contain flowers.

 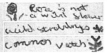

1: The number is 1. Look for flower 1, even you no (know) its name.

2: Creaping Buttercup.

3: White Dead Nettle does grow a head.

4: There is 5 flowers.

5: Goldon Rod, Wild Dafadil, Wood Sorrel, White Dead Nettle, Bugle.

6: Wood Sorrels.

7: Common Vetch.

8: Wild Strabberys.

9: Shoots.

10: Forget-me-not, which is my favourite flower. It is drawn roughly so the question is harder.

11: Wildflowers

12: Roots are brown.

13: Popy and (Pansy?)

14: Rose is not a wildflower.

15: One 10th of an inch.

16: Wild Dafodils.

17: Forget me-not.

18: Blue.

19: You can eat Wild Strawberry.

20: They do.

Chapter 9: Aurther Weather

The following summarises the codes found in weather terms.

Clouds	Others
Cirrus (misspelt Cirrius) Us-cries	**Evening**: Envying
Cumulus: Me-clues	**Mist**: Missed.
Nimbus: Us-numb.	**Rain**: rein
Stratus: Straight-us-stain.	

Juniperus Communis

Chapter 10: Wildflowers of the Pyrenees

The following are Pyrenean flowers not shown in the main book.

JUNIPERUS COMMUNiS SSP NANA

Dwarf Juniper. Family: *Cupressaceae*. June-July.

'A dense spreading scrub with wittish green nettle-like leaves. The globular fruits change from green to bluish-black. Grows on rocky, stony places, covering borders with a mat-like growth.'

Notes: I notice the lower-case 'i'. This plant is me and I was 'come-on' (reared-over). The 'Dwarf' means a small person. A toddler.

230

Nana means my rapist's mother and she stopped concurrent with her son in 1968. Communis-ssp means is-come-on. Juniperus means the same. Connect the central 'peni' (nipe) to the final 's' to bring penis-juus (juice).

The 'leaves change from green to bluish-black'. My plural is grassing on the penis but keeps getting hushed. Black means be-lack. My plaeses mean pleases. A plea to make the horrible thing go away.

ASPHODELUS ALBUS VAR PYRENAEUS

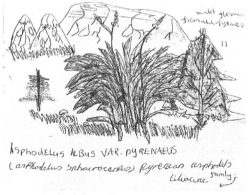

Asphodelus Sphaerocarpus. Family: *Liliaceae*. Pyrean endemic: June-August.

'Leaves long, narrow and stiff, forming large clumps. Flowers are whight with brown bracts in large spines on stems, usually single but sometimes branched. It grows on rocky slopes and mountain-sides.'

Asphodelus Albus var Pyrenaecus

Notes: This plant has lie-lack (Lilac-eae) for a family. My plural feels no-belonging whilst her oblivious-self lives a lie.

I had written that the leaves of this plant form 'large clumps'. My handwriting looks like 'dumps'. This means my past. My 'leaves' means to desert.

I keep spelling 'white' oddly. So far, I have spelt it wight, wittish (meaning whitish) and now whight. This word means we-tie and 'sh' about the down below. I mustn't know about it.

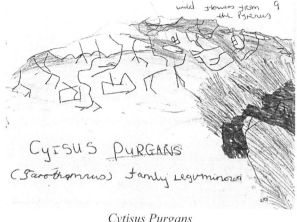

Cytisus Purgans

CYISUS PURGANS

Sarothamnus. Family: *Leguminosae.* May-July.

'A small bluish-green shrub. Leaves, undivided and alternate. Flowers, golden-yellow in terminal clusters, scented. Widely distributed in the esten Pyrenees, particularly on the Spanish side. Grows on steep stony mountain-sides.'

Notes: I have written 'Esten' again. This means seat-on. My Pyrenees looks like 'pyenus'.

I have suffered a tic here, for I had omitted the 't' in Cytisus. This word means us-sit. The 'bluish-green' reinforces the be-loo, but the I-sh keeps hushing the grass. Mountains means mounting.

Aquilegia Pyrenaica

AQUILE GIA PYRENAICA
Pyrenean Columbine. Family: *Ranunculaceae.* (Pyrenean Endemic) July-August.

'Grows to 20-40cm. Leaves are three-segmented, deeply-divided, and large of pale blue. Spur (is) slender and curved. Grows on steep, partly-shaded meadows and mountain-sides at the edges of woods and amongst boulders.'

Notes: The Latin name declares the ran-uncle. He chased me. Columbine means I am locked and numb to the thing he did afterwards. (I-lock-numb). The leaves are 'deeply-divided'. *I* am deeply divided. This plant grows in deep shadow. I can't see what Uncle Dan did and I am stuck on the boulder ('amongst boulders').

Codes of the Pyrenees

The following provides a list of codes found in the Pyrenean flowers.

The Alpine Pyrenees and Derivatives

The Pyrenean Alps has provided a wealth of opportunities for my plural. Pyrenees has morphed into penis. But derivatives of these words would create further codes.

Alpines: Alps and Alpine mean the same thing. Combine to find 'Alpines'. Penis can now be seen at the end of this word. 'Lie' threads through: A-**L**-p-**I**-n-**Es**. A-penis-lie.

Alpina: Nap-lia: The nap (coma) is a lie. Nap-liar.

Pyrenaica: The word beings with pyre. This means the burning. The 'aica' can be arranged to I-caa. (I-*car*). This means me for the Rac. Pyre-*on*- I-Rack means I am on fire. Pyre-on-Rack.

Pyrenaeus: Pyre-na-us. Pyre-anus. The burning sensation of rape from behind.

Pyrean: Pyre-rear-on. The burning sensation whilst being reared into. My 'Pyrenean' would morph into this spelling.

Seven times, I had used the phrase 'Pyrean endemic'. Endemic means me-end-I-see. I can no longer remember the rape.

Morphing words showing other meanings: numb, being deeply cut, the lowers of rape and my past stolen.

Latin Names

ADONIS PYRENAICA: Is-done-a pyre-on, I-ache. The burning rape made me ache.

AQUILE GIA PYRENAICA: An inverted 'T' can be seen in my capital 'I'. Aquile means a-quite – to be quiet about something. It's about the Pyre-on-Rack (of Pyrenaica). I mustn't know about the burning.

ANTIRRHINIUM MaJUS: Notice the final 'I-numb' (I-nium). The first part, antir means 'I-rant'. 'I-rant-I-numb'. The liar's mantra promotes oblivion. Majus means am-J-us. The central J is French for I. On either side is am-us. I am plural.

ASPHODELUS ALBUS VAR PYRENAEUS: See 'face' in 'asph' (phas). Read back from 'us' to find us-face-holed. Oral-rape left a hole in my face. I am now all-be-us (albus). And 'far (var) pyre-anus. The rape is far away.

CROCUS NUDIFLORUS: I-nude floor-rock-us. My lower part was stripped, and I was raped on the floor.

CYISUS PURGANS: This should be *Cytisus Purgans*. I-see-us. (Iy-c-uss). But I hadn't put 'sit (in Cytisus). I can't see a thing. Purgans means purge-san. Purge the stain.

DAPHNE CNEORUM: Daft-neck-room. (Daff-necne-room). I wasn't orally-raped in that room at all (apparently). It's 'daft'.

GENiTANA LUTiA: You-giant-liar. See the U-lia in 'Lutia'. Line up the Gentiana letters to find giant (giaannte). There are two lower case 'i'. The liar has severed me.

JUNIPERUS COMMUNiS SSP NANA: Juniperus means semen. The central letters Peni connects to the final 's' to bring 'penis'. Penis-juus (juice). Communis-ssp means come-on-piss. Nana means my rapist's mother. She stopped concurrent in 1968.

MERENDERA PYRENAICA: Me-render-a-penis, pyre-on, I-ache.

NARCISSUS PALLIDIFLORUS: (N)-Rac-is-us-Pa-lied-floor-us. My plural sees the liar as in with my narcissistic rapist. Hence, Rac-is-us-Pa. We lied. Florus means rape on the floor, and I lied about it.

NARCISSUS POETIC-US: (N) Rac-is-us, poetic, tic-us. My plural (who knows why I tic) drives my poems.

233

PAPAVER SUAVOLENS: Papa-Suave forms the start of each word. This means a suave father-figure. What's left is verolens: over-lens. In dissociation, my plural can see (over-lens) the suave-papa from above during rape.

PULSATILLA ALPINA: Pulse-sat-liar (pulse-sat-llia) nap-liar. The liar in my head insists the flashbacks to the pulse in my head during the 'sit' (suffocation) are lies.

I had elaborated on two varieties of this flower.

The SSP-Alpina sort grows on acid formations. Acid means 'said' (asid), for the 'al-pinass'.

The SSP *Sulphurea* grows on lime. Lime means lie (me-lie) and remain I-e/m (torn). Sulphur means suffocate.

RHAPONTiCUM CYNAROIDES: The opening 'Rhap' means rape (rahp). The word becomes rape-on-it-come. The lower case 'i' means me. Cynaroides means see-naro-ides. See-a-Nor-dies. The Nor had almost murdered me.

RHODODENDRON FERRUGIN-EUM: The first part means rode-end-Nor (rhoodd-end-ron). I was ridden on. The second part means you-fearing you-me. (Feerr-ing-u-me). I fear what my plural knows.

SILENCE AQUAULIS: This plant should be *Silene Acaulis*. The meaning is silence-a-call. My plural's calls are being silenced.

TUPILA ASTRAiLiS: Two-lip-liar is-all-sat. This should be 'Tulipa Australis'. I have written it with two lower-case 'i's. This means plural. I have a second-lip (tu-lip). This belongs to the liar. Tup-*lia*. She is hiding the 'sat-liar' (of Astralis) from me.

Families

Most of these words end in 'ceae'. For my plural, this means 'see'. ('c'). The pronunciation: ceae is the same. The two e's are like 'eye': e-a-e. To *see*.

Amaryllidaceae: Am-a-liar-see. Notice the central liar-formations: lli, lliyd, llyr. This means lie, lied, liar. What's left is am-a. But I can't 'see' (ceae-see) for the lie.

Caryophyllaceae: Rac-of-liar-lac-see. I can't see the truth for the lie. (Car-oph-ly-lack-see).

Compositae: Comatose-sit-pee. I was raped whilst unconscious.

Cupressaceae: Notice rapes in the middle: Cu-*pressa*-ceae. You-see rapes.

Gentianaceae: Line up the letters to find 'giant'. Giaaanntee. The Great Yellow Gentian belongs to this family and means great giant yellow. A big coward.

Iridaceae: I-rid-a-see. I have shut my eyes to the truth.

Liliaceae: Lia-see. (Lliia-ceae). The liar sees the truth. I can't

Leguminosae: (Le)-mug-I-no-see. I'm a mug for not seeing the truth.

Parueraceae: Par-rue-Rac-rape-see. (The word 'rape' knits the end with the beginning – ae-par). Rearrange the words to Rac-rue-see-Pa-rape. I rue the truth about the rape and wish I couldn't see it.

Ranunculaceae: Ran-uncul-see. Rearrange to 'see-uncle-ran'. My plural remembers an uncle running after me.

Scrophulariaceae: The '*ophul*' means fool (phoul). What follows is liar-see (lari-ceae). The message runs back to the beginning, scr (r'cs). Liar-fools-racs-see. The liar has fooled me, and I can't see.

Sulphurea: My *Science* book has shown sulphur means suffocate. But the opening sulph means fools. I'm a fool for not seeing the suffocation.

Thymelaeaceous: The sounding is 'Time-lays-us'. This means the time I was laid and made a plural.

Var Pygmea: This should be 'Var Pygmaea'. The meaning is twofold: pygmy means a small person – a toddler. It also means me-a-pig. The liar, borne of my toddlerhood is like the pig (policeman), my rapist's once-job.

Common Names

Alpina Anemone: Nap-liar, a-me-noe. Part of me knows about the coma.

Alpen-rose: All-penis-sore. Penis begins with the pen and jumps to the final es. Al-penes-sor

Cardoon Knapweed: Rac-done-nap-weed. I was used whilst unconscious.

Dwarf Juniper: Dwarf means a small person. Juniper is of the *Juniperus* and means penis-juice.

Garland Flower: Dagger-land-lowers. Rag is short for ragged and backwards is literally' dagger'.

Great Yellow Gentian: Great-giant-yellow. My oblivion has made me a big coward.

Moss Campion: I have written 'moss' like 'mass'. This means amss (plural). My drawing shows a p-R morphing to bring Camrion. An anagram for caim-Nor. Ams-came-Nor. I am plural for the Nor that came over me.

Pheasant-eye: Eye-the-penis. I had seen it. Pheasant means th-penis (penaas) and my eye. I had painted a pheasant for Mum in August 1981. These codes run through my artwork.

Pyrenean Columbine: Pyre-rear-on, lock-I-numb. I am numb to the rape from behind.

Snabdragon: My misspelled 'snapdragon'. Bans on-gard (guard). Garden means the same: guard-on. The liar in my head is guarding the truth.

Yellow Alpine Anemone: Coward, penis-lie, me-know. Yellow means coward. Alpine(s) means a-penis-lie. And anemone means a-me-noe.

Other Names

Asphodelus Sphaerocarpus: See 'face' in 'asph' (phas). Rotate backwards from 'us' to find 'us-face-holed'. Oral-rape left a hole in my face. Sphaer means 'fears'. The final 'carpus' means up-Rac. Something went up me.

Up-Rac-fears us-face-holed. I am frightened of the rape.

Coldicum: A misspelt 'Colchicum'. This deviation means I-locked-come (I-loc'd-come). My memory has locked the thing that came over me.

Lilium Pyrenaidcumlorus: I-llie you-me. Pyre-on-I-add, come-law-us. A lawman (policeman) came on me and I lied to myself.

Sarothamnus: The-man-sore-us. A man made me sore. Notice the central th-amn (the man). Saro (soar) means sore and the final 'us' means plural.

235

Chapter 11: Green Flowers

This section summarises the codes found in a green book of wildflowers. The flowers have been placed alphabetically. What follows are other commonly-used words found.

Blossom: This means be-loo-ss-me. I lost part of myself for the loo. The final 'm' means me. The Pear sort means 'rape'. The apple sort means 'appal'.

Bluebell: Be-loo (again). Bbell-lue. I was used like a loo.

Buttercup: Be-utter-book. In my Aurther Books, I had written about the 'Buttercub'. This book is uttering to me.

Deadnettle: Deaden-tell. The telling has been deadened by the liar. 'White Deadnettle' means we-tie the 'tell'. Red means read (past tense), but the 'red' has been removed.

Forget me Not: A plea not to forget my toddlerhood.

Forsythia: I-scythe-for-her. Part of me has been sliced off.

Groundsel: The word 'uncle' can be found in my spelling: 'Gro-uncel'. My other spelling, Grounsel, provides the 's' to bring 'uncle's'. I was used.

Gypsophila: See the Gypsophila-paedophilia echo. It ends with liar (Gypsoph-*ila*). The code begins with 'gyp. Backwards, this is pig, my rapist's once-job. Pig-paedophile's-liar.

Pansy: Pansies mean a-penis. (a-peniss). Pansy brings panys and also payn (pains). Penis-pain.

Polyanthus: I-lop-th-anus. This means rape from behind (not anal rape).

Poppy: This flower symbolises Remembrance Day. The Corn Poppy and Corn Rose contain the Nor and sore.

Wallflower: Wall-lowers – to wall-off the lowers. My slashed 's' (ẟ) brings: ẟlower. I am walled from seeing the lowering of rape.

Frequently-used Phrases and Other Words

Garden beds: Guard-on beds: I was raped on more than one bed, and I mustn't know about it.

Grassy: I-grass. This means to tell.

Soil: To sully.

Weedy/weed: To be weed on. This means semen.

Parts of the Flower

Flower: Lowers. My 'f' resembles a slashed 's'. I was lowered. Flowerhead means lowers-head.

Leaves: To desert.

Petal: (spelled pettle). Pee-tell. To tell about the semen.

Roots: Toors. Tores. I am torn.

Seeds: Semen.

Stalk: Talk-sat, to tell about the mounting.

Stem: Me-stain.

Colours Mentioned

Blue: Be-loo. How rape made me feel.

Purple: You-repel. My toddlerhood repels me.

Red: Read (past tense). To understand these codes.

Yellow: Coward. How my plural sees my oblivion.

Chapters 12 and 13: Garden Reports 1978 and 1979

My plural has inserted meanings behind the plants, just like she has the clouds. The following combines the plants mentioned in both years and are given alphabetically.

Antirrhinum (Popular name, Bunny Rabbits or Snapdragon): Herbaceous plant with bilabiate flowers. Notice the final 'numb'. The first part, antir means 'I-rant'. 'I-rant-I-numb'. The liar's mantra brings oblivion to the 'rabbits'. (Upend the 'b' to bring rap(p)ist.

Ash: Deciduous tree that gives flowers and berries. Ash is residue after the burning.

Apple tree: Tree bearing edible fruit. Appal. My toddlerhood is appalling.

Cuckoo spit: Froth exuded from the froghopper larvae. The cuckoo symbolises an imposter that left 'spit' behind. This means semen.

Cypress (dwarf): Coniferous evergreen shrub. I spelt the word, Cyprus (like the country). With the 'd' flipped, Cypr means cry'd. 'Us-cried'. It's like my misspelling, cirrius.

Hawthorne: Hardy hedgerow. The-Nor-whore. I'm in with my rapist for letting him get away with it.

Holly: Hole-I. I have a hole in me.

Laburnum: Tree with hanging yellow flowers. All-burn-me. I am all burned for the rape.

Laurel: Shrub with dark green, shiny leaves. Aurell. Oral.

Lavender: Aromatic evergreen shrub with blue flowers. The word begins 'alve (slang for halve) and ends 'rend' (tear). Halve-rend. I have been torn in half.

Lilac: Shrub of the olive family with blue-violet flowers. 'I-llac'. I lack an 'I'.

Pansies: Hybrid plant with rounded flowers. 'A-penis(s).'

Poplar (Golden): Fast-growing tree with golden leaves. Popular. Living the lie is a popular choice.

Rose: Prickly shrub with fragrant flowers. This means sore. The sensation after rape.

Sunflower: Plant of the daisy family with large yellow-red heads. Sun-son-lower. I was lowered and the burn was woe-ful.

Willow: Deciduous tree. Weeping willow for my lost toddlerhood. I-lloww. I was forced low and I woe over it.

Chapter 14: Krakatoa (Mt St Helens and Santorini)

The following provides a list of the Krakatoa codes and the other two.

Krakatoa: Volcanic Island in the Sunda Strait. My nickname had been Rack (sounded Rak). Krakatoa could be spelled Krrakatoa. This provides two raks. The word ends with 'to-a' (meaning a-two). A two-rak results. I am two.

Mount St Helen's: This volcano contains the stain of saint and the mount. The enhel (in hell) of Helen follows. Mount-stain-in-hell.

Santorin(i): Stain-tore (*sant*-tor-*ini*). A stain tore me. On either side of the 'tor' is a stain anagram. An 'I' is missing.

Anjer: Coastal town in Banten (formerly West Java) destroyed by a tsunami. Anjer means anger, how my plural feels about the rape.

Java: Island in Indonesia. The 'J' is a French 'I' with a dropped 'e' for the following vowel (J'ava). A-va means 'alve-her (with a dropped 'h' as in slang). I halve her. I have been halved.

Lighthouse: A Krakatoa tsunami reportedly washed one up a valley. The lighthouse means enlightenment about a house in the dark and a force (symbolised by the tsunami) wants to destroy it.

St Elmo's Fire: Glowing plasma seen on the mast of a British naval ship during the eruption. This means stain-fire-elm. I have been (so) sullied and burnt during rape that I am now a plural.

Sunda Strait: Straits between Java and Sumatra. Sunda means 's'under,' for being 'under'. My body position was straight, for I was restrained, arms to the sides. I was 's-under-straight. In vaginal rape, the son was straight. In both cases, I am forced under.

Tsunami: Oceanic waves caused by displacement of the seabed. The word is sounded, sue-nam-me. This means use-man-me. Man-use-me.

Chapter 15: Astronomy

The following explains my plural's meanings in my Astronomy project. My Aurther *Earth* has shown the meanings behind the planets.

The sun: This means sun-son. My burning face and the cause. Depending on the viewpoint, the sun can be used to express either.

Mars (Are-ams), its Moons and Features

Nix Olympica: Normally known as Olympus Mons. Nix is skin backwards (niks-skin). The following 'O' brings on-skin.

Read back within the olympica to find ly-me-caip (ly-m-pica). My lying self is caping the on-skin (Nix-o) from me. My skin was 'on' by something.

Phobos: One of Mars' moons is sounded fobos. This means 'of boss'. My children's stories contain a heartless boss that symbolises Uncle Dan. To my plural, this lying asteroid is working for the boss.

Demos: Sodme meaning sodomy. This pertains to rape from behind. Codes for this body position can be found in my stories and novels.

Asteroids and Comets

Ceres: Also pronounced 'Ceris'. This means 'cries'. This echoes with Mercury.

Vesta: The 'St' means saint, anagram for stain. What's left is 'eva' meaning 'ever'. Ever-stain.

Pallas: Apalls. Appals. My plural is appalled at what has happened.

Eros: Sore. (Like rose). What Uncle Dan did made me sore afterwards.

Icarus: I note the word 'scar' embedded within. What's left is 'I' and 'u'. I-you scar. We are severed.

Encke's Comet: Enck is an anagram for neck. This forms a trauma site during oral rape and 'it-come' (comet) on me.

D'arrest Comet: Wishful thinking: the arrest of my rapist who come-it on me.

Halley's Comet: Sh-yells, the muted cry about the thing that 'come-it' on me.

Jupiter (Us-writer) and its Moons

Amalthea: The first of Jupiter's moons. Am all heat. This is the burning sensation during assault.

Io: This moon is sounded 'I-o'. The 'o'-part is a homonym of 'owe'. This is an anagram of 'woe'. I-woe. My plural woes for what has happened.

Europa: Jupiter's third moon. An anagram for rape-u surrounds the central 'o-woe. Pa-rape-you-woe. Uncle Dan was like a father figure.

Ganymede: I am first alerted by the 'gan' syllable, anagram of ang. Ang'y and ange'ed can be found in this word meaning angry and angered but the 'r' is missing. Europa is Ganymede's neighbour and is saying 'you-r-(opa)'. The 'r' is for you. The missing r can now be placed in Ganymede. The result is 'angry me' or 'angered me'. These silent moons have been exchanging messages with one another.

My plural is limited by the proper nouns available, but she finds ways round these problems. Anger, rage and envy proliferate in proper nouns of my stories and novels.

Calisto: I had spelled this word 'Callisto' in my project book. Two-call-sit. My plural is calling out about the sit and when I was made still in the cot. (Still-cot). Double-meanings are rife in these codes.

Saturn (Sat-on) and its Moons

Janus: Saturn's closest moon. J'anus. I (am) an us. I was raped from behind.

Mimas: Saturn's second moon. I amms meaning I have two ams.

Enceladus: Notice the encel, at the beginning, anagram of 'encle' meaning uncle. The remainder of the word is 'ad-us' meaning add us. An uncle made me a plural.

Tethys: The-syt. This means the-sit.

Dione: Saturn's fifth moon. Die on. I had almost died.

Rhea: Saturn's sixth moon is sounds like Rea, an anagram for 'are'. An expression for being a plural.

Titan: Saturn's seventh moon. An anagram for taint. I have been tainted by the rape.

Hyperion: The first part of the word is 'hyper'. Rearrange the letters to 'phyre' to find a word that is sounded 'fire'. The rest is 'I on'. I-on-fire. I feel on fire during the rape.

Iapetus: I am first alerted by the 'Pa' word spelled backwards. The remaining letters are 'suite'. This means 'use it'. Pa-use-it.

Phoebe: Saturn's furthest moon. Sounded *fibi*. I-fib.

Uranus (You're-an-us) and The Five Greats Removed

The five moons of Uranus have been used to express the process of creating a plural.

This is what my plural has done to these five moons.

Oberon: is the trauma. 'O-beronn'. Bern-on means 'burn on'.

Titania: Eliminate duplicate letters from the taaiint anagram to find taint. It's just like Saturn's seventh moon, Titan.

Miranda: The words 'I ran mad' can be found in this moon. I have run away.

Ariel: The words lie and liar can be found in this moon.

Umbriel: is the oblivion that takes over. Dum-lier can be found. Dumb liar.

Neptune (Pen-tune) and its Moons

Triton: Neptune's closest moon: The part after the 'T' sounds like 'write-on'. The initial 'T' can be omitted for being a duplicate. I 'write on' this project.

Nereid: Neptune's second moon. This word begins 'neer'. This means 'near'. Read backwards from the end to find 'die'. Near-die. I had almost died during the smothering.

Finally, **Pluto** Lop-Loo-top. and the Outer Reaches.

The Far-Reaches

Galaxy: Sounded 'galaxi'. The word rotates on itself, beginning with 'g' (expressing the French 'I') and ending with the English 'I'. The result is I-alax-I. I-lacks-I. I am lacking an 'I'.

The Milky Way: The milky yaw. A mouth forced open, and the residue left behind.

Andromeda: This word contains my rapist's name and his mother's married name. This large galaxy is advancing towards the Milky Way.

The Black Hole: The blackout of coma. 'B-lack whole. Be-lack (a) whole. A part of me is lacking.

Supernova: the 'ova' of the word means 'over'. The super-over means being overcome. My rapist's name can also be found within this word.

Galaxy 3C-295

Near the end of this project, I mention a galaxy known as 3C-295. This remote galaxy is receding from us at half the speed of light. What does this galaxy mean? At first, I am stumped. I decide to spell out the figures. This is what comes out.

Three-see-two-nine-five.

The first bit is three-see-t. I was used like a seat when I was three.

The rest of the sequence is won-inef. This means ownnife. Own knife. The remaining ive means I've. I have (own) the knife.

Three-seat, I own knife.

I have cut away the seat and I am plural. The seat is hurtling away at half the speed of light.

The Under-meaning

With the identity of the stellar objects now revealed, my astronomy project takes on an entirely different slant. I have replaced the names of the celestial objects with the codes within. The following results.

Mercury: Me-you-cry is the closest object to the 'son'.

Venus: The atmosphere of Knives consists of carbon dioxide which traps my rapist's heat in a thick smothering layer. The surface contains lakes of tar or asphalt which boil and bubble. Knives is known as the hell planet.

Mercury Envies 'my' oblivion.

Mars: Am-ares has a painfully thin atmosphere. Am-ares has two moons: Of-boss and Sodme. Of-boss and Sodme are invisible to Am-ares' higher awareness.

Jupiter: It-tears-up is an alien world.

Jupiter's Moons: I-woe, Rape-you, Angered-me and A-still-cot are the largest moons of It-tears-up. Am-all-heat is the closest moon to Knives.

Saturn: Sat-on is flattened at the top. The inner moons of sat-on look like rapes. They are called Die-on, The-sit, Pa-use-it and I-ams. Taint is the largest moon in the solar system.

Saturn's outer moons are called I-on-fire, Pa-use-it and I-fib.

Uranus: the five moons of You-are-an-us are called Burn-on, Taint, I-run-mad, I-liar and Dumb-liar.

Neptune: Pen-tune is a remote planet and has a moon called Write-on.

Pluto: Loo-top is just a speck of light to the most powerful telescopes.

The Asteroids: Cries, Ever-stain, Sore, Appals and I-you-scar are remnants of a past disaster. It was known as the seat-'orid.

Chapter 16: The Sun and Moon

Chief codes for The Sun and Moon.

Boxer: workhorse in George Orwell's book, *Animal Farm* (1945). I painted Boxer on 22 Sept 1982 on the same day I began this project. Box-her. My plural has been boxed up and hidden away.

Corona: A recurring proper noun. The sun's outermost atmosphere which extends to the planets. Onca-Nor. Onca is a child's way of saying 'uncle'.

Lysimeter: An instrument that measures plant evapotranspiration. I had misspelled the word, 'lysemeter'. This means measuring lies.

Photosphere: The sun's innermost atmosphere: So-fear-hot. (The 'p' falls outside the phrase). I fear the burning pressure during assault.

The other spheres mean the same: fears and have been explained in the main book.

Notes on the images: (regarding book covers): provision 17 USC 113 (c) states it would not be an infringement of copyright to use images for "useful articles" or "articles having an intrinsic utilitarian function that is not merely to portray the appearance of the article or convey information."

Mt St Helens images copyright free. The owner of others couldn't be identified.

This book ends with two poems I had written in 1978. My Pyrenean flower, *Narcissus Poetic-us* says I am Rac-is-us, poetic, for my plural drives my poems. Both illustrate her obsession with the Moon and the sea. I was twelve and thirteen respectively.

Two Poems

Moon Mystery (written 23 March 1978)

Opening the hide out of the sky,
Breaking a path of light on high
Looking at the moon that shone
Wondering what there is beyond.

The moon is cracked by the boughs
Showing the teeth of the clouds
Curious operas of history
No answer for this mystery.

But there is one thing that I know,
That when the clouds come over low
No more of the moon it would seem
But it's always there with watching beams.

The Sea (Written 31 October 1978)

Stroking and stealing from the sands
Grabbing pebbles like watery hands
Singing its watery everlasting song
With its salty watery tongue

Sitting here as far as can see
The sky can meet with the sea
The strong blue line across its does send
Forever and ever without end

It can be calm but never still
But can have waves like a hill
It can have life of plants and fish
But can be death with one big swish.

Books by the Author

Tales from Daler Cottage: Unearthing the Hidden Codes within my Children's Mysteries

Mirror Image Shattered: A Twin's True Story

The Locked Door: The Hidden Novel Behind the Kidnap Thriller

The Lessons: The True Story of a Parasitic Novel

North Window: The Stranger behind the Reflection

Nadia: Testament of the Ghost Girl

Blood in Water: Eight Short Stories

Blood on the Corn: Uncovering the Assault Sites of my Toddlerhood

World of the Torn Eye: Messages within my Childhood Projects

The author lives in the UK and writes under a pseudonym.

243

Printed in Great Britain
by Amazon

82360615R00139